THE ROSE THEATRE

Christine Eccles

THE
ROSE THEATRE

NICK HERN BOOKS
A division of Walker Books Limited

ROUTLEDGE
A Theatre Arts Book
New York

A Nick Hern Book

The Rose Theatre first published as an original paperback in 1990 by Nick Hern Books, a division of Walker Books Limited, 87 Vauxhall Walk, London SE11 5HJ

First published in the United States of America by Routledge/Theatre Arts Books, an imprint of Routledge, Chapman and Hall, Inc, 29 West 35th Street, New York NY 10001

British Library Cataloguing in Publication Data
Eccles, Christine
   The Rose Theatre.
   1. London.   Theatres, history
   I. Title
   792.09421

   ISBN 1-85459-076-6

Library of Congress data available
ISBN 1-87830-107-0

Cover illustration: detail from John Norden's panorama of London, made in 1600 (Royal Library, Stockholm)

Printed and bound in Great Britain
by Biddles Limited, Guildford.

ACKNOWLEDGEMENTS

This book would not have come about if Nick Hern had not asked me to do it and in turn he would not have asked me to do it had not a popular demonstration led by Ian McKellen, Dame Peggy Ashcroft and Simon Hughes MP, formed a human chain to protect the vestigial remains of an Elizabethan playhouse against the damage threatened by property development on the site. Writing it was a daunting task for one who has not thought twice about Elizabethan playhouses since student days, and it could not have been done without the many people who have been incredibly generous with their time, expertise and knowledge in helping to collate all the information that is necessary to tell the story of the Rose Theatre and the Campaign that tried to save it. Any errors are entirely my responsibility.

My thanks mainly go to those who served on the Committee of the Rose Campaign for allowing me to observe their meetings. Although I followed the Campaign closely this is not an 'authorised' version of events, so their brave decision to let me be an independent observer is all the more appreciated. In particular, I would like to thank Nicholas Armstrong, Lauryn Beer, John Burns, Eileen Chivers, Martin Clout, James Fox, Dr Anthony Grayling, John Griffiths, Simon Hughes, Martin Kramer, Pat McDonnell, Philip Ormond, Heather Pickering, Dr Ruth Richardson, Barbara Todd, Martin Village and Alex Wilbraham.

I am indebted to Harvey Sheldon, Head of Greater London Archaeology at the Museum of London, Julian Bowsher and Simon Blatherwick who co-directed the excavation of the Rose for the Museum, George Dennis, the Museum's archaeological planning officer and to all the other archaeologists for the many long hours they spent interpreting the site for me. Thanks are also due to John Hinchcliffe at English Heritage for explaining their part of the excavation of the remains.

I am grateful to Jon Greenfield, Professor Andrew Gurr, C. Walter Hodges, Michael Holden, Iain Mackintosh and Professor John Orrell who have allowed me to quote from their informal and private correspondence concerning a small-scale model reconstruction of the Rose Theatre.

At the International Shakespeare Globe Centre I must thank Sam Wanamaker, Jennifer Jones and the architect Theo Crosby of Pentagram for talking to me at length about their project.

At Southwark Council I owe thanks to Cllr. Hilary Wines, Cllr. Geoff Williams and planning officer, Mark Dennett for explaining the planning needs and policies in North Southwark.

Caro Newling and Ralph Fiennes at the Royal Shakespeare Company provided me with an essential perspective on the events leading up 14 May. I must also thank the RSC's production manager, Roger Howells, for showing me research he has undertaken on correspondences between the Rose and the RSC's new auditorium at Stratford-upon-Avon, the Swan Theatre.

I am grateful to Margaret Slythe, Head of the Wodehouse Library at Dulwich College for writing to my publisher and drily remarking that she found it 'difficult to believe anyone could produce a book on the Rose Theatre without seeing the source material here', because as a result I did and it was well worth it. Southwark's Local History librarian Nicola Smith also made many suggestions which saved a lot of time.

Alleyn's School were enormously helpful in setting up an experiment to determine the capacity of the Rose and I would like to thank Eileen Chivers, Major Eric Randall and the team of sixth-formers: Christine Boyce, Barnaby Cole, Federico Forcolini, Ben Godwin, Louise Hopkins and Tamara MacFarlane who organised it all.

I would also like to express my sincere thanks to Simon Jenkins, former deputy chairman of English Heritage and Martin Myers, chief executive of Imry Merchant, for agreeing to talk to me.

I think I am grateful to Nick Hern and Jackie Bodley, his assistant, at least for their patience, sympathy and draconian editorial judgement.

Finally, I would like to thank my son Jack Thompson who put up with a most peculiar life whilst all this was going on and to whom I dedicate this book with love.

CONTENTS

LIST OF ILLUSTRATIONS

The drawings and photographs are reproduced by courtesy of their copyright owners who are listed in the captions.

CHRONOLOGY OF THE ROSE THEATRE

(Bold type indicates key dates)

Pre-Rose

1558 **Elizabeth 1 ascends the throne.** Thomas Kyd born.
1561 *Gorboduc* written by Thomas Sackville and Thomas Norton.
1563 Plague returns.
1564 **William Shakespeare and Christopher Marlowe born.**
1566 **Edward Alleyn born.**
1572 Ben Jonson born.
1574 **Royal Patent granted to Leicester's Men.**
1576 **James Burbage opens the Theatre.**
1577 James Burbage opens the Curtain. Philip Henslowe living in the Liberty of Clink.
1579 Edmund Tilney appointed as Master of the Revels.
1582 Edward Alleyn begins acting career.
1587 **Philip Henslowe builds the Rose Theatre.** Shakespeare arrives in London. Marlowe writes *Tamburlaine*. Mary Queen of Scots executed.
1588 The Armada.
1589 Martin Marprelate controversy.
1591 **Edward Alleyn quarrels with the Burbages.**

The Rose Period

1592 **Henslowe rebuilds the Rose Theatre and starts to keep a Diary. Alleyn and the Admiral's Men become resident company at the Rose. Henry VI premiered.** Alleyn marries Joan Woodward. Riot among feltworkers in Southwark. *Groatsworth of Wit* controversy. Thomas Nashe writes *Pierce Pennilesse*.
1593 Plague severe. Alleyn's company disbands. Marlowe killed. John Norden engraves a map of London.
1594 *Titus Andronicus premiered*. Kyd dies. Alleyn buys the Bear Garden.
1595 Francis Langley opens the Swan Theatre. Henslowe redecorates the Rose. Butter riots in Southwark market.
1596 Johannes de Witt visits London.
1597 *Isle of Dogs* controversy. Alleyn retires.
1599 Richard Burbage opens the Globe Theatre.
1600 **Henslowe opens the Fortune Theatre. Nottingham's Men vacate Rose Theatre.**
1602 Worcester's Men play a brief season at Rose Theatre.
1603 Elizabeth I dies. James I ascends throne.
1605 Lease for the Rose Theatre expires.
1609 King's Men move into Blackfriars Theatre.
1613 Henslowe opens the Hope Theatre. Globe Theatre destroyed by fire.

1616 **Henslowe and Shakespeare die.**
1619 Richard Burbage dies.
1625 James I dies. Charles I ascends throne.
1626 **Edward Alleyn dies.**
1642 **Parliamentary Ordinance closes all theatres.**
1649 Charles I executed.

CHRONOLOGY OF THE EXCAVATION AND CAMPAIGN

Pre-Rose Excavation

1987 Nov. Interland Estates Ltd. (Heron) apply for planning permission.
1988 Jan. Museum of London requests excavation.
        Oct. Interland sell site to Imry Merchant.
        Dec. Planning permission granted. Excavation begins.

Rose Excavation

1989 31 Jan. Chalk wall found in south west.
        15 Feb. *The Times* publicises the discovery of Rose Theatre.
        19 Feb. **Last day of excavation.**
        2 Mar. Ten week extension granted to Museum of London.
        22 Apr. Symposium organised by International Shakespeare Globe
            Centre.
        9 May Simon Hughes makes an adjournment speech in House of
            Commons.
        11 May **Margaret Thatcher makes a statement in support of Rose.**
        12 May Media overtaken by story of Rose.
        14 May **Last day of excavation. Vigil on site.**

Rose Campaign – The Moratorium

        15 May **Confrontation with sand lorries. Nicholas Ridley agrees a
            month's moratorium. Campaign Committee elected.**
        18 May First Committee meeting.
        26 May Campaign launched at Stringfellows Night Club.
        27 May Committee plans to launch a 'Bard Bond'.
        29 May Bank Holiday. Elizabethan Fair held on site.
        30 May Huggin Hill backfilled. Campaign committed to acquiring
            the whole site.
        31 May Simon Jenkins, of English Heritage, discusses details of the
            re-designed office block with some Committee members.
        1 Jun. Imry Merchant Annual Report announces record profits.
        2 Jun. **Imry Merchant unveils its re-design. Campaign announces
            plans to buy the site at a press conference.**
        4 Jun. Rally on site with RSC performance of *Dr Faustus*.
        7 Jun. Campaign seeks counsel's opinion.
        9 Jun. **Museum of London sacked.**
        11 Jun. **Rally on site and all-night vigil. Moratorium ends.**

Chronology

Post-Moratorium

13 Jun. English Heritage convene seminar on site.

15 Jun. **Nicholas Ridley announces that he will not be scheduling the Rose Theatre.**

16. Jun. Site of Rose backfilled with sand.

19 Jun. Keyhole excavation begins.

22 Jun. **Leave for judicial review is granted.** Southwark holds a Public Consultation meeting.

23 Jun. Rose Theatre concreted over.

30 Jun. **Campaign serves injunction on Imry Merchant.**

3 Jul. Injunction lifted. **Southwark Planning Committee defers decision.**

4 Jul. Date set for judicial review. Rumours of Imry Merchant takeover.

10 Jul. **Judicial review begins.**

11 Jul. **Judicial review ends.** Olivier dies.

17 Jul. **Judicial review fails.** Imry Merchant takeover by Marketchief is official.

25 Jul. **Southwark Council grant planning permission.**

Post-Rose Campaign

1 Sep. Section 52 agreed.

3 Oct. Southbridge House re-named Rose Court.

4 Oct. Committee receives bill for legal costs.

9 Oct. Symposium on preserving the Rose.

11 Oct. Formal elections to the Committee.

12 Oct. Press conference on the partial excavation of the Globe Theatre.

PREFACE

In June 1989 for the first time in nearly four hundred years the mighty line of a Marlowe play echoed around Bankside. Gerard Murphy in Edward Alleyn's famous role consigned his immortal soul to Hell from the stage of a flat bed truck, parked opposite the site of the newly excavated Rose Theatre. Evensong bells rang out from nearby Southwark Cathedral. Children clustered on fire escapes to get a better view. Groundlings threw their cash into waiting collection buckets and, the following week, for the main rally, camera crews paid considerably over the odds for the privilege of a place in the upper storeys of Bear Gardens Museum, from which to film a procession of megastars strutting their stuff in London's newest – and oldest – performing space.

The Rose Theatre, the only Elizabethan outdoor playhouse whose remains were known to have extensively survived, had been excavated by archaeologists from the Museum of London during the early months of 1989. In May, office development for the site threatened the remains with at best, partial damage, and at worst, total destruction. The bare bones of the Rose Theatre's geometry, barely two inches high in places, overturned a great many assumptions about the sort of theatre with which Shakespeare would have been familiar, but it was to prove unable to vanquish entirely the commercial imperative of land prices in North Southwark. The Campaign to Save the Rose, established at the very last moment, was granted just four weeks to put its case.

Unwittingly and ironically, the Campaign relived many moments from the crowded years of the Rose's history. Bankside then was the Shaftesbury Avenue and Reeperbahn of its day. Shakespeare must have had it in mind when he dramatised the suburbs of Vienna in *Measure for Measure*. Brothels, bear-baiting and the new playhouses all flourished across the river safe from the jurisdiction of the City's Puritan fathers. Maintained by favour at the court of Elizabeth I, and surrounded by internal conspiracies, the cross fertilisation and collaboration of the Bankside writers produced well over two thousand plays in the fifty-year period before the 1642 Parliamentary Ordinance forcibly closed all theatres.

The tension created by state control was as much responsible for the flowering of British drama in the 1590s, as the Puritan legacy of theatrical censorship in post-war Britain was instrumental in the renaissance of British drama during the 1950s. The twin glories – and rivals – of that latter era: George Devine's English Stage Company at the Royal Court and Joan Littlewood's Theatre Workshop at the Theatre Royal, Stratford East, may be said to compare with those twin glories of an earlier age: Shakespeare's Globe and the rival Rose, owned by Philip Henslowe and home to the celebrated actor, Edward Alleyn. Like the Royal Court and the Theatre Royal, both Elizabethan theatres were devoted to new writing – indeed the notion of anything other than new plays would have seemed quite baffling – but Henslowe's Rose (like Littlewood's Theatre Workshop) emphasised a collaborative way of working. Overshadowed by Shakespeare's genius, its repertoire suffered complete neglect until relatively recent times. Yet such is the measure of its rehabilitation that it was no coincidence that extracts from three of its plays could be performed on site during the Campaign. Deborah Warner's *Titus Andronicus,* Adrian Noble's version of the *Henry VI* trilogy and Barry Kyle's *Dr Faustus* were all triumphs of the 1988/9 theatrical season.

The Rose, probably built in 1587, established a repertoire which was dominated by Christopher Marlowe until his early death at the age of 29 in 1593. After that the Rose flourished for a while, but without finding another crowd-pulling writer it lost momentum and was not able to compete with the Globe, erected in 1599, exactly 100 yards from Henslowe's theatre, down what is now called Park Street and was then called Maid Lane. In the same way that the crowds in 1599 abandoned the Rose for the Globe, the media lost interest in the fate of the Rose once the Globe's partial excavation was presented to the world later in 1989. It was a brilliant public relations exercise, quite unlike the confused public confrontations provoked by the Rose; and Hansons plc, who masterminded it, had obviously learnt their lesson from that experience. Perhaps the ghost of Philip Henslowe was there to see the crowds once more abandon his theatre, and disappear down Park Street tempted by a rival attraction.

One aspect of the Rose which got the most comment from scholars and laymen alike, was the surprisingly small scale of the theatre and the intimate relationship it must presumably have afforded both actor and audience in Elizabethan London. At the Campaign's main rally, Ian McKellen was there to remind us, every time the PA broke down, that Alleyn & Co had no artificial aids acting as a barrier to direct communication, although, it was twentieth-century technology which allowed Lord Olivier's disembodied voice to make its last public statement. Out of, for once, a *functioning* speaker, he asked if a muse of fire could exist under a ceiling of commerce.

Unfortunately, Philip Henslowe would almost certainly have answered 'yes'. Henslowe had a number of property interests on Bankside and there is no reason to suppose that at the time he built the Rose he viewed it as anything other than a straightforward business venture. His deed of partnership with John Cholmley has little to say about plays, players or policy and is mainly concerned with confirming Cholmley's concession on the fast food trade. 'He . . . will not permitte or suffer any personne or personnes other than the saide John Cholmley . . . to vtter sell or putt to sale in or aboute the said parcelle of grownde . . . any breade or drinke other than as shalbe solde to and of the vse and behoofe of the saide John Cholmley.' John Cholmley's ghost should certainly have taken an advisory role on the sub-committee which organised the main rally, as he would never have let them lose the financial advantage that could have been extracted from the many ice-cream vendors who made a packet out of the thousand-strong crowd thronging Park Street that day.

A thousand or so – who's to say? Crowd estimates tend to reflect the vested interests of the person doing the estimating. *The Times,* for example, who had been the first in the field to report the story back in February, came up with a figure of 5000 for the rally. *The Independent,* sceptical as ever of anything that involves actors going over the top, put the crowd at a mere 1000. The actual size of Elizabethan audiences has, in much the same way, long been a contested issue. Contemporary eyewitnesses suggested a capacity house of 3000 people, but they had good reason to bump up the numbers. Faced with the actual physical dimensions of the Rose Theatre, actors and directors disenchanted with the large auditoriums of the National Theatre and the Royal Shakespeare Company, found equally good, but equally unreliable, reason for suggesting a much smaller capacity for the Rose.

But Philip Henslowe was too hard-nosed a businessman to have settled for the equivalent of an Elizabethan studio space. Indeed, when his lease came up for renewal in 1603 and the parish of St Mildred's in Bread Street tripled the rent because there was a profitable theatre on it, Henslowe stoutly declared that 'he wold Rather pulledowne the playhouse the . . . do so'. There is no evidence that he actually did pull it down but it's quite possible that much the same sentiment was shared by Imry Merchant, the property company who wanted to develop the site in 1989. Nicholas Ridley, the Secretary of State for the Environment, also demonstrated a sixteenth-century sensibility by proving he had much in common with his namesake, the pro-Reformation Nicholas Ridley, Bishop of Rochester. That Ridley achieved notoriety through the destruction of a major piece of medieval sculpture, the Holy Blood of Hailes: '. . . torn, broken in pieces bit by bit, split up into a thousand fragments' and Dame Peggy Ashcroft threatened to throw herself in front of Imry Merchant's bulldozers rather than witness a similar fate befalling the Rose Theatre. At the eleventh hour, the latter day Nicholas Ridley was persuaded to offer a million pounds to Imry Merchant to re-think their scheme.

A bit like the parish of St Mildred's, Imry Merchant also acquired the habit of tripling its sums every time the question of compensation came up. Still, whether £100 million or £30 million, it was a sizeable sum for the Campaign to have to find. Sizeable enough to embarrass its chairman, Simon Hughes, Democrat MP for Southwark and Bermondsey, the socially-deprived constituency in which the Rose remains were sited. On more than one occasion he suggested that a proportion of any funds raised ought to be donated to his needier constituents. Edward Alleyn would have been familiar with this argument. Anonymous Puritan complaints about the 'proud players' who 'jett in their silkes' whilst the 'pore people . . . sterve in the Streetes', finally led the local church to 'talk with the players for tithes for their playhouses within the liberty of the Clinke, and for money for the poore'.

Actors turned out in overwhelming numbers to save the Rose Theatre, the only tangible relic of that golden age in British drama. As Olivier said, 'It seems to me *terrible* that one's heritage can be swept under concrete, as though it had never existed'. Seemingly from diverse backgrounds, an unlikely cast met on the temporary stage erected in Unisys car park. Yet the Campaign illustrated that though members of British Equity are now part of the international jet set, the fraternity of actors is as close as in the tight-knit days when Edward Alleyn and the handful of players that made up the Elizabethan theatre world, set about defining the acting profession. At some point in their careers all of today's stars had worked with one another, and of course most had first met doing Shakespeare.

Perceived by the press largely as 'proud players' jumping on a bandwagon, actors gave way to the men in wigs as the Campaign sought redress in law. How Philip Henslowe, in that litigious age under Elizabeth I, would have loved a legal remedy like today's judicial review! This increasingly popular measure for overturning administrative decisions would have been a godsend to any theatre proprietor in the days when between them the Queen's Privy Council and the aldermen of the City of London issued a bewildering series of commands and counter-commands designed to limit the unstoppable growth of theatre. The Campaign sought to overturn the Secretary of State's de-cision not to schedule a monument which even he admitted was schedulable.

Geographically, the Campaign touched a nerve in all the most sensitive places. From the rate-capped Inner London Borough of Southwark, who were landed with the international respon-sibility of making the final decision, to a third-floor office above leafy St James' Square, where developers awaited the go-ahead. From the Palace of Westminster, the High Courts and Fleet Street, to the heart of the City in a conference room penetrated by the Rose Campaign. From meeting rooms at RADA with the background noise of students limbering up, to the stages of the West End with applause ringing in the ears, the case for the Rose was debated.

The waves made by the Campaign mean that the relationships between archaeology and planning, between con-servation and progress and between the claims of a living culture and the legacy of the past will never be quite the same again. The Rose, a brave powerhouse in its day, shone a spotlight on the divisive nature of art within contemporary culture. Once, the bemused building workers and the equally bemused

Campaigners would have formed one audience, questioning, popular and democratic. Now they stood on opposite sides; the theatre-goer a member of a privileged élite. Even those in government with the power to have effected a solution for the Rose, are usually conspicuously absent from the theatres that the state subsidises today. For the campaign to succeed, the living tradition of the Rose became subsumed under that powerful iconic figure, William Shakespeare. 'The Rose Theatre?' asked a young Australian hairdresser, 'isn't that where Churchill once performed?' And, in a way, he was right. Shakespeare, colonised as a symbol of national unity, has a moral force far greater than his plays. Yet without enlisting Shakespeare into the Campaign, the Rose would never have been saved. But if the tradition of the Rose, 'our heritage', means anything at all, it should mean that a theatre like the Royal Court's Theatre Upstairs will never again have to go dark, as it was in the summer of 1989.

The discovery of the Rose Theatre foundations, and the ballyhoo that surrounded it, was one of the big news stories during that heatwave. Thousands rallied around the chalk white skeletal geometry unearthed in the dark Southwark mud. People talked emotionally about the 'tingle factor', but there were hard facts to learn from the excavation of the Rose. The world of Elizabethan theatre scholarship is small, and to scholars the significance of the Rose's discovery was incalculable and needed no justification. It may be that in the same way that a handful of physicists speaking, in the main, just to one another, inadvertently gave the world Teflon saucepans, that one day research on the Rose will improve the daily lot for all. In the meantime, a concentration on detail brings the entire world of Shakespeare's contemporaries into closer focus. The canvas too often appears painted with broad brush sweeps. It is sometimes hard to think about it – or write about it – without heavy reliance on words like 'rumbustious' or 'gusto' and 'vigour': terms which tend to obscure the way in which this essentially English vernacular art form developed alongside the emerging neo-classicism of Renaissance Europe and reached out into the lives of all. By not being Shakespeare's theatre, Henslowe's Rose has much to tell us about context and practice, how traditions are made and how traditions are broken.

CHAPTER ONE

The Rose Theatre 1587–93

'. . . unexpectedly one of them hit the jackpot'.

The history of the Rose Theatre tells the short-lived history of popular theatre in England. Stagecraft traditions in the 1580s still looked back to the days before playhouses, when strolling players set up for business on village greens or outside inns, and performed to everyone from the artisan to the aristocrat. In 1587 when Philip Henslowe built the Rose Theatre, drama was in a state of transition. During the 1590s the Rose was in its heyday and, spurred on by professional rivalry, its rapid turnover of plays meant that it was able to respond immediately to the events of the day. By the end of the 1590s, the experience of performing in permanent theatres had led to more complex writing and production skills which anticipated an eventual need for indoor theatres, with their smaller audiences drawn from a single class. The years of the Rose Theatre's decline were years when the authorities finally had to come to terms with the challenge posed by this still rather new phenomenon in London life.

London's first playhouse had been built north of the City's boundaries in 1576 so theatre-going was a recently acquired, and growing habit by 1587. It was something of a risk, however, for Philip Henslowe to think that the habit could be encouraged south of the City when he entered into partnership with John Cholmley to finance a playhouse on Bankside. Elizabeth I had granted a licence back in 1574 to ' a James Burbage and four fellows of the company of the Earl of Leicester to exhibit all kinds of stage-plays during the Queen's pleasure in any part of England'. James Burbage's troupe, the Earl of Leicester's Men, founded in 1559, were firm favourites with Elizabeth. Until the Theatre was built, playing in London was on an occasional basis and confined to a series of inns: the Cross Keys, the Bull, the Bel Savage, the Red Lion and the Bell. The

1574 licence meant that the days of arduous touring were over and, for Leicester's Men at least, the establishment of a permanent base. Two years later, Burbage took advantage of the phrasing, 'any part of England', to locate his classically named Theatre in the capital itself.

The exact location of the Theatre was wisely chosen. It was sited in Shoreditch within the 'liberty' of Holywell, just outside the City's boundaries, close enough to where the potential audience lived and worked, yet outside the City's jurisdiction. The City's Council of 26 aldermen was a bastion of diehard Puritanism, implacably hostile to playhouses, players and plays. Their prescient complaint that the Queen's Patent of 1574 set a 'precedent farre extending to the hart of our liberties' acknowledged both their own jealously guarded autonomy and the monarch's indisputable sovereignty. In Elizabethan England, Elizabeth was the law. The City was in no position to countermand the edict of the Queen. If it was her wish that players should settle near her Court, ready and available to perform for her at Royal Command, then the City was powerless to resist.

The powers that the City did have gave them scope for interference and they exerted maximum pressure on the Queen's Privy Council to place theatres under restraint. The political brinkmanship employed by City, Church and Privy Council during these years, for control of the proliferation of playhouses that followed Burbage's Theatre, resulted in a complicated array of proclamations and counter-proclamations, petitions and counter-petitions which, no doubt, were designed as much to test one another's nerves, as to prove, in the absence of a police force or standing army, that one's own house was in order. Each aimed to demonstrate that under its management, the playhouses were under control. The situation though, in effect, was very much out of control and was to stay that way until the end of the century.

In 1577, only a year after the Theatre opened, James Burbage opened the Curtain in the same neighbourhood, and went on to enjoy a near monopoly on theatre in London for the next decade. It proved profitable and it was inevitable, given the expansionist ethos of the age, that a speculator, like Philip Henslowe, would be attracted by the profits. James Burbage had once been a carpenter by trade, and Henslowe, too, had begun his working life as a tradesman, apprenticed to a dyer.

However, unlike James Burbage who had then become an actor and thus, had every reason to plough his capital back into his profession, Henslowe had no other reason than the profit motive when he speculated in this new and still somewhat uncharted form of property development. He did not have the protection of the Queen's Patent, and Bankside had yet to establish itself as a focal point for theatre in London leisure. Building the Rose Theatre in 1587 was a risk, but a calculated risk.

London's landscape had been gashed during the Reformation and the dissolution of the monasteries had increased the availability of land. London was the largest town in Europe, a major centre for trade and navigation, and, out of the country's total population of just under five million people, over 300,000 had settled in the capital. Half of them lived in the crowded City where the wealth was concentrated, but the other half, the poorer citizens, lived in what were then the outlying suburbs, such as Southwark. Maynard Keynes said of this period that 'never in the annals of the modern world has there existed so prolonged and so rich an opportunity for the businessman, the speculator and the profiteer.' Philip Henslowe was all three. As a youth, he had come to London in 1577 to be apprenticed, but now, ten years later, he was in possession of his wealthy wife's fortune. At some point in the mid 1580s, Henslowe had married Agnes, the widow of Harry Woodward, his former master. 1587, the year when Henslowe ventured his capital in property development on Bankside, was a year that seems to sum up the whole perceived romance of the Elizabethan era. Mary, Queen of Scots had been executed at the start of 1587 and by the end of the year, William Shakespeare had arrived in London, while on the Continent Philip II of Spain was building up his navy which the following year would set sail as the Armada.

Yet political tensions lurked beneath the surface of public life and were to find expression on the stages of the playhouses. The Great War with Spain (1585 – 1604) was an early forerunner of the 'Falklands factor', apparently uniting the country when, socially, its internal divisions threatened explosion. During the first 25 or so years of her reign, begun in 1558, Elizabeth had managed to turn her realm around. From being queen of a small island nation isolated from Renaissance Europe and torn apart by its own Reformation, she had built an empire and established a more subtle form of Protestantism than her father, Henry VIII. But by the end of the 1580s, despite the seeming progress, the economy was nearly bankrupt, plague was endemic, the Queen was ageing and the national mood had swung. As a remedy against food and hunger riots, two statutes in the summer of 1588 fixed wages and prices. In 1588 a clothworker, for example, earned £5 a year, a brewer twice as much. A schoolmaster might expect £20 a year and a barrister, as much as £600 (litigation was a growth industry). After 1588, though prices were reviewed yearly and continued to rise, wages under statute remained pegged at the 1588 level. During the years of the Rose's heyday, civil disorder, fuelled by the economic malaise, was an uncomfortable reality for authority to face.

The volatility of civic life had for the first time found a regular focus. Londoners now had a public forum – the playhouses, whose plays, were, as Andrew Gurr says, the 'newspapers of the day'. As the theatre developed from its stable London bases, poets fired by the New Learning of the universities latched on to the new drama. Their plays, however obliquely, commented on and made sense of this difficult period of transition. Popular entertainment, the old mummers' plays, the street ballad, the jig, continued to hold their place in the life of the people. The Queen, at Kenilworth in 1572, had been entertained not only by the professional players who formed Leicester's Men, but also by the local men from Coventry in a 'storial show', no doubt much like the Mechanicals' play in *A Midsummer Night's Dream*. The claims of traditional play-making continued to co-exist alongside a new form of drama emerging in the mid-sixteenth century with Nicholas Udall's Plautine comedy, *Ralph Roister Doister* (1553), and Thomas Sackville's and Thomas Norton's Senecan play, *The Tragedy of Gorboduc* (1561), which were distinctly English renderings of their classical models.

The writers of these plays were educated men. Education was essential for the consolidation of the Tudor regime. Scholars had to be persuaded into public life, and courtiers had to be persuaded back into school. The concept of public life had an extraordinary hold on the Elizabethan mind and explains the dominant role played by rhetoric and play-making in the curriculum of the public schools and the universities. Memory was highly cultivated. Public speaking, as an art, was emphasised. The Queen herself was an acknowledged star performer at competitive set orations. In addition, her magnificent processions were unrivalled street theatre. Given such a context, it was inevitable that the university-educated, professional writer would carve his niche in the world of the playhouses.

Their new drama was fostered because of, rather than despite, Puritanism. The Puritans had created a culture where the spoken word was, on its own merits, a major source of entertainment. Stripped of all visual distractions, their churches had become, in the words of Sir Roy Strong, 'preaching boxes'. Revealingly, when the City petitioned the Privy Council to close the playhouses, they spoke of people doing their bad deeds 'under colour of *hearing* a play' (my italics). In the main, audiences were illiterate. Hearing words and seeing pictures was the only way of gaining any information. Andrew Gurr says that the Elizabethans had to invent the words 'spectacle' and 'spectator' to describe the novel experience of watching a play. Playhouses, unlike churches, had words to be heard and pictures to be seen. Nevertheless, when church bells rang from steeples and trumpets sounded from the roofs of the playhouses, a real competition for both audience and congregation was going on. Sermons were popular. They gave the mind something to feed on. Crowds packed the churches when Donne, Andrews or Hooker were at the pulpit. During the span of a century, William Tyndale's early translations of the scriptures, the Authorised Version of the Bible and the book of Common Prayer, had addressed themselves to the task of rendering the vernacular with a majesty worthy of its subject but in an idiom which could be understood by the masses.

Poetry was the dominant mode of literary expression, and theatre provided the meeting ground for the emerging human-ism of the Renaissance and the age-old customs and traditions of popular entertainment. In the 1580s, a wave of writers came out of the universities to take up a professional career writing for the stage. Financial considerations came into play. It was difficult on its own for a poet to make poetry pay. Patronage could not be relied upon. Publishing was a bit of a gamble. Copyright remained vested with the publisher who paid the writers an average of 40s. for a pamphlet. In contrast, playwriting, whilst not the way to make a fortune, was a way of making a living. The demand for plays was insatiable: Philip Henslowe paid from £6 to £10 for a finished script, more than a clothworker made in a year. Thomas Lodge and George Peele came from Oxford to make the theatre their career. Christopher

Marlowe and Thomas Nashe, from Cambridge, followed soon afterwards.

By 1587, theatre had already evolved into a discrete and distinctive new art. London audiences in their thousands had supported Burbage's playhouses in the north, nothing – not plague, pickpockets nor the Puritan curse of everlasting damnation – was likely to break the habit. When Henslowe entered into his deed of partnership with John Cholmley in that year, Bankside, largely because of its accessibility, was a good location. Close by was the only bridge spanning the Thames, London Bridge. Access to the Rose could also easily be gained by river. The Thames was London's main arterial highway: the ferries that plied their trade moved traffic fast and efficiently and Henslowe obviously expected a good proportion of his audience to come by boat. Indeed the fortunes of the Rose Theatre and the men who worked these river taxis were inextricably tied – and Henslowe was to go on to make political capital out of that relationship.

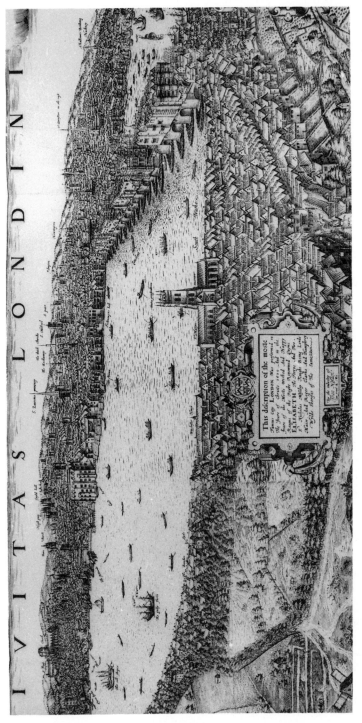

1. View of London, 1600, from *Civitas Londini*, drawn by John Norden. Note the boats on the Thames and the heavily wooded landscape of Bankside. (Royal Library, Stockholm)

Some of the Rose's audience would however be local, drawn from Southwark's thriving community. Southwark in the sixteenth century was an administrative mess, and Philip Henslowe was able to take advantage of this confusion when he built the Rose. Nominally all of Southwark came under the auspices of the Justices of Surrey. On a day-to-day basis, its component parts were effectively governed by one of three manors which comprised the borough. The manor belonging to the Abbey of St Saviour's, which included Bankside, had been granted to the Bishop of Winchester in the twelfth century and was known to Philip Henslowe, who had lived there since the end of the 1570s, as either the Bishop of Winchester's Liberty or Clink Liberty, named after the infamous prison run by the Bishop.

Clink Liberty – like the Liberty of Holywell which housed Burbage's theatres – was an anomalous jurisdictional area, so called after the days when it had once been monastic land. A 'liberty' enjoyed a certain amount of autonomy from both the City of London (and Clink Liberty anyway was outside City boundaries) and also from the Justices of the county – in this case Surrey – who technically had overall jurisdiction. The Bishop of Winchester within his Liberty had his own court to try law-breakers and his own prison in which to incarcerate them. Even by the standards of the day, the Clink (still slang for gaol) was particularly unpleasant. It was low lying, close to the river, underground and formed part of the common sewer. John Stow, a contemporary archivist, wrote in 1598 that the Clink 'was a prison for such as should brabble or frey, or break the peace of the Bank'.

The reality, as Philip Henslowe would have known, was that Bankside was mainly a law unto itself. The noxious Clink should have been a deterrent to law-breakers. So too should the spectacle of the many severed heads stuck on poles aloft the Southwark end of London Bridge. Nevertheless Southwark was outlaw country. It was close enough to the City to be an attractive bolthole for those on the run, yet outside the close organisation of its civic life and the long arm of its law. Southwark had always been a place for the dispossessed and the outcast; for fugitives from justice or religious persecution; for unlicensed traders and masterless men. Wat Tyler came through Southwark in 1381, and Jack Cade in 1451 made the White Hart Inn in Borough High Street his headquarters. Even as late as 1848, the Chartists were to find Southwark a place where few questions were asked.

One of the besetting problems for the City was that the Privy Council had made it clear that the City would be held accountable for all disorder in the capital, even in the liberties and suburbs outside the City walls where the Corporation had no power to impose its will. Failure to do so might result in the Privy Council unilaterally snatching away the City's historic rights. The City had tried in the past to meet the Privy Council's expectations for a quiet life in Southwark, by buying all of Edward VI's royal properties in the borough in 1550, thus gaining certain rights from the more lenient Justices of Surrey. Indeed, the City's jurisdiction might then have prevailed in Southwark were it not for the presence of the 'liberties'.

It does seem extraordinary, given the huge social and revolutionary turmoil in the years after the Reformation, that these ancient and contentious anomalies should still have been preserved to bedevil civic life. Rather typically, A.L. Rowse says that this 'is so like the conservatism of the English'. The result of such 'conservatism' was fortuitous anarchy for any prospective theatre owner. This impossible situation probably accounts for the City's constant nagging complaints to the Privy Council about the new playhouses, whose building the Privy Council had actively encouraged in the first place. It would appear that almost the first duty of an incoming Lord Mayor was to pen a letter to the Privy Council objecting to them.

Bankside, then, had a lot going for it as a location for Henslowe's proposed playhouse. It was accessible. In winter, it had the edge over Burbage's theatres. Burbage's audience always thought of the Theatre and the Curtain as being 'in the countrye' and found the way muddy and unpleasant in that season. Bankside was as free from harassment by City authorities as any part of London was likely to be. And Southwark already had a long established tradition of purveying entertainment. In the Middle Ages, its churches were centres for performing Miracle and Mystery plays. Pilgrims travelling to Canterbury stayed the night in the many inns on Borough High Street and were no doubt diverted indoors by jugglers, clowns and the like, while buskers were quick to seize an opportunity to pass around the hat outside in the yards.

South London even had its own theatre before Philip

Henslowe came along. In 1576 Peter Hunningborne established a playhouse, of sorts, at Newington Butts, a mile down the Kent Road. Not much is known about this venue except that it did not find much favour with any players. It was probably in completely the wrong location. Indeed, the Privy Council sympathised about the 'tediousnes of the waie' for audiences having to trek so far south of London Bridge.

Purpose-built arenas for bear-baiting located on Bankside were much closer to London life and were already in existence when Philip Henslowe negotiated a lease for the Rose messuage. The first reference to this grisly spectacle on Bankside is found predictably enough in an order of 1546 banning it. Consistent with the Tudor ability for having it both ways, in the same year, one Thomas Fluddie was granted a licence to 'make pastime' with the king's bears 'at the accustomed place in London', i.e. Bankside. By 1598, John Stow reported that 'there be the two Beare Gardens, the old and the new places . . .'. He described the arenas as 'plottes of grounde, scaffolded about for the beholders to stand safe'. What with severed heads on poles and bears baited to death, we have enough evidence of the Elizabethan taste for barbarity. Yet the Renaissance was also a time of great cultural change. Set against the barbarity of bear-baiting, one has to consider the voices raised in protest. In 1550, for example, the poet, Robert Crowley, wrote that bear-baiting was 'a full ouglye sight' and that those who paid a penny to watch the 'terrible tearynge' were 'the mooste fooles of all'. When it came to entertainment, the Elizabethan public, not all of them fools, were ready to accept an alternative.

By the end of the 1580s, Bankside had developed a professional interest in all the diversions of the flesh, and the area had emerged as the Reeperbahn of Tudor London. As early as 1528, Bishop Richard Fox wrote a letter to Cardinal Wolsey, to deny all accusations of lawlessness within his diocese, and added revealingly, 'except at Southwark', as if that were only to be expected. Indeed, successive Bishops of Winchester enjoyed an income from Southwark's taverns and stews. They specified the opening hours (not when Parliament was sitting) and laid down the rules. Any attempt to entice men into a brothel was punishable by the substantial fine of 20s. (or twice that if the brothel-keeper's wife did the enticing) and no whore was to remain within the Liberty on Holy Days (except at lunchtime). The popular slang for London whores became 'the Bishop of Winchester's geese'.

A pious wish lay behind the various ordinances aimed at controlling this red light culture, and it aimed at reducing the 'gret multiplicacion of orrible synne unpn the single woman'. Attempts, however, by either the Privy Council or the City to clean up the area existed side by side with the almost palpable sense of relief that brothels were, after all, better off confined south of the river. The tolerant, not to say cynical, jurisdiction of Church authorities in 1576 had already turned a blind eye to the fact that by selling the former convent of St Mary Overie to the Montagues, an old Roman Catholic family, it had provided a refuge and nest for recalcitrant recusants. If the Church could put up with Roman Catholics as its neighbours, it could easily continue to live cheek by jowl with the Bishop of Winchester's geese. For Philip Henslowe, who also owned, if not brothels, then at least buildings in which brothels were housed, exploiting the potential of Bankside was a calculated gamble that turned out to be a shrewd business move. The time was ripe for someone to tackle James Burbage's monopoly.

Philip Henslowe is a frustratingly enigmatic man as his Diary reveals. The Diary first belonged to his brother, John, who used it to keep accounts of his mining and smelting affairs in Ashdown Forest during the years 1575 – 1581. John Henslowe died in 1592 and Philip inherited his book. It is at this date that Henslowe started to keep a record of his own business operations. On Henslowe's death in 1616, it passed to his son-in-law, Edward Alleyn, and thus it came to form part of the library of the College of God's Gift, the charitable foundation established by Alleyn in Dulwich. For centuries, the Diary was kept inside a chest in the College's Big Hall whilst generations of school boys played leapfrog over the collection of priceless manuscripts. 'Neglect,' says Margaret Slythe, the college librarian, 'has a way of preserving things.' In the later years of the eighteenth century, the literary critic Edmond Malone, 'discovered' the Diary. His researches with Shakespeare's original cultural context are largely responsible for the industry of scholarship which has overtaken English Studies in academia. Henslowe's Diary, despite its name, is, in fact, not a journal of daily events but a record of accounts. Interspersed with the various box office receipts and the company loans are a number of strange recipes and charms; 'To make a fowle fall dead' and 'A Rewle to Knowe vnder what planet A chillde is

11

borne in'. They indicate that secret superstitious side which so often is found in the man of business. The Diary is one of the few extant pieces of hard evidence about Elizabethan theatre and thus a major document of primary source material. 'My Bible' is how the Diary is described by John Barton, Associate Director of the Royal Shakespeare Company.

During his life, Henslowe adopted many identities so it is not surprising that the first sheet of his Diary is given over to doodles and experimental signatures – sometimes his own, sometimes other people's. Among the scribbles is the sardonic comment, 'when I lent I wasse A friend & when I asked I wasse unkind'. It is as well to bear in mind this reflection of Henslowe's when attempting to assess his character.

Henslowe recorded the life of the Rose Theatre after 1592 almost daily on 242 pages wrapped in limp vellum. Whilst theatre workers are grateful that Henslowe kept his profit and loss sheets up to date, scholars have been quick to condemn the man for so doing. The Diary has given rise to a lineage of interpretation which Carol Rutter traces to F. G. Fleay's character assassination in 1890. Fleay then described Henslowe as 'an illiterate moneyed man . . . who regarded art as a subject for exploitation'; a crushing judgement in Victorian England, when serious writing for the theatre was in a state of terminal decline. This interpretation of Henslowe then went on to cloud criticism of the repertoire produced at Henslowe's theatre, obscuring its claim to attention whilst allowing sometimes excessive praise of the undoubted achievements at the rival Globe. Where Shakespeare and his fellows at the Globe 'sought to produce plays of lasting interest', Fleay opined that Henslowe's only 'object was to fill his own pocket'.

Both theatres would have been taken aback by Fleay's praise and vilification alike. Given what was then the extremely short history of professional drama in England plus the exigencies of getting any play on, even Shakespeare would have been as dumbfounded at the notion of 'plays of lasting interest' as he would have been baffled by the notion that there was anything wrong with filling his own pocket. This image of Henslowe as a *parvenu,* a man on the make, a ruthless exploiter of sensitive artists, persisted. Walter W. Greg who first edited the Diary in 1904 took up the baton from Fleay, and successive generations of scholars have embroidered their own variants of 'illiterate' and 'moneyed'.

Even in fiction, the character of Henslowe has been traduced on the basis of the undisputed historical fact that the man kept accounts. Caryl Brahms and S.J. Simon in their jointly written novel, *No Bed for Bacon,* imagine a Henslowe inseparable from his accounts. '. . . in his bedroom, Philip Henslowe awoke to find his pillow hard and pressing into his head. He moved it. It turned out to be his account book.' The same image of 'Henslowe with his eternal cash book' is deployed by Anthony Burgess in the novel, *Nothing Like the Sun.* Burgess calls him a 'brothel-keeper who would brood over a lost farthing'. Both novels set up the added joke that Henslowe, for all his obsession with making money by exploiting writers, lets the young William Shakespeare slip out of his sight as if Shakespeare was on a par with the unfortunate Henry Chettle, an over-commissioned writer in his day who is now understandably condemned to total obscurity.

It is true that Henslowe's handwriting, even by Elizabethan flexible standards, is appalling. Robert Bower, a much later citizen of Bankside and amateur author of a revealing history of Southwark, tactfully if complacently says, from the perspective of 1902, that: 'In those days writing was not so good as in mine'. However, by comparison, companion documents at Dulwich College written in the hand of Henslowe's son-in-law, the actor Edward Alleyn, are quite legible and prove that in those days, writing was possibly as good or as bad as at any other time. Henslowe's spelling lacks consistency, even in the ways in which he spells his own name, but it is not much more inconsistent than Elizabethan spelling in general. Sometimes, Henslowe forgets to change the date at the start of the year and uses the old year's date well into the new, an understandable slip of the memory. Whilst reasons abound to explain Henslowe's motivation in keeping a Diary, the one motive that can safely be rejected is Henslowe's wish to explain himself to posterity. Most probably all the Elizabethan theatre landlords kept account books – it is only Henslowe's which has survived. The recent editors of the Diary, R. A. Foakes and R. T. Rickert (1961) warn against 'doubtful assumptions and dubious interpretations'. 'Clearly', says Carol Rutter, 'Philip Henslowe has suffered at the hands of the scholars.'

The image of Henslowe as grasping, mercenary and uncultured has a stubborn life of its own. C. Walter Hodges at a symposium held to discuss the excavation of the Rose Theatre in April, 1989, said, 'I have always gone along with the common understanding that he was a colourful semi-underworld figure who lent out money – it fitted the rumbustious, rather old-fashioned view of Elizabethan theatre as a colourful place in the underworld.' Andrew Gurr at the same symposium admitted that Henslowe had suffered from a bad press although, as Carol Rutter points out, Gurr was one of those scholars who contributed to the bad press by conflating Henslowe's loans to the company with the company's separate commissions to writers. Gurr then went on disapprovingly to describe Henslowe as someone who deliberately 'kept in close touch with several hack writers'.

Once the story of the discovery of the Rose foundations had broken in the press, the media tended to treat Henslowe as a wholly admirable, even an heroic, character. Perhaps a more democratic age can respond sympathetically to the story of a basically unlettered man who turned a straightforward business venture into one of the most successful playhouses in Elizabethan London. It may be, however, that the rehabilitation of Philip Henslowe is yet another recasting of the man in the image of its age. These days, a Philip Henslowe at the helm of subsidised theatre, would seem an attractive proposition in the face of cutbacks in funding and the subsequent increasing need for business sponsorship.

Literary and theatrical tastes have changed as well. The writers at the Rose were virtually inventing the form of a five-act play as they went along. For centuries, their plays, which included Shakespeare's early works, remained unperformed. Dr Johnson, for example, called *Titus Andronicus* 'a barbaric pageant'. T.S. Eliot called it 'one of the stupidest and most uninspiring plays ever written'. A revival at the Old Vic in 1923 was greeted with hearty laughter. *Henry VI*, in all its parts, was similarly neglected. The RSC finally introduced it, heavily adapted, in the repertoire as part of their 1963 *Wars of the Roses* package. Effectively the RSC's 1976 production of the whole trilogy was like a second premiere and casting was problematic because few actors or agents were familiar with all the parts.

Beyond the Diary itself, little is known about the man whose theatre gave Shakespeare his first break. Even Henslowe's date of birth is unknown, but he grew up in the Ashdown Forest as the younger son of the Master of Game. By 1577 he was living in the Liberty of Clink apprenticed to Harry Woodward, upon whose death he remained as servant to the widow, Agnes. Sometime in the mid 1580s, 'she havinge a likinge or affection (for him) did . . . marrie and take him to husband.' Agnes was older than her husband, and there were no children of that marriage. She had, however, if not a fertile womb, then wealth enough, which under Henslowe's management could go forth and multiply. Almost immediately, he started on a series of financial adventures. In 1584 he and Richard Nicolson, a leather dresser, entered into a partnership to convert goatskins into Spanish leather. Henslowe also acquired an interest in starch manufacture, diversified into farming interests in Gloucestershire, kept up an involvement in his brother's mining affairs in Ashdown Forest, but mainly, he concentrated on building up a portfolio of properties in the Liberty of Clink. Unexpectedly one of them hit the jackpot.

On 24 March 1585, Philip Henslowe took a lease on the Rose messuage for a period of twenty-one years and at an annual rent of £7. This estate, bounded to the south by Maid – or Maiden – Lane, and to the west by Rose Alley, can be traced back to 1552 when its then owner, Thomasyn Symonds, widow of a fishmonger, in keeping with the charitable instinct of the age, gave it to the parish of St Mildred in Bread Street. It is described in this deed as a 'messuage or tennement . . . with twoe gardens'.

2. Deed of Partnership between Philip Henslowe and John Cholmley, 1587. It measures about 2' x 1½' (Dulwich College, by permission of the Governors)

A messuage then was a portion of land intended as a site for a dwelling house and its appurtances. A 'tennement' in Tudor times could embrace anything held in tenure from freehold on the land to actual buildings. Neither the messuage known as the 'little rose', or the later Rose Theatre, gave the name to Rose Alley. It had long been called thus after the large and notorious brothel which had existed on the north-western side of Rose Alley since the Middle Ages. E.K. Chambers said that Thomasyn Symonds's bequest, referred to as the Rose messuage, consisted by then of an actual rose garden. M.C. Bradbrook, however, asserted that the rose garden was attached to an inn. Both may be right: from 1574 until 1587, the land was leased out to vintners and it is likely that they ran a tap house of sorts on the site. Maybe at times, entertainment may have been provided for customers in the rose garden. This may have alerted Henslowe to the site's real potential. The Deed of Partnership drawn up by Philip Henslowe and John Cholmley on 10 January 1587 assigned to Cholmley the use of a 'dwellinge howsse' situated at the 'sowthe ende' to keep his victualling in. Perhaps a house in the south had long existed for this purpose.

John Cholmley is described in this document as a 'citizen and grocer'. The Deed, in itself, is evidence that Henslowe had substantial backing already and had no need of further financial aid to realise his scheme of building a playhouse on Bankside. His partnership though with Richard Nicolson (the goatskin converter) had perhaps accustomed him to working in tandem and Henslowe was not necessarily to know that opening a playhouse south of the river – opening *any* new playhouse in Tudor London – was to prove so successful. He also had the example of James Burbage. Burbage had built the Theatre in partnership with John Brayne who was also a grocer. Henslowe assigned to Cholmley all the profits from the sale of 'any breade or drinke', whilst Cholmley agreed to pay Henslowe a total of £816, in quarterly instalments of £25. 10s, over an eight-and-a-quarter-year period. This may be Cholmley's contribution towards the overall costs of building the playhouse or it may also include an allowance towards the catering concession.

The Deed of Partnership has little to say about policies to do with the theatre and concerns itself almost entirely with the distribution of profits and the assignment of financial responsibilities. Philip Henslowe accepted all charges relating to the playhouse, 'now in framinge and shortly to be erreckte'. The Deed, obviously a result of much hammering out, resulted in a joint agreement between them to share the task of appointing 'such personne & personnes players to vse exersyse & playe in the saide playe howse'. Both should either be present at performances, or make sure a deputy was, in order to agree on the take.

Allowing for complimentary tickets to their personal friends, Cholmley and Henslowe agreed to split their portion of the box office fifty-fifty. So, provided that Cholmley's share of the box office plus his proceeds from bread and drink, equalled his quarterly instalments of £25. 10s, he was in clover. Anything over and above this represented pure profit. The agreement was not due to expire until 1595 but it may well be that Cholmley himself had expired long before this date, perhaps during a recurrence of the plague. Or it is possible that Cholmley had fallen behind with his quarterly payments in which case Henslowe had the right to take full possession: 'To renter And the saide John Cholmley ... vtterly to expell.' Perhaps Cholmley was not the first caterer to discover that he had been over optimistic about an audience's eating and drinking capacity. Either way, the Diary, begun in 1592, does not record any mention of the grocer, Cholmley. The monies that Henslowe and Cholmley divided fifty-fifty between them would not have been the *total* box office revenue. Generally, it was only the income generated by admission to the galleries which went to the proprietor(s) – and even then he retained only half, the other half going to the players. Much later on, long after Cholmley ceased to figure in the life of the Rose, Henslowe in his Diary recorded when he began to take his receipts for *all* of the gallery. The entry marks a change in practice from the traditional half share for reasons which will be discussed later on.

The pennies raised from audiences in the yard, on the other hand, went directly to the actors. Thomas Platter, a visitor from Basle in the year 1599, reported that at the Globe, 'whoever cares to stand below pays one English penny but if he wishes to sit he enters by another door, and pays another penny. Whilst if he desires to sit in the most comfortable seats which are cushioned where he not only sees everything well, but can also be seen, then he pays another penny.' The Globe which was built in the year of Platter's visit, no doubt based its three-tier pricing policy on the neighbouring Rose.

17

With the exception of the clause which allowed Henslowe's and Cholmley's friends 'to go in for nothinge', the Deed is significant for its lack of enthusiasm about plays themselves. Henslowe, as a businessman, had, no doubt, observed that money could be made out of theatre audiences and, why not by him? The Deed is casual in the extreme on the matter of negotiating any usage of the Rose and in no way does it indicate the future impressario that Henslowe was to try to become. It could be any business document. At the time of signing the magnificent and impressive Deed of Partnership, the Rose Theatre was being built in prefabricated sections ('in framinge') and about to be erected and furnished. Since Henslowe did not start to keep his Diary until 1592, we do not know what happened in its first five years.

There are, however, possible clues to the Rose's early history to be found in a number of other documents collated by Carol Rutter. For example if the Rose was open for business in the spring of 1587, it might have been the cause of the Privy Council Minute dated 7 May 1587. This Minute issued a restraint forcibly closing all theatres on the pretext of the weather getting 'hotter and hotter' at a time when there was a 'danger of infection'. 'Certain outrages and disorders' committed 'in certaine places and Theaters erected' were, however, cited as further reasons. As the Rose was the only theatre to have recently been erected, then it is fair to infer that the Rose was one of the theatres forced to close that summer.

When the plague was at its height, playhouses were closed. Plague scythed its way through England with unaccustomed ferocity beginning in the year 1563. It never really went away and recurred every second or third year. Medical science offered no solutions. It was generally seen as God's judgement and most remedies were based on nothing more than superstition. The actor, Edward Alleyn, advised hanging herbs in the windows and watering the doorsteps daily – a token stab at common sense hygiene. Philip Henslowe knew of 'A good dryncke for the pestelence'. (The recipe involves a lily root boiled in white wine.) Plague was carried by fleas living on rats, and the thatched roofs of the playhouses were, no doubt, home to colonies of them. Nothing much really could be done to avert plague, and, when it struck, London became a necropolis. When deaths exceeded more than thirty a week, the Privy

Council and the City made common cause and looked to the theatres as a major source of infection. 1587 was not however a particularly bad year for plague, so it seems all the more likely that these unspecified 'outrages and disorders' lay at the heart of the Privy Council's edict. Despite the rallying patriotism of the coming war on the high seas, the mood in London was unsettled.

During the 'lost' years of 1587 to 1592, the Rose most probably was used for putting on plays, rather than animal-baiting or simply standing empty. Although the 1587 building was crude in some respects, it had some significant touches. The rake of its yard was audience-friendly and the carpenter, John Griggs, responsible for building the Rose, had erected a fixed stage.

The probability that Henslowe had installed players in his theatre is heightened in another Privy Council Minute addressed to the Justices of Surrey, written later in the same year of 1587. It passed on complaints from local people on Bankside about plays in general being performed on the Sabbath, and in particular, it mentioned plays 'within the libertie of the Clincke', presumably, therefore, at the new Rose Theatre. Objections to playing on the Sabbath were to be expected (indeed they still carry weight today). On the matter of ungodliness, the City could – and did – muster any number of objections to the theatres. The City argued that its youth was 'greatly corrupted, their manners infected with many evils and ungodly qualities by the wanton things they saw onstage, apprentices and servants were withdrawn from their work, to the great hindrance of trade and religion; besides harlots, cutpurses, cozeners, pilferers etc. did their bad deeds under colour of hearing a play'. Puritan sensibilities were outraged at the noise of playhouse trumpets cutting through the solemn tolling of church bells to entice congregations away from prayer. But the City was always on a stronger wicket when it stuck to arguments concerning either plague or the playhouse's potential for riot and disorder.

A month after the Privy Council's Minute reminding the Surrey Justices to enforce observance of the Lord's Day, a law student, called Philip Gawdy, wrote a letter dated 16 November 1587, which perhaps gives us another glimpse of life at the Rose in its first year. Gawdy described a disastrous accident. He had witnessed, at an unnamed playhouse, a stage effect for an equally unnamed play. It called for an actor to be shot onstage. The actor with the 'devyse' for shooting, swerved and inadvertently killed a child and a pregnant woman in the audience. Could this have taken place at the Rose? On the one hand, Gawdy said that the actor who should have been shot was tied to a post, and we now know that the 1587 Rose was a relatively simple structure and amongst other things, it did not have stage posts (though that would not prevent a resourceful stage manager providing a post specifically for this purpose). On the other hand, Gawdy did name the playing company responsible for this tragedy. It was the Admiral's Men, a company that in the years to come was to be primarily associated with the Rose.

Philip Gawdy ended his letter by pointing the sad moral that 'never comes more hurte than commes of fooling' and draws the familiar conclusion that the tragedy was God's judgement on an ungodly profession. Shortly after this incident, early in the New Year of 1588, Richard Jones, a member of the Admiral's Men who might have taken part in that tragic performance, sold to Edward Alleyn, a fellow member of the same company, all his 'playinge apparrelles playe Bookes, Instrumentes, and other commodities', for the sum of £37. 10s. Alleyn's brother, the innkeeper John, helped finance the deal. Robert Browne, another player with the Admiral's Men, was at that time touring Europe with part of the company, and perhaps Richard Jones planned to join them, leaving those remaining in England to re-organise their future. Edward Alleyn was to go on to become the most celebrated actor of the day with a re-formed company under the patronage of the Lord Admiral, creating a succession of parts, mainly written by Christopher Marlowe, which made the Rose famous in the coming decade.

Edward Alleyn was born in 1566, the son of a Bishopsgate innkeeper. Described as one, 'bred a stage player', he took up the acting profession in 1582 with Worcester's Men. By invest-ing in Richard Jones's theatrical assets, Edward Alleyn at the age of 22 was taking a leaf out of James Burbage's book. At a year younger, James's son Richard was to be Alleyn's main rival but in 1588, he had the backing of a theatrical dynasty in the making. Leicester's Men, the chief company of the 1570s had, by the 1580s, given way to the Queen's Men (with Richard Tarleton, the clown). The 1590s, however, would see two rival companies battle it out for prominence: the Admiral's Men led by Edward Alleyn, and the Chamberlain's Men led by Richard

Burbage. Personnel frequently interchanged, and the company's name changed as the patron's fortune changed. At times, the comings and goings of the various companies and their patrons makes the movements of individual actors almost too confusing to follow. It is probable that in 1588 Alleyn's purchase of theatrical stock indicated that he was keeping a very watchful eye on developments south of the river.

A playing company in Tudor England mixed the best characteristics of the Elizabethan trade guilds and the later communes. A sharer was the best position for an actor to be in. As the name suggests, a sharer was one who had invested his money in the company and shared in its profits. Sharers collectively decided policy and took all the major roles. Sharers were financially responsible for the costumes, scripts, wages of the hired men and fees for play licences (though not theatre licences – they were the responsibility of the landlord). Rental of a theatre was usually a percentage of the gallery income.

Shares had a precise value, and they could be high. In 1595, £50 was the price of a share in each of the two leading companies, the Admiral's Men and the Chamberlain's Men, which should be compared to the £60 that Shakespeare paid for New Place, a substantial house in Stratford that he bought in 1597. To prevent an actor making off with important assets (playscripts or costumes) a former sharer would be reimbursed for his share when he left. Although there were lean seasons, when times were good the sharer benefited far more than the hired actor. Sharers sometimes made as much as £1 a week although this would only mean an annual income of £52 in the unlikely event of continuous work being available. In addition, there were extra fees to be made from performances at Court and in private houses.

The core group of sharers usually featured about eight men. The entire company would be at least twice that. Intelligent doubling in an all male troupe can cope with the large cast demands of the Elizabethan play. Hired men and boys made up the numbers. The hired men were as experienced and probably as talented as the sharers and earned a fixed rate. E.K. Chambers gives this as between 5s. and 8s. a week. William Kendall, for example, was taken on by Alleyn's company in 1597 for 10s. a week in London, and 5s. a week when on tour, 'in the Cuntrie'. As theatre in London proliferated, companies became keen for hired men to commit themselves for long periods. Rivals were quick to poach good actors, and Kendall had to sign up for an exclusive two-year contract. Reneging on the deal was punishable by a substantial forfeit. At that point in time, Kendall was also expected to be 'redy att all Tymes' without any retainer. Later on, Alleyn's company was prepared to pay half wages if the hired men were forced to 'lye stylle' for over two weeks.

The boy apprentices represented the company's stake in the future. Their apprenticeships were not legal and binding and they were personally indentured to an adult actor, not the company. The actor treated the boy as part servant and part pupil and, in Edward Alleyn's case, took on a parental role. Alleyn's wife took a motherly interest in the boys when they were on tour and, in her letters to Alleyn, asked if 'Nicke and Jeames be well & commend them'. John Pigg, another boy, wrote her back an affectionate, joking reply. The account in Henslowe's Diary of the boy, James Bristow, 'Bowght' by Henslowe from the actor, William Augusten in 1597 for the sum of £8, was avidly seized on in 1989 by journalists following the story of the Rose. It made for sensational reading. In effect, the sale meant that Bristow's indentures were transferred from one to the other rather than that Henslowe was indulging in a little slave-trading. For his £8, Henslowe received the boy's wages of 3s. a week and in turn, he provided the boy with bed and board. Boys played the women's roles and, if the company was fully stretched, also some adult roles. The boys filled in as spear carriers, messengers and the rank and file of armies. Scholars who focus on the Rose tend to challenge Elizabethan theatre orthodoxy and Carol Rutter, for example, has a theory that mature female roles such as Cleopatra were played by young adult male actors, rather than boy apprentices.

Actors valued their comrades. In their wills, they bequeathed one another money, jewellery, musical instruments and choice costumes. Thomas Towne, a member of Alleyn's company, left the magnificent sum of £3 'To make them a supper when it shall please them to call for it.' The players were thrown into each other's company a lot. It was a volatile time for the playing companies as the 1580s came to an end. Many of them broke up and re-formed as plague was ever present, exiling players from London for long touring periods. Although Alleyn in 1588 had aligned himself with Lord Strange's Men, he continued to refer to himself as 'seruant to the lord Admiral'. Charles Howard, who had commanded the fleet against the Armada, was appointed Admiral in 1585, the year he first patronised a company of players. The Admiral's Men temporarily disbanded in 1588 with some players crossing the Channel leaving others, like Alleyn, forced to amalgamate with other companies.

Alleyn's loyalty to the Lord Admiral never wavered. The relationship between the player and his men was necessary under statute but it was a purely formal arrangement. The 'lords Rome' is an echo of a patriarchal connection which had little grounding in the reality of the arrangement. Technically the players came under their patron's protection but most of the

3.   A portrait of Edward Alleyn, preserved at Dulwich College which he founded. The agate ring prominently shown on Alleyn's right hand is worn by the Master every Founder's Day and until the 1870s, it was the custom for the Master to adopt the surname, Alleyn or Allen, in honour of Edward Alleyn. (Dulwich College. By permission of the Governors)

time, they were on their own. It is a measure, perhaps, of the personal friendship between Lord Howard and Edward Alleyn, that Howard much later on, in 1600, intervened directly in the players' affairs. One of the advantages of friendship for an aristocratic patron was the off-duty relaxation he could find with a man socially his inferior, but culturally, his equal. Although the players in *Hamlet* are not Hamlet's Men, their free and easy way with the Prince, and the Prince's free and easy way with them, suggests the sort of relationship enjoyed by Edward Alleyn and his patron which accounts for Alleyn's steadfast identification with the Lord Admiral.

The Martin Marprelate controversy of 1589 involved actors, writers, Puritans, the Master of the Revels, the Star Chamber itself and, no doubt, the Rose Theatre. The Master of the Revels was a position set up in 1494 and further strengthened in 1545 when it became part of the 'standing offices' under the Lord Chamberlain. He acted as censor. Edmund Tilney held the post from 1579 until his death in 1610. Scripts had to be approved by him after payment of a reading fee of 5s., which by the end of the century, had increased to 7s., an extortionate amount compared to the £6-£10 that a writer might expect to receive – at the very most – for having written the play in the first place. Seven shillings represented almost ten per cent of the writer's commission. Tilney also collected licence fees for the playhouse buildings, which like the reading fees, increased as the century waned. A proprietor like Philip Henslowe at first paid £2 a month for his licence for the Rose. By 1599, he was paying £1 more. In its way, the licence fee was a form of protection money. Other perks came Tilney's way. Henslowe in his Diary records that in 1601 he had to grease the palm of the 'clarke of the cownselle's' hand with 7s. before the clerk coughed up the performance fee earned by Worcester's Men for appearing at Court that Christmas.

In the early months of 1589, an anonymous group of radical Puritans conducted a literary war against the episcopacy, signing their satirical pamphlets under the pseudonym of Martin Marprelate. The war spread to the stages and exchanges became more embittered and vitriolic as playwrights like John Lyly, Robert Greene and Thomas Nashe (all later to be associated with the Rose in Henslowe's Diary), weighed in against the Martinists. The Privy Council were alarmed thinking that people who were vehement about disposing of their bishops, if provoked further from public platforms, might well go on to think about disposing of their Queen. In February, they called for the suppression of all material relating to Martin Marprelate, including the 'staie of all playes'. The Lord Mayor of London, Sir John Harte, was given the unenviable burden of carrying out this thankless task. In a letter to Lord Burghley, dated 6 November, he reported that he had sent for 'suche players as I coulde here of', but that only two had bothered to turn up. The Admiral's Men obediently agreed to 'forbere playinge', but Lord Strange's Men openly defied the Lord Mayor and played that very afternoon at the Cross Keys Inn. Six days later the Privy Council ordered that all scripts should be surrendered. The Star Chamber was brought in and asked the Archbishop of Canterbury to join forces with both Edmund Tilney, and a nominee of the Lord Mayor, to read the plays and 'stryke oute or reforme' anything which offended against either divinity or the state. Failure to comply with this edict would result in a total ban on playing 'forever hereafter'.

The Admiral's Men were evidently in business at the time of the Martin Marprelate controversy, perhaps staging provocative works by Lyly, Greene or Nashe. If Alleyn was with them, and treading the boards of the Rose at this time, he might also have been in a less provocative play, Thomas Kyd's *The Spanish Tragedy*. Kyd wrote the play sometime around 1585-9 and the part of Hieronimo was made so famous by Alleyn that later, in Henslowe's Diary, the play is always referred to by its hero's name, 'Jeronymo'. Evidently, Alleyn's impact was such that, in a tale recounted by F.P. Wilson, a young woman who had caught the theatre-going habit so badly that she saw a play a day, cried out on her death bed – she died young – 'Oh Hieronimo, Hieronimo, methinks I see thee, brave Hieronimo' and 'fixing her eyes intentively, as if she had seen Hieronimo acted, (sent) out a deep sigh . . . (and) suddenly died.' By 1589 'Jeronymo' had created enough of a stir in literary circles for Thomas Nashe to cast a cold critical eye on this 'English Seneca', whilst also administering a passing blow to that other up and coming Rose writer, Christopher Marlowe.

4. A statue of Edward Alleyn in his famous role of Barabas in Christopher Marlowe's *The Jew of Malta* erected in Dane John Gardens within the City of Canterbury. (Dulwich College. By permission of the Governors)

At the beginning of the 1590s, Edward Alleyn joined forces with the Burbages at the Theatre in a company that probably consisted of Lord Strange's Men (formed in 1589) and whoever was left over from the disbanded Admiral's Men, and together they played under the name of Strange's Men. James Burbage had, by 1591, two grown sons in the business. Richard, the actor, was 24 and his brother, Cuthbert, who went into theatre management was, at 25, the same age as Alleyn. James Burbage was a tyrannical landlord at his Theatre, prepared to use fisticuffs and broomsticks in defence of his rights. He was an enthusiastic litigant and equally enthusiastic about outwitting the law. He passed on this quarrelsome gene to both sons. In 1591 an argument took place 'in the Attyring housse or place where the players make them ready'. James Burbage took issue with Alleyn about the division of money and ended up insulting the Lord Admiral to Alleyn's face before driving the actor from his theatre. John Alleyn, Edward's brother, was witness to this disgrace to family honour. It is possible that the quarrel marked a new phase in the Alleyn/Burbage relationship. From what looks like a friendly rivalry between two actors contending for the laurel wreath (shades of the young Olivier and Gielgud), a family-based vendetta may have sprung up, which eventually was to prove fatal for the long-term future of the Rose.

In the meantime, however, it meant that Edward Alleyn and Lord Strange's Men were without a theatre base in London at a time when Philip Henslowe, after what no doubt seemed a chaotic start to his career as a theatre proprietor, lacked a resident company. Lord Strange's Men were clearly at the zenith of their fortunes and it must have been something of a *coup* when, on 19 February 1592, Edward Alleyn triumphantly led his company to Bankside. It was at this point that Henslowe started to keep an account of his income and expenditure in the Diary. He may have done this for any number of reasons. Perhaps Alleyn's arrival with a resident company had something to do with it. Alleyn, after all, had just fallen out with the Burbages about the way in which the box office had been shared out at the Theatre, and Henslowe would be anxious to avoid similar conflicts at the Rose. R.A. Foakes and R.T. Rickert think that the record of performances and income was for the benefit of the Master of the Revels. On a more practical level, 1592 was the year that Henslowe's brother died and Henslowe inherited the book which already enshrined his brother's regular accounts. But 1592 was also the year in which Henslowe embarked on an expensive building programme and perhaps, as is natural, he wanted to check income against expenditure.

That very same year, 1592, the Rose Theatre was enlarged and the stage was roofed at the not inconsiderable cost of £105, only five years after it was built. Why did Henslowe do this? The 1587 structure had been relatively crude as it was built at a midway stage in the development of London theatres, but more importantly, Henslowe may have been making ready for the arrival of Edward Alleyn with his bigger plays and bigger audiences. Henslowe's new stage roof could now incorporate the new stage technology – the 'heavens'.

The accounts for February 1592 registered by Philip Henslowe are exhaustive. They itemise the cost of nails, lime, thatch, sand and deal boards. They list wages to the workmen, the thatcher, and the bricklayer. They detail just about everything, but they do not specifically mention a 'heavens'. However later in the Diary, accounts dated December and January 1595 do mention that Henslowe then paid carpenters for 'mackinge the throne in the heuenes'; this suggests that the 'heavens' were already in position but either throneless or in need of a new throne in 1595. The 'heavens', which by 1616 Ben Jonson had come to deride for its creaking cumbersomeness, was, in 1592, the very latest thing. It was a hoisting device which enabled a throne or other vehicle to be lowered from the roof above the stage. Ernest Rhodes quotes a stage direction from the Rose play, *Alphonsus of Aragon* (1594), which has Venus confidently descending from the heavens and is followed by the less confident direction: 'Exit Venus. Or if you can conveniently, let a chair come down from the top of the stage and draw her up.' Coming down from the heavens was evidently one thing, but going back up quite another.

Henslowe thatched the hut which contained his 'heavens' and provided the actors with shelter from either the pelting rain or glaring sun. He also paid for a shed at the tiring house (dressing room) door to store costumes and props. He had both the room over the tiring house and the Lord's Room plastered. (Was my Lord Admiral expected to visit?) He painted the stage. He bought a ship's mast to fly his flag emblazoned with the sign of a rose, which John Norden, the panoramist, later mistook for a star. He paid for a barge, which Peter Thomson suggests may have been used to advertise the plays, in much the same way that today's buses trundle round the metropolis with posters reminding Londoners what's on in the West End.

Lord Strange's Men opened at the end of February 1592 and played a prolonged season which extended until 23 June. At first they relied on old standbys in the repertoire, like Robert Greene's *Friar Bungay and Friar Bacon* and *Orlando Furioso* and Marlowe's *The Jew of Malta*. Before the initial month was out, new plays had been rehearsed and were ready for performance. Shakespeare's *Henry VI* proved an instant crowd-puller on 3 March. Any play that made Henslowe more than £3 was considered a hit, and *Henry VI* on that wintry afternoon made £3 16s 8d. It was a play very much of its period. The few years before and after the Armada were a flourishing time for the chronicle-history play which celebrated the values of patriotism by showing 'the ill success of treason, the fall of hasty climbers, the wretched end of usurpers, the misery of civil dissension'. Against the challenge of a new work, an old favourite like *The Jew of Malta* still brought in a fairly respectable box office. Its 39s. compare well with the 30s. made by *Henry VI,* once the novelty had worn off.

Business boomed until mid-June 1592, when the Lord Mayor successfully petitioned Lord Burghley to close the playhouses due to riots in Southwark. The actual flashpoint had been ignited over an attempted arrest of a feltmonger for debt, and the riot had begun in Blackfriars, north of the Thames. It involved a great number of 'lose & maisterlesse men', who then made their way south of the river and 'assembled themselves by occasion & pretence of their meeting at a play'. By eight in the evening, they had created 'great disorder & tumult' in the vicinity of the Rose. The Lord Mayor admitted that the apprentices had been provoked by the quite unnecessary violence offered by the marshal's men, but nevertheless he imprisoned the malefactors and asked for the Privy Council's advice. The Privy Council took action. Fearing that Midsummer Day (21 June) would be an occasion for 'lewd assemblye' in Southwark, they set up a night-watch that extended all over London and ordered that 'there be noe playes' in any of the usual venues until Michaelmas (29 September). The Justices in Surrey were charged with carrying out this command in their area.

The City was anxious lest the feltmongers' affray caused the

Privy Council to take over City affairs. Disorder within the vicinity of a playhouse was yet another weapon against the playhouses as playhouses were places where the multitude gathered; had not 'the horrible rebellion of Kent and his complices' broken out during a stage play in the days of Edward VI? The City's paranoia about an Elizabethan audience erupting into a mob seems, with hindsight, to have been groundless, though not at the time irrational. The playhouses were commercial, secular venues in which perhaps three thousand people, from across the class divide, could be crammed together in a potentially inflammatory social promiscuity. In an undemocratic age, a servant was thus afforded unusually easy access to his master. Henslowe's audience, though emotionally susceptible, was possibly not as disorderly as was commonly perceived in either his day or in later years.

Ben Jonson called the audiences a 'rude barbarous crue, a people that haue no brains'. He was not the only writer to litter his plays with contemptuous references to the groundlings. Yet these 'insults' cannot be taken at face value. Dame Edna Everage is just as insulting to her audiences who seem to relish the quite unjustified abuse she pours on them. The innumerable Elizabethan references to constant nut-cracking amongst the audience have to be taken in the same way as today's allusions to chocolate munching in the stalls. If the Elizabethan groundling was as impossibly behaved as some of these insults imply, it would be a brave actor indeed who would challenge them further. It is almost impossible to believe that the actors at the Rose projected the heart of their great plays to the discerning few in the galleries across a barrage of noisy indifference from the yard.

Various writers have likened the experience of Elizabethan theatre-going to, among other things, a rock concert or football match (Peter Thomson), a funfair (M.C. Bradbrook), a public meeting (Glynne Wickham) or a circus (Alfred Harbage). It obviously had little in common with a night in the 1990s at the Royal Court, yet it is arguable that it had more in common with a Royal Court experience than any of those mentioned above. Set against Jonson's dismissal of the groundlings, Thomas Dekker, after all, wrote that 'from rare silence' his audiences would 'clap their brawny hands, T'applaud what their charm'd soul scarce understands'. Despite the fog, mud and damp, the rain or snow, the charmed audiences flocked to the Rose. Elizabethans may have been hardier than us, but they were not weatherproof. The playhouses, whilst open to the air, were not without some kind of protection. The actors had shelter provided by the 'heavens'. The 'Two-penny Clients' sat under the roofed galleries. Perhaps on really bitter or wet days, everyone crowded under their eaves.

The attractions of the yard – the cheaper price, the proximity to the action – were, perhaps, outweighed by the disadvantages – exposure to extreme cold in winter, exposure to extreme heat in summer, the possibility of rain in all seasons and the discomfort of standing for two hours. Thomas Platter, the visitor from Switzerland in 1599, reported a distinction between the two-pence patrons who sat and the penny-paying patrons who presumably stood. There are many punning references concerning the 'understanding gentlemen' in the plays, and this reinforces the accepted idea that these gentlemen of the yard stood under the actors' noses. But did they, in fact, stand? Ernest Rhodes thinks not. Rhodes, another scholar who has focused on the Rose and come up with a challenge to Elizabethan theatre orthodoxy, suggests after textual analysis of the plays that the groundlings actually *sat*. The 'understanding gentlemen', as well they understood, were not supposed to be standing, but sitting down.

Ernest Rhodes argues that lines such as the prologue's 'Sit downe' in *The Battle of Alcazar* (1593) were addressed not to the two-pence clients, who would already be seated in the seats provided, but to the jostling crowd in the yard, who might not yet have sat down. Placed like that, without any territorial security, there is always an imperative to push to the front. Without organisation, such a crowd would be a distraction to themselves and a nuisance to everyone else. It would be in the actors' best interests to sort them out at the beginning of the performance. Henslowe's receipts rarely indicate a full house in the galleries, so it is likely that, generally, there would be enough space in the yard for an audience to sit down. Rushes would protect them from the mud, and the really well organised, according to Dekker's *Gull's Horne Book,* would have brought along their 'Tripos or three-footed stool'. Given the probability of a usually well behaved theatre-going public, the City's response to the feltmongers' dispute which, in any event, had no tangible link with a theatre, was a mighty over-reaction. The Rose closed for the summer of 1592 and by end of September, plague had once more made its way back to London with unabating virulence.

Philip Henslowe was unable to make any income out of his empty theatre. Edward Alleyn and Lord Strange's Men, however, were able to survive financially by taking to the road in that summer of 1592. It was an exceptional group of men that went on tour. Perhaps Thomas Nashe had them in mind when he wrote *Pierce Penilesse,* a pamphlet published that August. In it he praised the actor's art to the sky and called plays themselves a 'rare exercise of vertue'. As well as Edward Alleyn, Lord Strange's Men fielded William Kempe, Thomas Pope, John Hemminges, Augustine Phillips and George Brian; five men who were eventually to make up the backbone of the Lord Chamberlain's Men – Shakespeare's future company. William Shakespeare himself may have even been on tour with Edward Alleyn. Either way, Shakespeare was to find out that summer that, like Thomas Kyd, it was now his turn to attract the bile of a jealous critic and an embittered rival.

Robert Greene, the vituperative anti-Martinist pamphleteer, was dying in abject poverty. His last work, a pamphlet entitled *A Groatsworth of Wit,* turned on actors for exploiting writers and warned his fellow scribblers of a certain actor-turned-writer: 'There is an upstart Crow, beautified with our feathers, that with his Tygers hart wrapt in a Players hyde supposes he is as well able to bombast out a blank verse as the best of you . . .' And just in case the reader did not pick up on the parodic reference to the line, 'O tiger's heart wrapt in a woman's hide' from the recently performed *Henry VI* Part III, Greene went on to give a further clue to this actor/writer's identity '. . . the only Shakes-scene in a countrey'. Greene also, *pace* Thomas Nashe on Kyd, administered the almost obligatory passing blow to Christopher Marlowe on the grounds of Marlowe's declared atheism. As if he had seen into the future, Greene warned Marlowe: '. . . little knowest thou how in the end thou shall be visited.'

Unlike Thomas Nashe's previous attack on Thomas Kyd, passions were sufficiently inflamed for Greene's attack to require a rebuttal. Henry Chettle, who lived off his wits and chased more commissions for plays than he could ever write, was responsible for the publication of Greene's pamphlet – possibly out of charity for the dying man. In his preface to a subsequent pamphlet, *King-Hart's Dream,* Chettle made an apology of sorts. 'With neither of them that take offence,' he said, 'was I ever acquainted and . . .' – here comes that passing blow to Marlowe – 'with one of them I care not if I never be.' Perhaps it was put to Chettle that the unsettled summer of 1592 was not the most politic of times to be savaging the new writer whose work boded so well for the future of Lord Strange's Men at the Rose Theatre – if the Rose ever re-opened.

In October 1592, Edward Alleyn wed. His bride was Joan Woodward, daughter of Agnes, and step-daughter of Philip Henslowe. Henslowe recorded this dynastic alliance in his Diary, dating the occasion with full solemnity: 'the 22 daye of october 1592 In the iiij & thirtie yeare of the Quene majesties Rayne elizabeth by the grace of god of Ingland france & Iarland defender of the fayth'. Even given the natural Elizabethan tendency to keep everything within the economic unit of the family, this generation of players and playhouse owners, who had in the main, come from solid backgrounds in trade, were not slow to inveigle their relatives into the profession. Philip Henslowe already had a nephew, Francis, on the stage. And Edward Alleyn's innkeeper brother, John, had for a while worked as an actor with Lord Sheffield's Men. Joan Woodward's sister, Bess, went on to marry Augustine Phillips, a player of many clown roles. The Burbages were, however, established as the most formidable family act in the Elizabethan theatre world. Was this in the back of Alleyn's mind when he married Joan?

In old age, Philip Henslowe wrote 'that he was much beholden unto . . . Allin. And that (he) could never had effected those things which hee did, but by the help and care of the said Allin'. From now on, the nature of the role that Henslowe played in the working life of his theatre becomes a contested issue. The business affairs of both Henslowe and his son-in-law, Alleyn, are inextricably intermingled, not only their dealings in the theatre but also in property. Alleyn had now started to diversify his interests, and he put to good use the fortune he was making on the stage. He would die the wealthiest of all the Elizabethan actors. Henslowe had often chosen to work in partnership and what better partnership for him than one that kept everything within the family? The 1587 Deed of Partnership with John Cholmley could be almost any business arrangement, a simple joint agreement by two landlords. Later, the entries in the Diary show Henslowe, almost casually, and with a proprietorial tone, referring to 'my players'. His relationship with the players had changed with this marriage.

No more was it to be just a clear cut matter of collecting his share of the take.

The marriage between Joan Woodward and Edward Alleyn may have started out as cold-bloodedly as Henslowe's own marriage to Joan's mother, but it seems to have settled into a warm and loving relationship. As in the long enforced tour of 1592, they were often separated when plague sent Alleyn into the country and a regular correspondence flourished. In his letters, Alleyn called Joan his 'good swett harte & loving mouse' and betrayed his anxiety for her welfare during the time of plague by begging her to 'kepe your house fayr and clean which I know you will'. A postscript to one letter chided her. 'Mouse,' he wrote, 'you send me no newes of any things you should send of your domestycall matters such things as happens att home.' His concerns appeared to centre either on his clothes – his 'whit wascote', 'orayngtawny stokins' – or on his bed of spinach, which Joan must be sure to remember to plant come September. With Joan, Edward Alleyn was able to relax and laugh at his reputation, dubbing himself a 'fustian king'.

In truth, the endless touring imposed a strain on players and was not nearly as lucrative as playing in London. An undated petition from the players sometime in the year of 1592 was sent to the Privy Council. It mentioned the possibility of 'division and seperacion' of the company on the road. It hinted, and none too subtly, that this might result in them being 'vnreadie to serve her majestie'. (Come Christmas, Lord Strange's Men were in fact sufficiently in readiness to play at Court, despite their enforced absence from Bankside.) Their petition went on to entreat all the 'verie good Lordes' of the Privy Council to re-open 'our plaiehowse on the Banckside'. In passing, the players remembered the plight of the watermen bereft of fares since the closure of the Rose.

The plight of the watermen had not gone unnoticed. Someone organised a petition appealing on behalf of their 'poore wives and Children' that the Rose be re-opened. Henslowe may well have had a hand in this. The syntax elides, 'Phillipp henslo, and others the poore watermen', leading M.C. Bradbrook to refer drily to Henslowe as 'that toiling sculler'. In the end it would seem as if a compromise was reached. Lord Strange's Men were allowed for a time to play half weeks at the unpopular Newington Butts venue until finally the Privy Council gave way and allowed the players to return to the Rose 'solonge as yt shalbe free from infection of sicknes'. Philip Henslowe started recording the resumption of business shortly after Christmas on 29 December 1592. It proved only temporary. In the five weeks allowed them, Lord Strange's Men premiered Marlowe's *The Massacre at Paris* – a £3. 10s success – gave 29 performances of a dozen plays and presented *The Jew of Malta* at Court on New Year's Day. The plague, though, had not been driven away by the wintry weather. Instead, at the zenith of Alleyn's career, plague returned with a ferocity unparalleled since the days of the Black Death. By 1 February 1593, the Rose was once again closed.

It was at this low point in everyone's fortunes that Philip Henslowe started his money-lending activities. Pawnbroking was a freely available credit facility and practised widely by the citizens of Bankside. In London as a whole, attempts to set up registers indicated that over 500 men offered this short-term financial expedient to their neighbours. Henslowe's clients ranged over the social scale from 'my Lord Burte' to the 'midwife's daughter' or 'the woman who sells herbs in the market' but they were usually women, trying to keep a roof over their families' heads. Most of the loans Henslowe made were for sums less than 30s., and the interest charged was high, sometimes as much as an illegal 50%. Loans were generally secured against items of clothing. Henslowe, for example offered money against an expensive violet coloured cloth cloak trimmed with a velvet cape, as well as the more humble doublet and hose: both items, no doubt, were riddled with plague-carrying fleas.

Despite facing another forcible indefinite closure at the start of 1593, Philip Henslowe had found the Rose Theatre a profit-able venture and he was in a good position to bail out those who came to him for help during the devastating days of the plague. His Diary shows that in an average year, Henslowe made some £250 profit from his share of the box office, and, as well as the Rose, Henslowe had other property interests on Bankside, collecting rents from thirty assorted properties (including his brothel).

Financially, Lord Strange's Men were strong in the spring of 1593. They had earned £30 in Court fees over Christmas and probably bided their time, hoping for the best until the reality of the continued closure forced them to embark on yet another tour at the beginning of May. Whatever tensions had existed in the previous summer were now probably exacerbated by their being thrown back into one another's company so soon after returning to London. At the end of the tour Edward Alleyn parted company with the other five leading players, whose talents had made the Lord Strange's Men the premier company in England. The 'division and seperacion' that Lord Strange's Men had threatened in the summer of 1592 now came to pass.

Edward Alleyn possibly felt in a strong position after the split. He was the leading actor in the land and he had the loyalty of the most formidable writer at the time, Christopher Marlowe. Alleyn's interpretation of Faustus, Barabas and Tamburlaine had made both their reputations. Marlowe's plays were always sure-fire hits, and the writer was still a young man. At 29, he was the same age as the relatively unknown and untried William Shakespeare, but Marlowe, unlike his exact contemporary, had already made his mark on the theatrical world and proved his worth. Alleyn eventually gathered together new players in 1594 to re-form a company under the patronage this time of the Lord Admiral. In that year, the former actors with Lord Strange's Men re-constituted themselves as the Lord Chamberlain's Men. William Shakespeare decided then to throw in his lot with them at Burbage's Theatre.

Alleyn had a commanding style and, as Carol Rutter suggests, he 'perhaps stamped his personality too forcefully on Lord Strange's Men'. Playing companies, despite the formal hierarchy inherent in the patronage system, were democratically run, and some of Alleyn's fellow actors on tour with him in the summer of 1593 might have taken exception to an actor sufficiently well known to be referred to as 'Ed. Allen and his Companie' on the title page of *The Knack to Know a Knave* (1594), famous enough for correspondence to be addressed to him simply as,
'To E Alline
on the bank side'

5. Edward Alleyn's autograph. (Dulwich College. By permission of the Governors)

They might also have suspected him of being too much in cahoots with the Rose's owner. Alleyn, evidently was as M.C. Bradbrook says, 'not an easy man'. The mass defection of Kempe, Pope, Hemminges, Phillips and Brian to Alleyn's long-standing rival would have seemed a blow to him but not, perhaps, a disaster.

Much worse was in store. Whilst Edward Alleyn was in the country, plague raged in London, and by early August 1593 total deaths reached over a thousand every week. The authorities were jumpy, nervous as ever of any potential disorder. A certain amount of panic had been generated at the expense of immigrants, by people seeking a scapegoat for the epidemic. Violence was in the air. A doggerel rhyme scrawled on a church wall betrayed militant xenophobia ('You Strangers') and hinted that the graffiti artist responsible for inciting racial hatred was a professional writer ('Note this same writing'). In mid-May, Thomas Kyd, a conspicuous playwright, was arrested for possible sedition, and, under torture, said that the incriminating papers, blasphemous and atheistical, found in his room, were the property of fellow writer, Christopher Marlowe. In a letter written by Kyd out of fear, he said; 'Touching Marlowe's monstrous opinions as I cannot but with an aggrieved conscience think on him or them.' Before the case could come before the Privy Council, Marlowe was dead, stabbed through the eye in a tavern brawl. The coroner's inquest on 1 June 1593 cleared his assailant, Ingram Frazier, whilst also providing a smokescreen which possibly covered up the fact that government agents were involved in the deliberate murder of London's leading playwright.

Shakespeare, if he had been killed in a tavern brawl in 1593, would be known today as he was known then; the author of some narrative poetry, a sonnet sequence and probably only the *Henry VI* trilogy. The loyalty of Shakespeare in 1593 would have meant little to Alleyn, but the loss of Marlowe meant everything. If Kyd's plays were at a mid-way point between the emblematic medieval morality play and the mature five-act Elizabethan drama, then Marlowe's plays, by addressing the audience through character not thesis, made the complete break. The discovery of dramatic objectivity in Renaissance drama, which Marlowe made possible, is comparable to the discovery of perspective in Renaissance art, and it led eventually to the development of more psychologically realised characters.

Marlowe's plays maintained their popularity immediately after his death and were revived in the Restoration. After that they sank into theatrical oblivion for two centuries. On 16 September 1881, Henry Irving unveiled the Marlowe memorial at Canterbury and the *Saturday Review* noted that the great actor was 'provokingly silent concerning the total banishment of (Marlowe's) plays from the stage'. In 1885, Irving essayed the part of Faustus on the professional stage and ten years later, achieved Alleyn's probable ambition by becoming the first actor to be knighted. Yet, what Robert Greene called Marlowe's 'bragging blank verse' and Ben Jonson called his 'mighty line', George Bernard Shaw said was responsible for 'the horrible worship of blank verse for its own sake which has since desolated and laid waste the dramatic poetry of England'. Shaw declared of Elizabethan dramatists in general: 'One calls (them) imaginative, as one might say the same of a man in delirium tremens; but even that flatters them . . . In condemning them indiscriminatingly, I am only doing what Time would have done if Shakespeare had not rescued them.'

The day after Boxing Day 1593, the Rose was allowed to re-open. The Admiral's Men had not yet formed and Sussex's Men, a combination of Pembroke's and Lord Strange's Men, benefited from the Christmas trade with their own repertoire. *The Jew of Malta,* a popular 'get-penny', was performed on 4 February 1594 and it is possible that Edward Alleyn, who had made the title role his own, was once more back at the Rose. In which case he might also, as leading player, have created the title part in *Titus Andronicus.* This was the big hit of the season, and the last play of Shakespeare's to be staged at the Rose. On 23 January 1594, *Titus*'s first performance, earned £3. 8s. The play was repeated straightaway and performed twice in the week that followed, bringing in £2 on each occasion. The revival of Marlowe's old play, *The Jew of Malta* by Lord Strange's Men, in contrast, made only £1. There would be no more new plays by Alleyn's favourite dramatist. The writing was on the wall but still so faint that no one at the Rose would have paid much heed. Shakespeare had not yet joined Burbage north of the river, although by the spring he almost certainly had.

CHAPTER TWO

The Rose Theatre 1594–1603
'. . . the cold, decaying noisome Rose'.

The decline in a company's fortune is always a protracted affair and, despite the low takings for *The Jew of Malta,* the box office at the Rose early in 1594 was particularly good. Theatre-starved Londoners flocked to the Rose, and the theatre was really getting into its stride when, once again, plague struck. A Privy Council Minute dated 3 February 1594 closed the theatres and banned all performances 'within the compas of five miles distance from London till vpon lykelyhood and assurance of health'. Assurance was not to be forthcoming until April 1594. Then a fragile alliance between the Queen's Men and Sussex's Men took to the stage when the Rose re-opened. They lasted for only a week as a combined operation. The companies then tried playing the Rose separately, alternating their performances.

Finally Edward Alleyn was ready to launch the newly formed Admiral's Men and they chose to open with, what else, but that old standby – *The Jew of Malta.* Henslowe recorded an income on 14 May of 48s., and no doubt he looked forward to a settled year for the rest of 1594. It was not to be. The season was cut short after just three days. No reason has survived. If it was plague again, then a five-mile *cordon sanitaire* did not apply this time as the Admiral's Men were allowed to perform only two weeks later at Peter Hunningborne's unpopular venue in Newington Butts. To make matters worse, Alleyn had to share it with that other new outfit launched in 1594, the Chamberlain's Men.

This would have been awkward for both companies. The previous year most of the leading players had worked together in one company. After the long tour of 1593, it was Richard Burbage, whose father had once so soundly trounced Alleyn, who went on to command the loyalty of Alleyn's former comrades. The Chamberlain's Men had gained not only the most experienced actors in London (including the popular clown William Kempe), but also a writer who had at last started to find his voice. Richard Burbage had made his mark in the title role of *Richard III* back in 1593. By 1594, Shakespeare had finished this first group of chronicle-history plays and had also written *Titus Andronicus, The Comedy of Errors* and *Love's Labour's Lost*. Plays then started to come thick and fast, *The Taming of the Shrew, Two Gentlemen of Verona, Romeo and Juliet, Richard II, A Midsummer Night's Dream* and *King John* were all written within about three years between 1594 to 1596. To the loss of Christopher Marlowe, the Admiral's Men had to add another the same year; Thomas Kyd died. What had Edward Alleyn got in his repertoire to match that of the Chamberlain's Men other than *The Jew of Malta* and *The Spanish Tragedy?*

The pursuit of novelty was all. Between the two companies, the demand for fresh material to stoke up the repertoire was almost insatiable. When they were allowed, the Admiral's Men performed a different play for six days a week, adding one new play to their repertoire every fortnight. Only eight or so new plays might last from one year to the next. A big hit would be repeated at monthly intervals. There was a direct relationship between a new play and the box office. Receipts shot up. Against the challenge offered them by Shakespeare's pen, the Admiral's Men encouraged writers to work collaboratively. On the basis, perhaps, that if they hadn't got one distinctive dramatist at their disposal, then perhaps teams of indifferent writers might, between them, come up with something whose overall sum would be greater than its individual parts. Play making like this has to be a hit-and-miss affair, and when a resulting play for the Admiral's Men turned out to be a hit, its success seemed due more to its topicality and immediacy rather than any innate literary quality.

The collaborative play, *Sir Thomas More,* which dates from this period, is one such play. It is not one of the plays mentioned in Henslowe's Diary, but the case for its being a Rose play has much to commend it. F.E. Halliday is confident that the play belonged to the Admiral's Men and was produced 'as a counterblast to Shakespeare's own work for the Chamberlain's'. Walter W. Greg says that the 'book-keeper' (prompter) who annotated the manuscript of another Rose play, Anthony

Munday's *The Wise Men of Westchester* (1594), was also the book-keeper on *Sir Thomas More*. A job which placed a man in the sensitive position of gaining access to an entire script would, presumably, put a premium on his loyalty to the company. Play piracy was rife and a play book was one of a company's most valuable assets. Writers were discouraged from publication, and actors were not allowed to have complete scripts. The 'book' would be inscribed with the official licence and from it, the individual parts would be copied out. It would seem likely then, on the basis of the book-keeper's involvement, that both *The Wise Men of Westchester* and *Sir Thomas More* were the property of the same company: of the Admiral's Men.

In addition, three Rose writers, Munday, Chettle and Thomas Heywood co-authored its first draft. It was another play which met the appetite for historical drama generated in the years after the Armada. The story of Sir Thomas More was recent history so, not surprisingly, it met with censorship problems, and Edmund Tilney, the Master of the Revels, returned it for revision. 'Leave out ye insurrection wholly, and the cause of it' was Tilney's characteristic command. Evidently, Tilney drew the line at provocative and topical dramas which explored the reasons underlying popular revolt. He was not fooled by the play's historical context. (Much later on, in 1600, the Privy Council was to complain about the 'obscure manner' of certain plays, 'yet in such sorte, as all the hearers may take notice'.) To help with the revisions yet another Rose writer, Thomas Dekker, joined Munday's team which was possibly even further supplemented by William Shakespeare.

Against F.E. Halliday's confident assertion that this play was in the repertoire of the Admiral's Men stands the widely held belief that the three-page revisions which show Sir Thomas More pacifying a riot (interpolated to pacify Tilney) are not only by Shakespeare but that the surviving manuscript is also in Shakespeare's very own hand. Why Shakespeare would then wish to collaborate on a 'counterblast' to himself is a mystery, as Halliday recognises. Either scholars will have to give up their belief in the authenticity of this manuscript (not easy – only six other specimens of Shakespeare's writing are known to exist and all of them are signatures) or the notion of the counterblast will have to go. If *Sir Thomas More* was written as early as 1593 (one of two dates offered by the *Oxford Companion to English Literature*, the other being 1601), then Shakespeare was still either a member or an associate of the Admiral's Men.

If the play was written just a bit later, say 1594, then Shakespeare's collaboration with the Rose dramatists could have come about during their shared season that summer at Newington Butts. Burbage and Alleyn may have been rivals but Shakespeare (and other writers) might have adopted a more detached stance. There was advantage to be gained for writers from the experience of seeing another's work. Besides London was big enough to contain two major companies, provided one stayed north of the City, the other south of the Thames.

The summer of 1594 was exceedingly wet and the season at Newington Butts, with or without the strained relationship between the leading players, disastrous. Henslowe records an all-time low of 4s. as his income from yet another revival of *The Jew of Malta*. In fairness to the *Jew*, all Henslowe's takings were down. The Privy Council had previously sympathised with players' complaints about this venue. The way to Newington Butts was indeed tedious. Furthermore it was a venue 'of longe tymes plaies haue not there bene vsed on working daies'. This suggests that Peter Hunningborne was used to opening up only on an occasional basis, at holiday time. The receipts may not even represent Henslowe's customary 50% of the gallery income, which was more properly Peter Hunningborne's entitlement. Precisely what Henslowe's involvement was with both 'my Lord Admeralle & my Lorde chamberlen men' is debatable. He may have been acting as agent or go-between. Fortunately for both companies, it proved to be a short arrangement lasting just ten days.

By mid-June 1594, the Admiral's Men were allowed back home, and Alleyn led his men back to the Rose Theatre. After the hiccough at the beginning of the year, this was their real launch on London's theatre-going public. The company during this nine-month season consisted of John Singer, Thomas Towne, Martin Slater (or Slaughter), Edward Juby, Thomas Downton, James Tunstall and Richard Jones, the actor who, back in 1588, had sold his theatrical effects to Alleyn. Making up the numbers were Charles Massey, Samuel Rowley and Richard Allen. From 15 June 1594, they played a long season which only finished because of Lent the following year. The Admiral's Men managed to mount 17 new plays during this season as well as dragging back *The Jew of Malta*. The old warhorse this time made 23s. on 23 June, 41s. on 30 June and 27s. on 10 July. It continued to stay in the repertoire and was played a further six times before Christmas. *Dr Faustus* makes its first appearance in Henslowe's Diary on 23 September and its box office suggests that it had been out of Alleyn's repertoire for some time. It proved to be a £3. 7s. hit.

Overall it was a profitable period, and Henslowe received £340. 11s. For a while the Admiral's Men had staved off the competition which in any case was, in 1594, entirely limited to the Chamberlain's Men. The pestilence of 1593 had had a catastrophic effect on playing companies. The Queen's Men, which Francis Henslowe had joined, were a broken troupe as far as London was concerned, relegated to provincial touring. Pembroke's Men had had to pawn all their theatrical assets. On the south bank, the Admiral's Men reigned supreme. Without a doubt, Bankside had proved itself a successful theatre location. So successful, that another theatre was being built in the neighbourhood. The Lord Mayor wrote to Lord Burghley, in some agitation, on 3 November with the news that Francis Langley 'intendeth to erect a new stage or Theater (as they call it) for the exercising of playes vpon the Banck side.'

Francis Langley is described in this letter as 'one of the Alneagers'. An alnager was a wool inspector, and, amongst other things, Henslowe's would-be competitor was also a goldsmith, money-lender and speculator. Carol Rutter calls him 'a land-pirate' and then goes on to describe him rather curiously as 'constructed upon the Cockney model'. Not many scholars have a kind word to say about Langley. Andrew Gurr refers to his theatre as 'Langley's unhappy Swan'. Peter Thomson says that Langley offered 'a motive of avarice besides which Henslowe's sharpness pales into insignificance'. It would seem, given the rehabilitation of Henslowe's character, that Langley is now fated to play the role of J.R. to Henslowe's Bobby Ewing. What little is known of the Swan's history, tells of many embittered sagas of money withheld, legal disputes (one even embroiling the far-from-litigious Shakespeare) and a major scandal of theatre history.

Christmas as a whole in 1594 was uncharacteristically slow at the box office, though trade did pick up in the peak holiday week. The Admiral's Men bested the Chamberlain's Men for the number of performances at Court, giving three or four shows to their one or two. The beginning of Lent in 1595 provided a natural break after nine months' continuous performing. It was in this year that Henslowe's partnership with John Cholmley was due to expire – if indeed the partnership had lasted beyond the signing of their Deed. Henslowe used the five-week break in early 1595 to refurbish and redecorate his theatre again. The Rose had been in use for nearly a decade and even in the two years since the major building works of 1592, the constant wear and tear by actors, the push and shove of the crowd would have played havoc with any timber-framed building in this low lying part of town.

The amount Henslowe spent was not enormous – about £15. Much of it went on 'the paynter'. Langley's Swan Theatre might now have opened, or if not open, it must have been nearly complete. Henslowe perhaps had seen or heard of its mock marble stage posts ('able to deceive even the most cunning'), which were to impress Johannes de Witt on his visit to London the following year. Maybe Henslowe wanted to add a few colourful painted flourishes of his own to the interior decor of the Rose. The Elizabethan theatre is often wrongly thought of as bare. Indeed this supposed feature was much admired in the late nineteenth century when the vogue for plush interiors and spectacular stage-effects had almost reached the point of self parody. 'The accessories in those days,' writes our Southwark friend, Robert Bower, harking back to less ostentatious times, 'were delightfully simple'.

Though the Elizabethans made do without what we know as scenery (a 'Here we are in the Forest of Arden' would generally suffice), their theatres were colourful buildings. Contemporary observers used terms like 'gorgeous' and 'sumptuous' to describe the interiors. The unabashed sensuous quality of the decor was another weapon in the Puritan arsenal directed against playhouses. The faked luxury of these playhouses must have been similar in effect and appeal to the opulent glamour of the early picture palaces of the twentieth century. Henslowe's new decor was not enough to make any big impression on de Witt. He conceded that the Rose was one of two magnificient theatres south of the Thames, but went on to specify that the Swan was 'the largest and most magnificent' of them. It was during the March refurbishment that Henslowe installed the throne in the 'heavens'.

The Rose re-opened its doors on 23 April 1595 and closed them again on 26 June. Plague this time was not an issue, and, though no restraint orders appear to have survived, more than likely the closure was due to civil disorder. A dispute over the price of butter had grown completely out of hand. From skirmishes in Southwark Market on 13 June between apprentices and traders, the young men's passions grew until they erupted on 23 June at Billingsgate Market. Southwark fishwives had bought up the entire stock – no doubt with the aim of fixing the price of fish – and the inflamed apprentices went berserk. As with the feltmakers' dispute of 1592, this fracas would have been a good pretext for the City to insist that the Privy Council and the Justices of Surrey close the playhouses.

By late August in 1595, the Admiral's Men were back at the Rose for an uninterrupted six-month spell. *The Jew of Malta* was temporarily put out to grass (it did not return to the repertoire until after Christmas) but *Dr Faustus* soldiered on and made 32s on 11 September 1595. A new version of Marlowe's *Tamburlaine* dating from the previous year remained in performance, but few of the new plays had whatever it took to ensure the same long life as Marlowe's veterans. *The Mack,* for example, completely disappeared from view after only one recorded performance earlier in 1595. By the end of 1595, the Rose was forced to go dark for half the playing week. The Swan Theatre was now open and pulling in part of the Rose's former trade. That year the Chamberlain's Men outdid the Admiral's Men for the number of royal command performances given at Court, although some consolation was to be found at Shrovetide when the Queen remembered her old favourite and commanded performances from the Admiral's Men, which equalised the score.

Lack of good new plays possibly accounted for the slump in the Rose's fortunes, but audience's tastes were also changing. The posthumous publication of Sir Philip Sidney's *The Defence of Poesie* in 1595, although relating to a much earlier generation of drama centred on the Senecan *Gorboduc* of 1561, made critical comments which could have still been applicable to the theatre associated with Edward Alleyn. Alleyn, that 'fustian king', was of the old school. As an actor his talents lay in rhetoric, whilst Richard Burbage, who also had the advantage of playing Shakespeare's more rounded characters, was developing a style of more realistic acting that was so revolutionary that the term 'personation' had to be coined to describe it.

Playing continued uninterrupted at the Rose until the

beginning of Lent in 1596 and began again on Easter Monday. By May, the Admiral's Men, their pockets hit by the three-day working week imposed on them in the run up to Christmas, as well as the loss of lucrative Court fees, began taking out loans from Philip Henslowe. At this point, Henslowe's Diary undergoes an interesting change as he starts to record the loans and what they were for, thus revealing much more about the working life of his theatre. The loans were, invariably, for costumes or play commissions and were never seriously large enough to put the company in permanent hock to Henslowe, and they all appear to have been repaid within a short period.

Early interpretations of these loans betrayed prejudice against the 'moneyed' and 'illiterate' Henslowe. The suggestion was that he deliberately ensnared the players by trapping them into debt so as to prevent them defecting from the Rose. It would appear that some time in 1596, the Admiral's Men began losing its players. Certainly come October, Richard Jones and Thomas Downton decamped to re-form Pembroke's Men, a new troupe based at the Swan. So if it had been Henslowe's intention to enslave the men, it would appear not to have worked. Carol Rutter provides Henslowe with a sterling defence on the matter of the loans. She suggests that Henslowe was acting as nothing more than an informal banker to the company, extending credit to meet production expenses. Bernard Beckerman, however, thinks that a series of internal crises, prompted by the defections, lay behind the company's insolvency. Sharers who left were entitled to take back their share or some of the company assets. So as well as losing men, the Admiral's Men might also have been losing capital or stock.

Francis Langley had instituted a system of loans to get things going at the Swan Theatre, and perhaps the players put it to Henslowe that it was in his best interests too to have a lavishly costumed company playing in brand new plays. Once Henslowe started the habit, he became increasingly more caught up in the affairs of the players who performed at his theatre. Initially a quarter of the loans he made seemed not to have been authorised by the company as if Henslowe was attempting to act more as manager than banker. Increasingly though, his Diary records authorisation from one or other of the players, who would not have been at all happy with Henslowe's attempts to taken on a managerial role.

The season that had begun in May 1596 lasted until July 1596 when 'increase of sicknes' closed the theatres and sent the Admiral's Men off on the roads with their skips. *The Jew of Malta* was given its last recorded performance at the Rose on 21 June, when it brought in 13s. George Peele, a popular Rose writer, died during 1596, but Thomas Heywood is mentioned for the first time in Henslowe's Diary as selling them a 'bocke' for 30s. in the same year – so, in the matter of writers, it was swings versus roundabouts, though Heywood's 'bocke' must have been an old play because a new play could earn a writer at least £6. By late October, the players were allowed back to Bankside and embarked on a hardworking schedule that took them well into the summer of 1597.

Despite their hard work they were up against even harder odds as Christmas 1596 approached. Earlier in the year, James Burbage had negotiated a long-term lease for performing indoors at premises in Blackfriars. This move was blocked by local citizens after petitioning the Privy Council who then extended its ban to all inn-theatres in the City. Unlike the Admiral's Men, accessibly situated on Bankside, the Chamberlain's Men found they lost most of their audience in winter when the trek to either the Theatre or the Curtain proved muddy and uncomfortable. Instead, Burbage & Co used to move closer to their audience by taking up residence at the Cross Keys, an inn in the City. This venue was now denied them, so instead James Burbage came to terms with Francis Langley and the Chamberlain's Men moved into the Swan. Shakespeare moved his lodgings from Bishopsgate to Bankside for the duration.

The Admiral's Men managed to stage twelve new plays at the Rose during the winter season of 1596. Only three of them, though, hit the magic target of £3, and they probably only did so because they were staged at the height of the Christmas season. At that time of year, even another revival of *The Jew of Malta* could not have failed to hit the jackpot. But the days of the *Jew* were over, though *Dr Faustus* was going strong. It made 27s. on 28 October and ever decreasing amounts thereafter (17s. on 4 November, 9s. on 17 December). Thomas Kyd's *The Spanish Tragedy*, however, turned up trumps on 7 January 1597 in a version so new it even required relicensing. It was one of the few plays to be a £3 hit, so not surprisingly, it was repeated four times that month. The Admiral's Men were not commanded to take part in the Court Revels at all that winter. They were completely eclipsed by the Chamberlain's Men who gave all six performances. All in all, dogged by the rival players, it was a dismal end to a highly fraught year.

In 1597, the Rose Theatre would have celebrated its first decade, but there can have been little good cheer. The future, now that the exclusivity of Bankside had been broached, would have been as uncertain to Henslowe as the historical record has subsequently become for historians. In this year, Henslowe started a new system of keeping his books which has never been satisfactorily de-coded. This means that box office figures are speculative, although the titles of plays with their dates of performances are still considered reliable. The editors of the Diary suggest that the new system indicates a shift in the relationship between Henslowe and the players stemming from the money-lending arrangement that had been in operation between them since May 1596. For a period, Henslowe may have taken all the box office, not just for the galleries but also for the yard. Weekly averages during the periods 24 January to 14 March 1597 appear to come to as much as £20. In the days when Henslowe recorded his half share of the gallery income, a £3 income on one afternoon was considered a hit. £20 would be the equivalent of a £3 hit each day of a seven-day working week. Such a sum would have been hardly likely even when Alleyn's company were at their zenith. So the £20 clearly represented more than Henslowe's usual 50%. If it represented the total income, then Henslowe was perhaps deducting any money owed him, before handing over to the players the residue to which they were entitled.

The season that had begun in October 1596 limped on until 12 February 1597. *The Spanish Tragedy* was the last entry under Henslowe's old system of accounting. After its successful revival on 7 January 1597 (the first recorded performance since June 1592) it remained in repertoire throughout 1597 but the box office after 22 January is uncertain. On that date, Henslowe tells us that it brought in 19s. On 24 January he adopted his new five column entries: the first two columns represent pounds and shillings, the second three columns pounds, shillings and pence. What the columns themselves refer to is a mystery.

Then some kind of internal crisis prompted the Rose to close abruptly for a fortnight. The Admiral's Men began losing players in earnest this year. Thomas Towne and John Singer, who were certainly missing for a time from the Admiral's Men during this year, may have abruptly joined Jones and Downton, who were already at the Swan. The Chamberlain's Men had moved on, and it was Pembroke's Men who were about to open the Swan season on 21 February. It is possible that at this point, the core group of sharers with the Admiral's Men numbered only four; Edward Alleyn, Martin Slater, James Tunstall and Edward Juby. This would have affected their financial status as well as their acting line-up. Somehow, the Admiral's Men were able to solve their internal problems and get the company back up to playing strength. All the old plays were fully rehearsed within that fortnight and the players re-opened on 3 March 1597. By 19 March, the Admiral's Men were even able to launch a new play, *Guido,* with the help of a £4 19s. loan from Henslowe towards its costumes ('sylckes & other thinges for gvido').

Matters would appear to be almost back to normal by April. In the period from then until the end of July, the company managed to give seven premieres and, apart from a short Easter break, they performed on a regular basis. A surviving stage plot, one of seven extant connected with a new play, *Frederick and Basilea,* which opened on 3 June 1597, names the following as members of the company: Edward Alleyn, Richard Allen, Edward Juby, Martin Slater, Thomas Towne (evidently he had returned from Pembroke's Men), James Tunstall, Thomas Hunt, Charles Massey, Samuel Rowley, one 'Black Dick', one just plain 'Dick', Edward Dutton's boy apprentice (and Edward Dutton as well), 'Will' and 'Griffin' (two other boys), 'Ledbetter', and unnamed guards and 'gatherers'. The appearance of John Pigg (Edward Alleyn's boy player), taking on an adult role, is perhaps some evidence that the company were still finding it hard to recruit the full complement of experienced actors. Even the 'gatherers' (people who collected the pennies at the door) had been pressed into service to fill out the crowd scenes.

Stage plots were in common usage. A large poster-sized synopsis of character movement hung backstage, giving the actors a breakdown of casting for each scene. Perhaps the new players with the Admiral's Men, many completely unused to the repertoire, were particularly in need of all the help they could get in remembering their entrances and exits. Patrick Tucker has a theory that rehearsals were minimal; there would be little time for even going through the play once, though if anything, his production of unrehearsed scenes from Shakespeare, staged at the anniversary Benefit for the Rose at the Haymarket on 13 May 1990 largely proved the reverse. Certainly the Elizabethan actor's ability to memorise had to be prodigious (even allowing for a blatant reliance on prompts). The impositions they placed on their writers to write a finished play within two or three weeks were impositions they placed on themselves. They rehearsed and learnt a part within the same time scale. Rehearsals would have been limited to the morning only. Afternoons were given over to performance. Given the dark and cold of an evening, it is unlikely that the cast would have met after a show to resume rehearsals.

The actor was at the heart of the Elizabethan theatrical experience, and the Rose plays, above all, are actors' plays. There was more prestige in being an actor than a writer, and this, perhaps, accounted for Nashe's bile at the actors, 'vain, glorious tragedians', and Greene's contempt of 'those Puppets'. Sir Richard Baker, however, reflecting from the position in 1643, a year after Cromwell's Parliament had closed the theatres, said that Alleyn and Burbage were 'two such actors, as no age must ever look to see the like'. Baker concluded that 'a Play read hath not half the pleasure of a Play Acted'. His comment is a far cry from subsequent scholarship, which privileges the text above the performance, and it is all the more poignant, given that in 1643, the only way Baker, or anybody else, was likely to experience a play was precisely by reading it.

Baker praised actors for the 'Ingeniousness of the Speech when it is fitted to the person, and the Gracefulness of the Action when it is fitted to the Speech'. An actor's chief requirement was the ability to speak verse. He had to induce his audience to respond to the words. Dialogue was like a map, or a musical score. It had a self-evident direction, and in this way boy actors were able to play complex and tragic parts. The boy had only to 'pronounce' correctly and the character formed itself around the words automatically. 'Character', as such, has only in recent years acquired the implication of psychological consistency, and the actor's search for sub-text is a twentieth-century development. In Elizabethan plays, the actor did not so much play the character through the text, as the text 'spoke' the character for the actor. It helped that audiences accepted that poetry was a natural mode of expression, and this allowed actors to emphasise rather than conceal the rhetorical devices of the plays. They used a recognised code of gestures which could be adopted as readily by a boy as by a grown man. To indicate anger, an actor might knit his brow, clench his teeth, fist his hand and stamp his feet. Audiences were much moved. Contemporary accounts tell us that the Talbot scenes of *Henry VI* at the Rose drew 'the teares of ten thousand spectators'.

On 18 July 1597, Henslowe scribbled in the margins of his accounts the familiar depressing news that 'marten slather went for the company of my lord admerelles men'. Slater had not, however, gone to the opposition at the Swan but into retirement and took with him five old play-books, representing the investment he had made in the Admiral's Men over the years. Still, it meant that the Admiral's Men lost an experienced player, familiar with the repertoire, as well as five reliable shows. The internal crisis probably caused by actors' defections in the spring of 1597 was, by then, over. It had nearly ruined the day. An external crisis, though, was brewing and, inadvertently, it was to save the day. The fortunes of the Admiral's Men were about to change, and at last the change would be for the better.

28 July 1597 was an important date in Elizabethan stage history, but Henslowe's Diary gives no indication of the turmoil that was about to engulf London's theatre world. On 28 July he recorded under his new system the usual mystifying box office receipts for *The Witch of Islington,* the second and last of two recorded performances. He also entered into a number of long-term agreements. Only the day before he had managed to secure the services of the actor, Thomas Herne, on a two-year contract. On 28 July itself Henslowe sold Thomas Towne a black cloak trimmed with silk lace for 25s. 6d. Towne agreed to repay this amount under a sort of hire purchase arrangement, which would extend for the better part of a year. Ben Jonson at 25, making his first appearance in the Diary, borrowed £4 from Henslowe to be repaid 'when so euer either I or any for me shall demande yt'. Jonson was not a member of the Admiral's Men, though he may have been thinking of joining them. On 28 July he was still only an actor with Pembroke's Men at the Swan. Maybe Jonson took out the loan because he anticipated his coming troubles. Maybe Henslowe lent it to him because he had

not. The Swan Theatre was poised to provoke one of the great scandals of theatrical history.

On that same day, 28 July, both the Lord Mayor and the Privy Council reached for their respective quills. The Lord Mayor's letter, arising out of a routine meeting of the Court of Aldermen before their month-long summer break, was the standard rehearsal of complaints against playhouses ('conteining nothinge but prophane fables, lascivious matters, cozeninge devises & scurrilus beehaviours' and so on, and so forth). It ended with the request for a 'fynall suppressinge of the saide Stage playes, as well at the Theatre Curten and banckside'. It is unlikely that the Privy Council would have responded in any way to this only too familiar and unspecified litany of complaints. But on 28 July they *did* issue a command concerning the playhouses. It cannot have been a reply to the Lord Mayor. Apart from all other considerations, both missives would have crossed in transit. The distance between Greenwich and Guildhall would have prohibited an instant response unless the matter were very urgent. Nothing in the Lord Mayor's letter indicated an emergency.

Yet on the pretext of 'greate disorders' (not mentioned at all by the Lord Mayor, who would almost certainly have mentioned them), the Privy Council not only issued a restraint order on 28 July against all performances that summer, but they also went on to order that all playhouses within three miles of the City of London were to be 'plucked downe quite the stages, Gallories and Roomes that are made for people to stand in and so to deface the same as they maie not be ymploied agayne to suche use'. Amongst other signatories to this unprecedented order was the Lord Admiral himself. What had the playhouses been getting up to to warrant such a draconian measure? A clue is given in the Privy Council's response the following week to a letter sent them by Richard Topcliffe, a man relentless in his witchhunt against those loyal to Rome and one adept in torture. He had been given a tip-off by an unknown informant and, on the basis of that, had informed the Privy Council that a subversive play, *The Isle of Dogs,* was being performed by Pembroke's Men at the Swan.

For how long this play had been in the Swan's repertoire is unknown. *The Isle of Dogs* is a lost manuscript co-authored by Thomas Nashe and Ben Jonson with the collaboration of certain actors. That it was satirical, we know, but other than

52

that, we know very little. It contained 'very seditious and sclanderous matter' together with 'leude and mutynous behaviour' (according to the Privy Council who responded immediately to Topcliffe's letter). Presumably though, the script must at some point have been read and licensed by the Master of Revels.

Had the actors then, wishing to respond to some sensitive political matter of the day, interpolated extra, unlicensed, improvised speeches? Thomas Nashe, writing some two years after the event, said he was responsible *only* for the first act, 'the other foure acts . . . by the players were supplied, which bred both theire trouble and mine to'. Two players, Gabriel Spencer and Robert Shaa, along with Ben Jonson, were jailed almost immediately. Had they had a hand in some impromptu 'devy-singe of that sedytious matter'? Jonson at this point in his career was an actor, and by all accounts, not a very good actor either. It was quite a spectacular debut, then, that Jonson made as a writer with *The Isle of Dogs*. After that, the name of Ben Jonson was unlikely to be forgotten. Thomas Nashe, more experienced and not wishing to take the rap for the offence, wisely fled to Yarmouth whilst investigations proceeded.

Richard Topcliffe, known as 'the cruellest Tyrant of all England' had previously broken another writer under torture. In 1593, his methods had forced Thomas Kyd to incriminate Christopher Marlowe. Now, in 1597, Topcliffe was to be given another opportunity to 'break' a writer. The Privy Council gave Topcliffe instructions on 15 August to make further enquiries. Indeed, they required him to make the players and writers 'deale trulie' with him, and they urged him to follow up the papers found in Nashe's lodgings. Despite being given such a wide brief, Topcliffe, in the end, was unable to proceed with anything that would stick. Perhaps all manuscripts were quickly destroyed. Besides, improvisations are rarely committed to paper. By early October, Spencer, Shaa and Jonson were quietly released from prison. The whole affair seems to have been based either on trumped up charges or irresponsible risk-taking, which was hastily hushed up. The question is, was *The Isle of Dogs* scandal behind the Privy Council's edict on 28 July commanding the demolition of the playhouses? And why, anyway, were the playhouses then not pulled down?

Philip Henslowe evidently was not that put out by the order to pull down his playhouse. From 28 July onwards, he kept his head down and got on with plans for the autumn as if nothing had happened – or, indeed, would happen. The Privy Council edict ordering the demolition of playhouses also ordered that all performances anywhere (inns, public places etc.) should be banned until All Hallows (1 November). Henslowe, however, anticipated being back in business by Michaelmas (29 September). Following the loss of so many players from the Admiral's Men earlier in 1597, he started to take a more active part in company affairs and, copying a practice initiated by Langley, he began placing actors on contract personally to him under bond. Henslowe spent much of August in negotiations with various men to start work at the Rose 'from mihelmase'.

In a typical deal struck on 10 August with the actor, William Borne, Henslowe referred for the first time to *The Isle of Dogs*. He directly linked the 'Restraynt' that had closed the Rose, with the 'playinge the Ieylle of dooges'. He blamed the events at the Swan for the closure of his theatre. Carol Rutter argues that Henslowe was wrong because the dates of the 28 July edict and the subsequent tip-off from Topcliffe a whole week later do not tally. For her the edict, despite Henslowe's contemporary explanation, therefore remains 'an enigma'. It is true that the dates do not tally and, in the light of no other surviving documentary evidence, it is possible that the 28 July Privy Council edict is completely unrelated to the later charge of sedition at the Swan. However, whoever tipped off Topcliffe may also have passed on their information to the Privy Council at the same time. Topcliffe may have been not so much informing the Privy Council as seeking from them some more of that sadistic work he found so agreeable. In the Privy Council Minute of 15 August, which gave Topcliffe the authority to pursue the matter further, it was the Privy Council who took responsibility for the arrest of the actors: '*wee* caused some of the Players to be apprehended' (my italics). This clearly indicated that the Privy Council were not only already apprised of the affair but had also taken their own action by arresting Ben Jonson *et al* before Topcliffe wrote to them.

Perhaps activities at the Swan accounted for the Privy Council's reference on 28 July to the 'great disorders'; disorders which may have emanated from outrageously satirical attacks delivered from its stage and which continued until the arrests of the principal players later in August. How else to account for the Privy Council's concern about disorder on 28 July? The

Privy Council was far more likely to be sensitive to political sedition concerning matters of state, rather than the moral considerations which so permanently affected the Puritan sensibility of whichever Lord Mayor was in office.

With hindsight, Thomas Nashe described this storm in a teacup as the 'straunge turning of the Ile of Dogs, from a commedie to a tragedie two summers past'. For storm in a teacup it had proved to be. Philip Henslowe was quite right in acting as if it would be business as usual once the uproar had died down. His playhouse was closed for two and a half months, but it was not pulled down. Not even the Swan Theatre was pulled down, though doubtless to Henslowe's joy it remained more or less permanently closed. The savagery of the Privy Council's command says more about its extraordinarily supple methods of government than about its impotence in executing its own imperative. Such a muscular threat, if backed up by flexible offstage negotiations, reminded the players and the playhouse owners of the line that could – and would – be drawn when things got out of hand.

Once the dust had settled, all the playhouses were back in business with the exception of the Swan. It stayed closed and thereafter only operated on an intermittent basis. Furthermore, it was ordered that playing companies be limited to the Admiral's Men and the Chamberlain's Men. The Chamberlain's Men, however, now found themselves without a base. Not only had they lost their winter residency at the Swan, but Giles Allen – or Alleyn, (Elizabethan spelling is so uncertain), who owned the ground lease for the Theatre, refused to extend its term. 'Is that Giles Alleyn from whom old Burbage got the land, Ned's kin?' asks the novelist, Anthony Burgess, floating a most attractive idea. Edward Alleyn's family did originate from this part of London. Both his father and his brother were landowners. Was Giles another member of the clan? Had he been biding his time since Alleyn's humiliating defeat at the hands of the Burbages in 1591, and chose this moment to revenge family honour? James Burbage was by now dead (he had died in January 1597) but his son, Cuthbert, fared no better with the intransigent Giles. The Chamberlain's Men were evicted and the Theatre was dark. Furthermore, the Burbage's capital was tied up in the Blackfriars venture which was still denied a theatre licence. For the time being, the Chamberlain's

Men had no venue other than the distinctly inferior Curtain. Sometime at this settled point in the Rose Theatre's history, Edward Alleyn, who had long topped the bill, decided to retire. The precise date of his last performance is unknown. Bernard Beckerman points out that after 11 October 1597, Alleyn, who had until then been acting as guarantor for loans to the Admiral's Men, ceased to take this responsibility, although did continue to act as witness to loans until 8 December.

Alleyn's fame and reputation cannot be over-estimated. Thomas Nashe said that not since Roscius nor Aesop, 'those admyred tragedians that haue liued euer since before Christ was borne, could euer perform more in action than famous Ned Allen'. On tour, at Court and at the Rose, Alleyn had made memorable the parts of Orlando Furioso, Tamburlaine, Faustus and, of course, the Jew of Malta. Other than continuing to revive these great parts, there were no further challenges left in theatre for him. Another Marlowe was unlikely to come along. At 31, Alleyn was still a young man in the autumn of 1597, and so the subject of Alleyn's retirement has attracted much speculation. Some say he felt tainted by a profession which provoked so much ire from the Church. Legends persisted that his nerve had never been quite the same since he counted an extra devil, or two, on stage during *Dr Faustus*. 'The truth of which', said William Prynne, the Puritan pamphleteer who spread this story in 1633, 'I have heard from many now alive, who well remember it.' However, his tone immediately suggests a false rumour. The woman who hallucinated and saw Hieronimo on her deathbed was not the only exemplar deployed by Puritan preachers in their attacks on theatre.

The truth was probably more pedestrian. Edward Alleyn had amassed a fortune. As well as being a sharer with the Admiral's Men, since 1594, he had also been the sole owner of the Bear Garden, where he and Henslowe jointly promoted the 'sport' under licence from the master, Ralph Bowes. Of the 468 recorded Elizabethan and Jacobean actors, only a handful accumulated real wealth and Edward Alleyn was one of them. Alleyn was no poverty-stricken player, and he was possibly hoping for a knighthood. After all, was he not the Queen's favourite? An actor's social status had risen in the course of the reign from the rank of beggar to the rank of a gentleman bearing his own coat of arms. Ben Jonson was quite amused by this turn of events and mockingly rendered Shakespeare's coat of arms, with its motto 'non sans droit', as 'not without mustard' in *Every Man Out of his Humour*. The hoary old show biz tradition of performers dying in harness did not originate in this period, when plague or poverty could so easily take an actor in his prime. Many actors got out of the profession altogether once they had accumulated enough money to opt for a settled bourgeois life. Alleyn sold his stock to the Admiral's Men whilst retaining a privileged involvement with the company. It threatened him with no responsibilities, and he continued to live as neighbour to the Rose Theatre, on Bankside. Eventually, he was to devote himself entirely to charitable work.

The Admiral's Men opened at the Rose a fortnight after Michaelmas 1597, as Henslowe had anticipated in the previous summer. Rehearsals no doubt occupied the actors for the first two weeks of their contracts. Many of Pembroke's Men had scurried down Maid Lane from the Swan, when it appeared that Langley's venture was sunk, and they signed up for lengthy periods against a forfeit of £40. The only problem was that they had also signed bonds with Francis Langley for more than twice that amount. The actors were not yet amalgamated into one company and the remnants of Pembroke's Men and the Admiral's Men played together but under both patrons' names. The Admiral's Men went on retaining their familiar name throughout the season despite the Lord Admiral's elevation to Earl of Nottingham on 22 October. Possibly Alleyn gave his farewell performances in *The Spanish Tragedy,* which started the season on 11 October 1597, and in *Dr Faustus,* the third production that followed. It was during this autumn that Henslowe instituted a system of lending money against writers' commissions on a regular basis. The ex-jailbird, Ben Jonson, secured 20s. for a scenario shown to the company on 3 December, and he promised delivery in time for Christmas – just three weeks later. The need of the Admiral's Men for a new Christmas hit was possibly greater even than the need of an impecunious writer for 20s. There is no evidence, however, that they received it. Jonson was never a fast worker and sometimes spent a year writing one play.

Francis Langley went to court against the actors who had broken their £100 bonds with him. Legal proceedings began in November 1597 and went on until May 1598. The actors retaliated by saying that Langley had brought about their defection when the Swan was refused a licence. Langley then counterclaimed that the actors had also defaulted on debts, totalling £300, which they had incurred by borrowing money for costumes. The actors defended the charge by saying that not only did Langley own these costumes but he was also making money on them by hiring them out at a profit. No wonder Andrew Gurr referred to this theatre as 'Langley's unhappy Swan'. Eventually, the cross suits were settled when the players paid Langley £35 against the debts and retrieved some of their property.

At the end of 1597, Henslowe and the players agreed to long-term financial arrangements which were completely independent of Alleyn. Henslowe started to list company debts in a systematic manner. Interest does not appear to have been charged, and his money-lending to the players was therefore not a business arrangement like his pawnbroking to the community. It was instead an indication of his increased managerial functions, possibly undertaken after Alleyn's departure. Another entry in the Diary, dated 29 December 1597, would appear to confirm this. Henslowe wrote, 'A not of all suche goods as I haue Bowght for playnge sence my sonne edward allen leafte (p)laynge'. Under this entry, he started to note what he anticipated would be his continuing investments in theatrical stock. However, the short list which then followed, perhaps signifies that the players put a stop to Henslowe's managerial ambitions.

His loans, however, were another matter: for Henslowe and the players, loans guaranteed some stability. Certainly by comparison with Christmas 1596, Christmas 1597 ended well with an invitation to the Admiral's Men to return once more to Court. It had been an eventful year and by its end, Philip Henslowe had turned the Rose around. He had seen off the opposition from the Swan, which had proved so fatal in the previous year. The main rivals to the Admiral's Men, the Chamberlain's Men, were threatened with homelessness, and the lesser rivals were a broken company. True, Edward Alleyn had retired, but in the quest for new players, new plays and new parts, the company had taken on Ben Jonson and Thomas Dekker. The Rose Theatre once again reigned unchallenged on Bankside. All was set fair for 1598.

Shortly into the new year, the Privy Council further clarified matters for the two official playing companies. An act was passed on 9 February 1598 ('for punyshment of Rogues Vagabonds and Sturdy Beggars') which repealed all other legislation affecting players and increased the penalties for unlicensed entertainers ('. . . be stripped naked from the middle upwardes and shall be openly whipped untill his or her body be bloudye'). Ten days later, the Privy Council issued an order against an unnamed third company which was playing in the capital without permission. They reiterated that only the Admiral's and the Chamberlain's Men were 'licensed and tollerated' and ordered the Justices of Middlesex and Surrey to suppress this illicit troupe. Like many of the Privy Council's directives concerning theatre, this one was not carried out. Still, it was there in the records, for all to see.

The accumulated debt of the Admiral's Men was acknowledged in a statement dated between 8 and 13 March 1598. Individual sums went back to 11 October 1597, and the total came to some £34. Amongst other loans, Henslowe had provided them with £3 to bail Thomas Dekker out of a debtors' prison. Against their deficit, the Admiral's Men listed all their assets on 10 March 1598, including those 'Gone and lost'. The assets included costumes, stage properties and play books. Costumes were a major item, reflecting the significance of dress in Elizabethan times. A man's place in society was designated by colour, fabric and decoration. Costume was also indulged in for its own pleasure, and this created problems. A statute, the year before, had laid down rules and regulations limiting certain sorts of apparel, to certain specified social classes. The idea was to confine 'inordinate excess' only to those entitled by their rank. An actor, offstage or on, wearing the 'payer of crymson satten Venysiones, layd with gowld lace', as listed by Henslowe, was a target for public criticism. Many individual actors also provided their own costumes. Worcester's Men once bought a 'womones gowne of black velluett' for £6 from Thomas Heywood who had just written *A Woman Killed with Kindness,* which, as it so happened, conveniently called for a woman garbed in black velvet.

Costumes had a strong emblematic function. One of the interesting items in Henslowe's inventories is the 'robe for to goo invisibell'. In *Dr Faustus,* Mephistopheles puts a charm on Faustus so that Faustus can 'walk invisible to all'. Girded with the charmed garment, Faustus upsets the Pope at St Peter's feast and hits him on the ear. Emblematic language was easily understood by an Elizabethan audience whose eye was trained

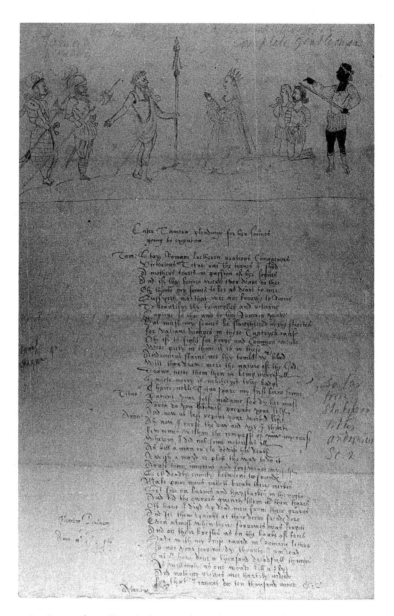

6. A scene from *Titus Andronicus* drawn by Henry Peacham in 1594.
(Marquis of Bath, Longleat)

in its vocabulary. The Peacham sketch made of *Titus Andron-icus* in 1594 represents a typical Elizabethan mix of the stately and the grotesque. There is some attempt at historical costume for the chief characters, but the soldiers look just like contemporary Elizabethan militia – an anachronism in our terms but, emblematically, the soldiers could be 'read' and understood by the Elizabethan spectators. Tokens, like spears, a chain, spurs and, of course, a crown, placed character. The boy playing the part of Tamara became his part when he put on that voluminous gown and enormous crown.

Emblematism was carried through in the stage hangings which draped the tiring house wall – black for a tragedy, cupids for a romance. Battles and executions were staged with gory, yet stylised realism. Drownings were managed symbolically with river gods appearing to carry off their watery victims. 'Three rustie swords', as Jonson deridingly said, were all that was needed to settle the fate of the houses of York and Lancaster. His derision, expressed in the 1616 prologue to the printed edition of *Every Man In His Humour,* was a sign that tastes eventually changed. The 'heavens', which Henslowe had had installed in 1592 and refurbished in 1595, were, twenty years later, another butt for Jonson's humour. He wrote that audiences now would be relieved that:

> . . . neither Chorus wafts you ore the seas;
> Nor creaking throne comes downe, the boyes to please.

Audiences at the Rose Theatre, however, loved such effects. They would have shrieked in terror at the devils streaming out of the 'Hell mought', a property listed by Henslowe in his inventories. Scenery, as we understand it, did not exist, though an early use of a backdrop is indicated by the 'clothe of Sone and Mone'. The stage, with large properties like the 'hell mouth', was not completely bare. There was a choice on offer to the boy who played Rose in Dekker's *The Shoemaker's Holiday.* When he came to the pretty speech, 'Here sit thou down upon this flowery bank', he could have pointed to one of the two 'mose banckes' in stock. Did the 'baye tree', suitably adorned, double up as the rose bush for the Temple garden scene in *Henry VI?* Plain and functional items, beds, tables, chairs are listed by Henslowe along with much more exotic props: chains of dragons, tombs, the entire city of Rome.

Sir Philip Sidney's *Defence of Poesie,* published in 1595, attacked the conventions of Elizabethan stage practice. If

'Thebes' is written above a door, 'What child is there,' he asked, 'doth believe it is Thebes?' As a classicist, Sidney harked back to Aristotle and the unities of time, place and action, but Elizabethans challenged the developments of European Renaissance theatre. Miracle and Mystery plays had accustomed them to the dramatic representation of all of Eternity or the Cosmos, enacted on the wooden slats of the old pageant carts. The stage of the Rose was an imaginary domain and a sign above a door was an aid to the imagination, not an inadequate representation of reality. Characters on stage indulged in all kinds of 'unrealistic' behaviour. They spoke poetry. They soliloquized. They indulged in apostrophe. The intermingling of illusion and reality was the primary aesthetic experience and visual signifiers and effects, an important theatrical asset.

On 13 March 1598, three days after the stock had been itemised, the Admiral's Men started borrowing again. One loan went towards paying the 'carman' in an emergency for 'caryinge & bryngen' new stuff to a private performance given in Fleet Street after the Admiral's Men's 'own stufe was lost'. Another was for 5s. spent at 'the taverns in fyshestreate for good cheare'. (Could the good cheer have accounted for the loss of the 'stufe'?). Most of the loans were, however, concerned with play commissions. The system of collaborative writing was by now well established. The writers were the employees of the actors and Henslowe loaned the actors the money to pay the playwrights. Down-payment based on a sample scenario formed the equivalent of a contract. The average going rate for a completed play was £6, which would then be shared on a pro rata basis amongst its contributors. In the years between 1598 and 1600, a writer like Thomas Dekker completed eight of his own plays, collaborated on another twenty-four and probably earned about £30 a year.

Up to five writers might collaborate on any given script and perhaps individuals specialised in certain sorts of writing; the comic bits (although those might be left to the clowns with their own individual specialities), the love interest, the big speech and so on. The playwright, John Arden, points out that all this would have been made very much easier by the constant repetition in Elizabethan plays of a whole range of stock scenes. 'I do not mean,' he hastily adds, 'that the *content* of the scenes is stock . . . any Playwright told the size of the company and the type of story they wanted dramatising would have at his disposal a complete series of received conventions into which he could fit his narrative.' Shakespeare started writing in this way. There are academic doubts about his involvement in *Two Noble Kinsmen, Sir Thomas More, Henry VIII* and *Pericles.* This might be because so many people, scholars in particular, are reluctant to believe that Shakespeare was capable of writing badly. This priority, though, had less to do with fine literature than getting the show on.

Once a script was delivered, production was rapid, and it must have been an intensive learning experience. Output was prolific. It has been calculated that over two thousand plays were written in the period between the 1574 Royal Patent and the Parliamentary Ordinance which closed the theatres in 1642. Inevitably some of these team-written plays were nothing better than hack work. Yet hack work often has the advantage of catching the pulse of the time. Durability in theatre terms is not the most reliable measure of a play's true worth in its day. Collaboration, according to RSC director, Trevor Nunn, was a method of work 'that the Elizabethans and Jacobeans enthusiastically embraced'. The golden age of Hollywood also relied on collaborative writing and, amongst others, the Marx Brothers worked in this way. Joan Littlewood's most successful productions were largely a result of collaboration between the writer, Joan Littlewood and the cast. Certain modern-day playwrights (notably Howard Brenton and David Hare) have, from time to time, chosen this method.

Henry Chettle features prominently in Henslowe's list of loans, chasing commissions in the summer of 1598. On delivery of one manuscript, Chettle usually immediately offered an idea for another. As only two to three weeks sometimes elapsed between taking the idea to the company and bringing back to them the completed script, a team of writers was necessary to fulfil the punishing schedule. In early May 1598, for example, Henry Chettle was given £1 on the strength of his idea for a play, *Black Batman of the North*: the title alone possibly justified the sum. On 22 May, Chettle, after collaboration with Thomas Dekker, Thomas Drayton and Robert Wilson, delivered the final manuscript of *Black Batman* and received a £6 fee to be split four ways. By 13 June *Black Batman* was up and running and evidently in rehearsal. On that day, Henslowe recorded loans of £5 towards 'divers thinges' for *Black Batman,* with an added £3 for more 'divers thinges' the following day.

On 14 June, whilst *Black Batman* was in rehearsal, Chettle secured a first payment of 5s. for a new play entitled *Richard Coeur de Lion's Funeral,* and went back the next day for a further 5s. Two days later, on 17 June, Chettle had added Richard Wilson and Anthony Munday to his team, and all three men got 15s. each. Money was dragged out of Henslowe against this play in dribs and drabs, no doubt as dribs and drabs of the play were dragged out of its authors. In the end, its originator received another 15s. on 21 June, whilst, final payments of 20s. went to Munday, 30s. went to Wilson and a further 30s. went to Thomas Drayton, yet another writer brought into the syndicate. Perhaps, for that larger sum, Drayton acted as a much needed script-doctor. Henslowe in the end settled with Chettle for a meagre 10s. towards Chettle's 'pte of boockes' (part of the book). Besides, Henslowe added, Chettle 'Reastes . . . in my Deatte the somme of xxxs'. (Chettle was forever in debt and once had to be bailed out of Marshalsea, with the help of another loan from Henslowe.) All in all, between 14 and 26 June, the entire script of *Richard Coeur de Lion* was written with the help of four writers at a total cost of £5. 15s.

No sooner had Chettle got *Richard Coeur de Lion* out of the way, than he approached Henslowe with a third idea – a sequel to the earlier *Black Batman of the North.* Sequels to, or adaptations of, plays which had proved popular were a standard way of spinning out the play's appeal. At Chettle's rate of production, it was no surprise that he had gained a reputation for failing sometimes to deliver. Harry Porter, on the occasion of *Black Batman II,* offered to provide a guarantee against default, as did Robert Shaa for Chettle's fourth idea later that summer. The sequel to *Black Batman* was delivered on 14 July. This time, Chettle appeared to have accepted major responsibility as the writer, for although Richard Wilson was brought in to add a 10s. contribution, Chettle received £4. 15s. in all.

Fired by his re-acquired ability to meet deadlines, Chettle, backed by Shaa, put forward the idea for *A Woman's Tragedy.* This time, Chettle was given the full fee of £5 in *advance,* 'eather to do the playe or els to paye the mony with in one forthnyght'. On the whole, the romantic comedies and tragedies and particularly the chronicle-history plays which featured so prominently in Henslowe's Diary from 1592–1597 were gradually giving way by 1598 to domestic comedy or tragedy. A title like *A Woman's Tragedy* is joined by William Haughton's *A Woman will have her Will* and Harry Porter's *Two Angry Women of Abingdon* (as well as its follow-up, *Two Merry Women of Abingdon*). All were written a year after *The Merry Wives of Windsor,* Shakespeare's only middle-class comedy.

The Elizabethans knew the faults of their own taste, which, in any event, was changing. Contemporary comment was every bit as withering as the later judgements of Robert Bower, that understanding citizen of Southwark and its enthusiastic chronicler who may not be as eminent as Shaw but is probably the more representative critic for all that. Bower was not alone in 1902, when he said that 'the plays of Elizabethan times had been barbarous, their plots full of horrors and one of the writers of the time afraid lest his massacre might seem insipid, promised that his second play would "greater murders tell"'. This unnamed writer was prepared to plumb the depths. However, he probably did not go as far as Cyril Tourneur did. In *The Atheist's Tragedy* (1607–11), Tourneur (not a Rose dramatist) came up with what has to be the most risible stage direction outside a Brian de Palma movie: 'As he raises up the axe (to chop off his enemy's head) he strikes out his own brains.' However, Thomas Nashe, back in 1589, had said of Thomas Kyd that he 'let blood line by line and page by page'. The Tourneur play is evidence that sensationalist writing lingered on as the new domestic comedy emerged. Both sorts of plays were features not just of the Rose Theatre, but of all the playhouses contemporary with it.

R.A. Foakes and R.T. Rickert, editing Henslowe's Diary in 1961, are critical of literary judgement based on prejudice against Henslowe. They single out R.B. Sharpe, who in 1935 described Henslowe as 'an ignorant man, whose spelling bears witness to a complete lack of acquaintance with literature'. Sharpe, given that premise, not unnaturally concluded that the Admiral's Men were forced to make a 'proletarian appeal' to lower-class audiences. G.L. Hosking in his 1952 biography of Edward Alleyn continued in this vein. 'The Lord Admiral's Men' he writes, 'served the popular taste for melodrama, the Lord Chamberlain's the taste of the more discriminating.' Foakes and Rickert are doubtful about such social division since it seems to imply that a more sophisticated class of people made their way to the Globe 'in anticipation', they mockingly say, 'of a kind of Third Programme'. The Rose staged *Titus Andronicus, Dr Faustus, Henry VI. Part III, The Jew of Malta, The Shoemaker's Holiday, Tamburlaine, The Spanish Tragedy,* and *A Woman Killed with Kindness*. Set against these classics are the perhaps forgettable, *Strange News out of Poland* and *The Blind Eats Many a Fly* (one of 'two hundred and twenty, in which I haue had either an entire hand, or at least, the maine finger' – Thomas Heywood's claim says it all).

Heywood, like Chettle, was a prolific writer for the Rose but not many of his plays reached publication. 'One reason,' Heywood gave, 'is that many of them by shifting and change of companies have been negligently lost. Others of them are still retained in the hands of some actors, who think it against their peculiar profit to have them come into print and a third, that it never was any great ambition in me, to be in this kind vol-uminously read!' Ben Jonson was alone in having the great ambition to be published in his lifetime. Shakespeare only ever wrote two works specifically for publication, and they were narrative poems. Jonson ensured Shakespeare's posthumous fame by helping to gather up his collected works for a printed edition in 1623. Whilst he was doing this, it probably occurred to him to achieve immortality for himself. In 1616, he brought out a folio edition of his own Works. It is rather telling that he entirely omitted from this collection his collaborative plays for the Rose (*Hot Anger Soon Cold* with Harry Porter and Henry Chettle in 1598, *Page of Plymouth* with Thomas Dekker in 1599 and *The Scots Tragedy* with Henry Chettle '& other Jentellman', also in 1599).

Jonson's move to seek publication would have been deemed vainglorious by his fellow writers and treacherous by the playing companies. In this way, however, Jonson ensured the survival of his best work. Many manuscripts by other writers have possibly been undeservedly lost. Some that survive would be no loss to anyone if they had not. Others, though, suffered an undignified end, the victim of John Warburton's unthinking cook. Warburton (1682–1759) was an antiquarian and a keen collector of old manuscripts. He bought the original 'books' of everything from early Jonson to Middleton and the later writers. In 1720, Warburton sold some of his collection to the Earl of Oxford to raise money for drink. His cook, Betsy Baker, then 'unluckily burned or put under pye bottoms' fifty-five manuscripts. A great deal of the Rose's repertoire went to line Betsy's pie tins. The survival of plays has been more a product of chance than critical evaluation. As Margaret Slythe, the Dulwich College librarian said of the survival of the Henslowe / Alleyn papers, 'neglect has a way of preserving things'.

Shakespeare, though his plays are no different in kind from those of his fellows, was recognised by both his peers and his public as being exceptional. Throughout the period of the Rose Theatre, the quality of writing improved overall, as the writers learnt from the experience of seeing their work staged. Their drama fed off the demands of the audience as much as being fed by the rivalry of so many writers. The Rose's audience were not only capable of enjoying something that was more than just the theatrical equivalent of today's tabloid press, they preferred it. Henslowe's Diary is evidence of that. The plays we now deem to be classics were the ones that people paid good money to see. Marlowe made more at the box office than his contemporaries, and Marlowe's better plays made more than his poorer ones. It was the lack of new plays by Marlowe that had largely forced the Admiral's Men into encouraging teams of writers to work together towards quick delivery of material.

Of the total debt of £120. 15s. 4d. incurred by the Admiral's Men from 13 March to 18 July 1598, £84 had gone on plays, either on new commissions or retrieving old plays. (The company pursued Martin Slater in retirement for the five books he held.) This substantial investment in writers, was not, however, reflected in increased takings. The Admiral's Men had reached the point where they were unable to repay their debts out of income. From 29 July onwards, Henslowe recorded that 'Here I Begyne to Receue the wholle gallereys'. A solution of sorts to an accumulating problem of mounting debts.

Without a doubt, even at the unfortunately located and by now, old-fashioned Curtain, the Chamberlain's Men had the edge when it came to crowd-pulling plays. In September 1598, a schoolmaster called Francis Meres published the pamphlet, *Palladis Tamia; Wit's Treasury,* which provides a contemporary critical commentary on the playwrights of the day and singles out William Shakespeare for excellence in both comedy and tragedy. Twelve plays of his were named and his 'fine filed phrase' was particularly commended. The Rose writers were not entirely neglected. Meres also recognised the tragedic gift in

Marlowe, Peele, Kyd, Drayton, Chapman and Dekker and the comedic gift in Lyly, Lodge, Greene, Nashe, Heywood, Chettle, Chapman and Munday (the latter acclaimed as 'our best plotter'). Jonson, who was in an ambivalent position with the Rose, was mentioned as one of 'the best for Tragedie'.

In the autumn of 1598, Jonson was to demonstrate something other than literary talent when it came to tragedy. On 26 September 1598, Philip Henslowe wrote to his son-in-law, Edward Alleyn, who was staying with friends in Sussex, with the 'harde & heavey' news that Gabriel Spencer, a member of the Admiral's Men since 1597, had been killed in a duel by Ben Jonson. Spencer and Jonson had both been involved in *The Isle of Dogs* affair and incarcerated together during the summer of 1597. The reason for their quarrel is unknown but Henslowe was furious. The news, he wrote, 'hurteth me greatley'. He referred scornfully to Jonson, the writer, as 'Jonson bricklayer'. It was well-known that Jonson's stepfather had refused Jonson a university education and instead had him apprenticed as a bricklayer. Jonson only escaped being one of the 800 felons to be hanged that year by pleading benefit of clergy and reading out loud the required Latin verse from the Psalms which proved a clerical vocation. Instead of swinging, Jonson was branded a felon and saw all his goods confiscated. On 23 October, George Chapman took over finishing the last two acts of a tragedy commissioned by Henslowe from Ben Jonson. Temporarily in Henslowe's disfavour, Jonson before too long was once again to be under commission at the Rose.

The letter which brought Alleyn the news about Gabriel Spencer and Ben Jonson was mainly concerned with Alleyn's business venture at the Bear Garden. Alleyn had bought the arena back in 1594 and apparently operated there under licence from the Master of the Royal Game of Bears, Bulls and Mastiff Dogs. Henslowe, in this letter, ingratiatingly offered his services as a promoter to his son-in-law, 'not as two friends but as two Joyned in one'. Soon, the two of them were to be joined in theatrical partnership once again because the problem of the Burbage's lease for the Theatre had not gone away. The Chamberlain's Men, unhappy at the Curtain, and unable to come to a deal with Giles Allen (who may or may not be Ned's kin), planned an audacious revenge of their own. The original twenty-one-year ground lease of 1576, said that the timbers of the Theatre belonged to James Burbage, if removed before expiry. The lease had now expired. Most of James Burbage's capital was tied up in the Blackfriars venture which had yet to pay off. But with the old timbers of the Theatre, his sons could build a new playhouse and the plan was to dismantle the Theatre, transport its timbers and re-erect it in that most successful of locations – Bankside.

On 28 December 1598, armed with axes and crowbars, the Burbages and twelve workmen invaded the Theatre. It had been empty since 1597 and stood 'in darke silence, and vast solitude'. Packing up the Theatre and taking it away was no moonlit flit. The men brazened it out in 'forcible and ryotous manner'. No amount of stealth would have provided sufficient cover to remove the large quantity of heavy timber from under the nose of Giles Allen (or Alleyn). He, of course, disputed the Burbages' claim to the timber and later took the matter to court, claiming that he had other uses for it. The Burbages, meanwhile, had effectively settled the matter. Under the direction of Peter Street, a master carpenter, they pulled down the playhouse, and transported it in segments across London and over the Thames. John Stow reported that the Thames was frozen over that Christmas so the task of transportation may have been made easier by sliding the beams across the ice.

Just one hundred years from the Rose, equidistant from Henslowe's theatre in Maid Lane and Henslowe's home in Clink Street, Peter Street started to erect the theatre that was to be known as the Globe. If Giles Allen (or Alleyn) was 'Ned's kin', as Anthony Burgess imagines, and his refusal to renew the lease was motivated by family revenge backdating to Edward Alleyn's eviction from the Theatre in 1591, then it had disastrously backfired. The delicate balance of playing companies, one in the north, the other in the south, was at an end. Although building work on the Globe would stretch until at least the summer of 1599, Philip Henslowe and the Admiral's Men would have known by the end of 1598 that all their hard effort and investment in writers that year would be undone by the permanent presence of their rivals, virtually on the Rose Theatre's doorstep. Despite an appearance once again at Court, there can have been little seasonal warmth in the hearts of the Admiral's Men to toast in the New Year.

The Rose enjoyed its last good box office this Christmas and the Admiral's Men performed as usual until Lent. They continued to hand over all their gallery income to Henslowe. On 21 February 1599, the Chamberlain's Men signed a thirty-one-year lease with Nicholas Brend, owner of the land on which the new Globe now stood, whilst Philip Henslowe's ground lease for the Rose messuage had only six years to run. The Rose's takings made a nose dive when the theatre re-opened on 26 March 1599, although it was too soon for the Globe to have been in business yet. By May, the building work may have been complete as a certain Thomas Brand referred to the Globe as 'de novo edificata' in this month. Competition from the Globe would have been formidable. Apart from anything else, it was the latest thing in theatre architecture. Although built with the timbers of the 1576 Theatre, the Globe was not a replica. Since 1576, a revolution in drama had taken place, which would have been reflected as much in theatre architecture as in theatre practice and writing. Peter Street's Globe must technically have outstripped Langley's Swan in much the same way as Langley's Swan outstripped Henslowe's Rose.

The Admiral's Men this year changed their name to Nottingham's Men, honouring their patron's elevation to the Earldom back in October 1597. Henslowe failed to enter anything to do with income in his Diary during the summer of 1599. Plague may have interrupted playing, though recorded deaths from plague in 1599 were low. Despite the lack of box office entries, Henslowe continued to record company loans which indicated that the Admiral's Men were in production somewhere in London. Carol Rutter suggests that the lack of entries might represent a new arrangement whereby Henslowe allowed Nottingham's Men to take all the box office to tide them over during this difficult period, when its rival first opened its doors. Thomas Platter, on holiday from Basle, wrote back a description of *Julius Caesar* which played at the Globe on 21 September 1599. 'An excellent performance,' he said. The Admiral's Men did their best to compete. They commissioned plays from 'the new poete' George Marston as well as from the old hands. The ubiquitous Henry Chettle was still chasing commissions with his fellows, George Chapman, Thomas Dekker and Ben Jonson (now obviously forgiven by Henslowe and co-writing *Page of Plymouth* and *The Scots Tragedy*). On 16 October, the Admiral's Men set out to exploit a situation which had brought the Chamberlain's Men into some difficulty in the past. The issue had once again become topical. They commissioned a squad of writers (Richard Wilson, Thomas Drayton, Anthony Munday and Richard Hathaway) to write *Sir John Oldcastle*.

Shakespeare's Falstaff had originally gone under the name of Sir John Oldcastle in the two parts of *Henry IV,* written in 1597. Calling a fat and cowardly buffoon by the name of Oldcastle was one way for the Chamberlain's Men to get at the present Lord Cobham (his ancestor had been the valiant anti-Papist, Sir John Oldcastle, Lord Cobham). For a short while back in 1596/7, his predecessor, the seventh Lord Cobham, had held the office of Lord Chamberlain and proved singularly unsympathetic to players, personally blocking the Burbages' plans in Blackfriars. (Henry Carey, Lord Hunsdon and the previous Lord Chamberlain, had died in July 1596, and his son, George Carey, was passed over for this position. The Chamberlain's Men had therefore to go under the name of Hunsdon's Men until the seventh Lord Cobham died in March 1597. George Carey was then appointed to the vacant office of Lord Chamberlain and the players once again reverted to their familiar name of the Chamberlain's Men.)

The seventh Lord Cobham was not a man easily amused. He had taken exception to the satirical use made of his family name. Under pressure, the Chamberlain's Men then renamed Oldcastle, Falstaff, and Cobham's enemies nicknamed Cobham, Falstaff. The current Lord Cobham in 1599 was a prominent courtier and actively involved in the humiliation of the Earl of Essex, following Essex's fruitless escapades in Ireland. In September 1599, the Essex affair was hot political gossip, and thus the Falstaff/Oldcastle affair gained new currency. The Chorus in Shakespeare's *Henry V,* the play which had possibly opened the Globe, toasted Essex's expected triumph in Ireland. Essex, however, had failed to quell the rebellion and, instead, he had made a truce with Tyrone, the rebel leader. Formerly the Queen's favourite, Essex was then arrested by the ageing Queen and, though now released, he was a dangerous man at a time when succession to the throne was still unsettled.

This was too good an opportunity to miss. The Admiral's Men seized it, and they got out their own version of the historical Sir John Oldcastle, 'Whose vertue shone above the rest'. The play which was written in the autumn of 1599, blatantly pandered to those audiences who were enjoying the spectacle of Essex's downfall. In such measures, players demonstrated their political allegiance. The Globe had sided with the rebellious Essex and, later, were to be asked to make a much more overt act of support. The more conservative Rose had either taken the establishment side at face value, or else had just capitalised on the political feeling in general which had been generated in the capital by Essex's misfortunes. Whatever the case, the box office at the Rose picked up.

Nottingham's Men, however, were not prepared to go on making shift in this way. A *succés de scandale* like *Sir John Oldcastle* might temporarily boost the box office, but a more permanent solution had to be found now that the Chamberlain's Men had moved south. The lease of the Rose was soon to expire; the theatre in 1·599 was an old-fashioned building, and altogether it made sense for the players to concentrate on another venue, north of the City. On 24 December 1599, Edward Alleyn came out of retirement and acquired a lease from Patrick Brewe on a plot of land in Golding Lane, close to Whitecross Street, beyond Cripplegate. Here the Fortune Theatre was to be built, using Henslowe's money and the experience of Peter Street. Alleyn and Henslowe acted quickly. On 8 January they jointly agreed a contract with Peter Street which specified reproducing all of the innovative features of the Globe, its seating arrangements, divisions and stairs. The stage, for example, was to be framed and proportioned 'like vnto the Stadge of the saide Plaiehowse Called the Globe'. In instalments, Peter Street was to receive a total of £880. Alleyn approached his former patron to use his influence at Court to expedite matters.

Charles Howard, Earl of Nottingham issued a warrant to the Privy Council and to the Justices and Officers in Middlesex on 12 January 1600. He justified the new building on the basis of the 'dangerous decaye of that Howse ... on the Banck', together with the improbable assertion, no doubt trumped up for the occasion, that the area was 'verie noysome ... in the wynter tyme'. And he reminded the Privy Council that Her Majesty had a 'greate lykeinge and Contentment' for the players and thus he entreated them to let building work go ahead without 'molestacon'. Confident that Nottingham's support would win the day, Henslowe allowed building work to begin at once. Henslowe, who had had some kind of hand in the waterman's petition of 1592, recognised the political advantage of organised support and encouraged the local community to register their approval of his plans. In January a petition was sent to the Privy Council from the inhabitants of Finsbury Park giving reasons why the 'Newe Playhowse . . . might proceede and be Tollerated'. Firstly, because the theatre was to be situated in fields, away from residential areas. And secondly, because Henslowe had promised to make weekly donations towards the relief of the poor which, otherwise the parish was unable to afford. It was signed by twenty-seven men including the constable, warden and two overseers of the poor. Suggestions that the ungodly playhouses should tithe a regular amount to parish relief were longstanding. As early as January 1587, an anonymous Puritan had written to the Privy Council comparing the 'proud players' with the 'pore people' and recommended that the players should 'pay a weekly pention to the pore.'

Players were not uncharitable and not without social responsibility. Edward Alleyn had left the stage largely to devote himself to good works and was to go on to found the College of God's Gift in Dulwich at a cost of £10,000. Like his father-in-law, Philip Henslowe, he was to end his days as a vestryman of St Saviour's, the Rose's local church. The continual railing against players was unjustified and led the actor, Nathan Field, to retaliate from the pulpit at St Saviour's. He protested at 'the extraordinary violence of your passion particularly to point att me and some other of my quality, and directly to our faces in the publique assembly to pronounce us dampned, as thoughe yow ment to send us alive to hell in the sight of many witnesses. Christ,' he reminded the Bible thumpers, 'never sought the strayed sheepe in that manner; he never cursed it with acclamation or sent a barking dogg to fetch it home, but gently brought it uppon his own shoulders.' By offering to contribute towards parish relief, Henslowe found a way for playhouses to secure quasi-official acceptance by the Church. The Church after almost two decades of failing to suppress playhouses, was probably by now quite happy to make this kind of accommodation. In March 1600, the Archbishop of Canterbury ordered St Saviour's, 'that the churchwardens shall talk with the players for tithes'. It was a tacit recognition that playhouses on Bankside were there to stay.

However, other residents near Golding Lane were not prepared to accept a new playhouse in their midst even with the offer of charitable alms. They too had the ear of the Privy Council. Lord Willoughby led a group of men who successfully objected to the proposed Fortune Theatre on 9 March 1600. The Privy Council then reminded the Justices of Middlesex of the Council's 1594 edict to 'pluck downe' the playhouses. The new Fortune, they said, was a 'scandall' which would 'greatly dysplease her Majestie'. The Justices were asked to stop all further building work and 'deface' what had already been built. The reference to the 1597 edict might, however, be a coded instruction to the Justices inviting them to ignore the request completely. After all, in 1597 the playhouses had not been plucked down – and neither, too, was that to be the fate of the partially built Fortune. A month later, the Privy Council reconvened and reversed their earlier decision, following, no doubt, some energetic backstage lobbying by Nottingham. The Warrant that resulted, dated 8 April, this time took on board Nottingham's earlier arguments. It began by acknowledging Alleyn's popularity at Court. 'Sondrye tymes,' the Warrant said, the Queen has, 'signified her pleasuer, that he should revive the same agayne.' Evidently, Alleyn had been persuaded to make the ultimate sacrifice in the best interests of this new venture and come out of complete retirement. The Warrant made direct reference to other details of Nottingham's argument ('the decaye', the 'verie noysome' nature of Bankside). It urged the Justices to permit building to go ahead without 'lett or interrupcion'.

It was not the end of the matter. On 22 June, the Privy Council returned yet again to the vexatious issue of a new London playhouse. They laid down certain stipulations in an order addressed to the Lord Mayor and the local Justices. Firstly, they stipulated, that only two playhouses should be in business, 'one shalbe in Surrey' and the other, in Middlesex. Secondly, they specified that the Curtain had to be pulled down and that the Globe was to be the only theatre allowed in Surrey. Thirdly, the players were allowed to give only *two* performances a week. Fourthly, it was up to the Lord Mayor and the Justices to ensure that this policy was carried out. By off-loading responsibility for these unenforceable demands on the Lord Mayor, the Privy Council was acceding to the City's longheld stance on theatres without changing the situation one bit. The final stipulation ('these orders will be of little force and effecte vnlesse they be duely putt into execution') revealed the Privy Council's quandary. Such was the popularity of play-going that, short of a restraint order, no system of control operated for long. In the past, when it had come to co-operating with impossible demands, the players blatantly went their own way.

As with the Church authorities, who were by now tacitly accepting the role of theatres in public life, the Privy Council's order can be interpreted as an official acceptance of the playhouses' right to exist. It was an advance on the position back in 1574 when only James Burbage was granted the right to build a theatre. Since then, with no Privy Council backing or Royal Warrant, theatres had proliferated. The Privy Council Order of 22 June 1600 now established the right for there to be more than one theatre in London; it legitimated what was, in effect, the unofficial status quo. It was a way of rescinding its negative position of 1597 and it was a positive way forward. It is ironic that the Privy Council came to terms with the situation just at the time when the evolution of drama meant that the large, democratic, outdoor playhouses, which the City feared, were about to give way to the exclusive, intimate, indoor theatres, which were more a matter of private conscience than public order.

Meanwhile back at the cold, decaying, noisome Rose, Nottingham's Men struggled on in the London winter until mid-February when the company may have voluntarily decided to go on tour in the country rather than continue hanging around Bankside for the small amounts of money that the box office was bringing in. Their final season at the Rose began on 6 April. On 10 July, the company made ready for their move across London and signed themselves to Henslowe for debts totalling £300. Building work on the Fortune was a little delayed and it was in the autumn that Nottingham's Men opened Henslowe's and Alleyn's new theatre. They took with them all the familiar Rose repertoire, including some really old favourites given fresh treatments.

In 1601, Ben Jonson was hired for £10 to provide 'new adicyons' to two plays, one of them was Kyd's ever popular *The Spanish Tragedy*. Shakespeare had originally paid *hommage* to Kyd in 1599 by writing *Hamlet,* a version of *Jeronymo*. In 1601, Shakespeare had probably completed a second version of the play, with new additions of his own. Jonson's adaptation, with Alleyn in the lead, offered strong competition. In the same year, Robert Shaa and Edward Juby were paid £5 towards the cost of re-staging the *Jew of Malta*. 'Divers thinge' were bought, and a further 10s. spent at the tailor. The following year, William Bird and Samuel Rowley, were paid £4 for their additions to *Dr Faustus*. The last recorded entry which represented Alleyn's involvements in the business affairs of Nottingham's Men was made on 3 November 1602 when Henslowe lent him 40s. to pay Thomas Dekker for re-writing parts of *Tasso*.

Henslowe's Rose would, in the future, see new plays and new players on its stage. Pembroke's Men played there for two dates in late October. Whilst business at the Fortune proved immensely profitable, business at the Rose seems to have ceased after Pembroke's two performances. They only earned Henslowe 11s. 6d. in all. Both Nottingham's Men and the Chamberlain's Men appeared at Court that Christmas, but so too did two other companies, the Children of St Paul's and the Children of the Chapel. These boy companies had a long-standing tradition of public performances since the early sixteenth century and had suddenly become wildly fashionable to the disdain of the professional adult troupes. The vogue did not last long, but it was not without impact. The boy companies attracted big audiences and took Court fees away from the adult companies, as well as enticing writers like the Rose veterans George Chapman and Ben Jonson to write for them. Jonson used the platform provided by the boys in their indoor venues, to launch the 'War of the Theatres'. This was an intensely incestuous 'war', which allowed Jonson to settle a few literary scores.

Meanwhile, there were matters of more political urgency on Bankside than Jonson's aggressive insistence on neo-classical concepts. The Essex controversy which had involved both Bankside theatres in 1599 resurfaced. Essex was still in disgrace and had finally turned against the Queen. He planned an insurrection which would 'liberate' her from her courtiers, though his hidden agenda no doubt involved regicide. To win popular support, a deputation of Essex's men approached the Chamberlain's Men on 7 February 1601, and offered them 40s. to stage an old hit, *Richard II*. They believed the revival of this six-year-old play which told the story of a deposed king, would sufficiently inflame the audience on the Saturday, who would then go on to support Essex's planned insurrection on the Sunday. However the Saturday audience refused to be inflamed and on the following day, the natural lethargy of a British Sunday prevailed. The Earl of Essex with his three hundred men stormed through the City but no one else joined in. The next day, Essex surrendered and was brought to trial. The Chamberlain's

Men were investigated about their involvement and although Essex was executed, the players were acquitted of all charges of sedition. Indeed at the Queen's command, they were invited to perform *Richard II* on the very eve of Essex's execution for the Court at Whitehall.

Two months later the Privy Council took action. They remembered their edict of 22 June 1600 against the Curtain, and wrote to the Justices of Middlesex to complain specifically about plays which dramatised 'gentlemen of good desert and quallity, that are yet alive, under obscure manner, but yet in such sorte, as all the hearers may take notice both of the matter and the persons that are meant thereby'. It may well be that Henslowe had anticipated that the recent political skirmishes of the players would draw attention to the Rose and he may wisely have kept his theatre empty during this period to prevent it being pulled down. On the very last day of 1601, the Privy Council looked again at the matter of London's official theatres. They wrote to the Justices of both Middlesex and Surrey to point out that their 'said order hath bin so farr from taking dew effect'. In so far as this Minute is concerned with illegal performances in Surrey theatres, it seems probable that in 1601 Henslowe did open the Rose, but on an occasional basis only.

The next sighting of the Rose is provided when Philip Henslowe started recording loan entries on 17 August 1602 under the name of 'my Lorde of worsters players'. Worcester's Men were a new company who would directly have benefited from Henslowe's system of loans. Henslowe celebrated the deal by taking them all out to supper. On 21 August, he spent a whole 9s. at the Mermaid Tavern. The Mermaid stood in Bread Street and hosted the Friday Street Club (an entrance was in Friday Street). Sir Walter Raleigh was the founding father and the club was frequented by Shakespeare, Donne, Beaumont and Fletcher. Beaumont apostrophised Jonson in these words:

'What things we have seen
Done at the Mermaid, heard words that have been
So nimble, and so full of subtle flame,
As if that every one from whence they came
Had meant to put his whole wit in jest,
And had resolved to live a fool the rest
Of his dull life.'

Capturing the same note of rhapsody, that unregenerate Bardolater, Robert Bower, apostrophises further: 'What a rare treat it would be to drop in at the old Mermaid and meet the happy coterie of the chief dramatic wits, to listen to the wit of Shakespeare, to note the courtly elegance of Fletcher, to catch the luxuriant Beaumont . . .' Would Worcester's Men have found it a rare treat to be at the Mermaid Tavern for a meal at 9s., all found? Thomas Towne's bequest of £3 towards a supper for his fellow players seems a far more generous spread. Besides, by listing the 9s. in his Diary, Henslowe obviously considered the meal only a necessary business expense, rather than any personal gesture of his own generosity.

The star attraction of the Rose's new company was Will Kempe who had left the Chamberlain's Men in 1599. Thomas Heywood and Thomas Dekker, old Rose stalwarts, joined Worcester's Men as did the newcomers, Thomas Middleton and John Webster. Heywood had now become a sharer with the company and his prolific output dates from this time, as does his sale of the black velvet gown and his script of *A Woman Killed with Kindness*. Henry Chettle, as usual, was working flat out and with Thomas Dekker, collaborated on twenty plays, some designed for Nottingham's Men at the Fortune. *Sir John Oldcastle* was revived in a new version, with £2. 10s. of alterations. Worcester's Men were less concerned with new writers than the Admiral's Men had been. They spent most of their borrowed money on lavish spectacular effects, particularly those that maximised the horrors of untimely and painful death. On 6 March 1603, the Queen watched her last performance at Court: Nottingham's Men, with maybe Alleyn giving his last performance to his greatest Royal fan. Word might have got back to Henslowe that she was dying. On 7 March 1603 he added up a final reckoning with the players, anticipating the public mourning that would close all theatres upon her death. The debts incurred by Worcester's Men had reached £220. 13s. 3d. of which nearly £100 had been repaid. On 12 March, they left London for a tour and on 19 March, the Privy Council closed the theatres. Five days later, Elizabeth I was dead.

It was 'by the kynges licence' that Worcester's Men started to prepare for a new season at the Rose. On 9 May 1603 they began a new loan account with Philip Henslowe. On 25 June, Henslowe negotiated to renew the ground lease for the Rose estate which was due to expire in 1605. Henslowe wanted the same £7 annual rent as was agreed back in 1587. The parish of St Mildred's in Bread Street had other ideas and suggested a lease of £20 a year with a further 100 marks (£40) service charges, towards maintenance. 'I sayd,' wrote Henslowe that 'I wold Rather pulledowne the playehowse.' Henslowe did not carry out this threat but after that date he seems to have let the theatre just rot. He recorded no further entries in his Diary about the Rose.

Plague had interrupted all public life in London since May 1603, and 30,000 citizens were to die before it abated, one of them being the improvident actor Robert Browne who had sold his share many years ago, and died 'very pore'. Edward Alleyn's final recorded public performance was given in a special ceremony during the coronation celebrations the following year. As the Genius of the City, he performed 'with excellent action and a well-tuned audible voice'. By then, the privilege of patronising playing companies had been centralised under the crown. The Lord Chamberlain's Men became the King's Men. Nottingham's Men became Prince Henry's Men and Worcester's Men became Queen Anne's Men. But as Queen Anne's Men, they never played at the Rose. The last recorded commission for a play for the Rose (a drama about Jane Shore, mistress to Edward IV), which had earned Henry Chettle, Thomas Heywood, John Day and John Duke, 10s. apiece back in May 1603, was not staged at Henslowe's Bankside theatre when playing finally resumed in 1604.

Worcester's Men instead went to the Curtain and the Boar's Head in April 1604. By 1604, Nottingham's Men, now the Prince Henry's Men, had reduced their debt to Henslowe to a manageable £24, and Philip Henslowe ended his Diary. The Privy Council's letter to the Lord Mayor lifting the restraint made no reference to the Rose although it specified that the Fortune, the Globe and the Curtain could now resume 'publicklie to Exercise ther Plaies'. Presumably the Privy Council had conveniently forgotten that back in 1600, it had asked the Lord Mayor to ensure that the Curtain was pulled down. On 25 February 1606, the Sewer Commission noted the final recorded appearance of Henslowe's theatre. The messuage was now 'out of his hands' and it was one Edward Box who owed the Sewer Commission tax for the site 'of the late playhouse in Maid Lane'.

Despite school history books, it is not often that the end of a monarch's reign coincides neatly with the end of an era, yet the death of Elizabeth I and the accession of James I registered the end of an era for popular theatre in English life. The 'university wits', the players and the groundlings had shared in common the same daylight, the same political concerns and the same language. The theatre they made thrived for a short time but, like the Rose Theatre itself, its time was short. Players saw their future in the private theatres. Under Elizabeth, a yearly average of half a dozen Court performances had been commanded, but under James there were usually at least twenty. Not only did this increase the players' incomes, it also gave them more incentive to focus on the different demands of indoor playing. The drama in the seventeenth century addressed a single social class, courtly and fashionable. The creative tension between player, audience and writer would never be the same again.

CODA

The story of the outdoor playhouses does not quite end with the last recorded mention of the Rose nor does the story of Philip Henslowe and Edward Alleyn. Both men persevered with their joint application for the Mastership of the Royal Game, a post which controlled all animal baiting in London. Under James I, bear baiting exhibitions at Court had increased. James I was particularly interested in the bravery and savagery of mastiffs and expressly asked for three choice dogs to be pitted against the lions in the Tower. The Master, Sir William Steward, took advantage of Henslowe's and Alleyn's position as promoters of the 'sport' at the Bear Garden by simultaneously denying them a licence whilst refusing to buy out their lease. Effectively this put the Mastership into a sellers' market and in 1604, Henslowe and Alleyn bought out Steward's patent for the enormous sum of £450. Alleyn recorded that on average, he made £60 annually out of his investment so it turned out to be a nice little earner. In 1610, Alleyn sold the Bear Garden to Henslowe for £580 and in 1614, he invested £10,000 in building the College of God's Gift at Dulwich, apparently now determined to devote himself entirely to good works.

The Fortune continued to provide a base for the players who

were now called Prince Henry's Men, and under that patent, Edward Alleyn's name is not listed. Subsequently Henslowe and Alleyn made over a quarter share of the profits to the eight leading actors in the company and invested them with greater managerial responsibilities. Alleyn's position as a father-figure continued within the company. In 1605, the company demonstrated that they had not lost their touch for anticipating theatrical trends. The *Consistory of London Correction Book* recorded that in that year, a woman called Mary Frith had appeared in 'a play about three-quarters of a year since at the Fortune in mans apparel' and had 'sat upon the stage in the public viewe of all the people there present . . . and played upon her lute and sange a song'. The well-known transvestite, Mary Frith, was the inspiration for Moll Cutpurse, heroine of Middleton and Dekker's later play, *The Roaring Girl* (1611). As Lesley Ferris says of Frith's illicit appearance on the 'male only' stage of the Fortune, 'the significance of this event . . . is not lost on the playwrights, who use it in their epilogue as a tantalising trailer, a sort of post-performance advertisement which promises that subsequent productions of his play will feature "the real thing" – that is, a woman.' In 1618 the company took over the lease. The Fortune, conveniently located for Court and the nobility, remained popular and was rebuilt in brick two years after a fire in 1621. Spasmodic business was reported even after 1642, when all the other playhouses had closed down. It was finally dismantled by Cromwell's soldiers in 1649.

Meanwhile in 1611, a new company, Lady Elizabeth's Men, had received a royal patent and entered under a collective bond into a contract with Philip Henslowe. For a while they played at the Swan. Middleton's play, *A Chaste Maid in Cheapside* was the last success for Langley's unhappy theatre. Two years later, in 1613, the company amalgamated with the Queen's Revels, and inherited Nathan Field as their leading actor. In this year, Henslowe's old Bankside rival, the Globe, burnt down and Henslowe seized the opportunity to build a new theatre in its stead. By demolishing the old Bear Garden, he could swiftly create a multi-purpose entertainment venue, suitable for both theatre presentation and animal baiting. The Swan now lost its resident players and thereupon fell into partial disuse. In 1620 it presented prize fights. The last recorded mention of it is in *Holland's Leaguer,* a pamphlet issued in 1632, which says, elegiacally for a theatre which had caused so much grief, that it 'was now fallen to decay, and like a dying *Swanne* hanging downe her head, seemed to sing her own dirge.'

Henslowe now entered into his last partnership for a third theatrical venture. He joined Jacob Meade in 1613 to contract Gilbert Katherens for the demolition of the Bear Garden and the building of the Hope, as this venue was to be called. The partners signed their Articles of agreement in 1614, by which time the Hope was completed and occupied by Lady Elizabeth's Men. One of its first big hits was Jonson's *Bartholomew Fair* and for a while it benefited from the gap on Bankside left by the gutted Globe. Unlike Henslowe's 1587 Deed of Partnership with John Cholmley, this document does take on board matters to do with theatre life. Amongst its nine points, one covers grievance procedures for players in dispute and three relate to company accounts. Together, the two partners accepted responsibility for supplying costumes and props for companies, resident or touring. This was a managerial role Henslowe had tried, but failed, to take up with the players at the Rose back in late 1597. Meade and Henslowe agreed jointly to advance money for play commissions of *their* choice, not the players.

Whilst the Articles accepted that four or five sharers had the right to veto Henslowe's and Meade's choice of play (and also the right to sack actors), control of the players at the Hope was clearly designed to pass from the sharers to the landlords. Despite the clarification of the relationship, dealings between Meade, Henslowe and the players were far from smooth. Within a year there were disputes over the share of box office. Further acrimony was generated when the actor, Robert Dawes, was brought in against the will of the players on a contract far more stringent than the briefly-worded deals signed by Henslowe at the Rose. Robert Dawes, for example, had to attend all rehearsals – or pay a fine of 12d.; he had to be properly costumed and ready for the 3 p.m. start – or pay a fine of 3s. Dawes was expected to be sober and if he 'happen to be overcome with drincke', he would have to pay a fine of 10s. If Dawes failed to turn up at all, he had to pay a fine of 20s. Henslowe even set himself up as a would-be *dramaturg*. Writers read their plays to him before they got script approval and when they did, Henslowe kept the final rights.

Philip Henslowe would appear to be more behind this new regime than Meade, who may just have been a sleeping partner. In 1615, the company drew up some articles of grievance specifically against Henslowe. They listed complaints about misappropriation of funds, abuse of hired actors and the withholding of certain scripts. On a more general basis, Lady Elizabeth's Men accused Henslowe of using his loans as a means of control, enslaving players further by insisting on exorbitant bonds and wilfully breaking up five companies by dismembering their personnel. In general, Henslowe stood accused of double-dealing and manipulation on a grand scale. The historical record does not provide us with Henslowe's defence but it does however tell us that whilst the actors demanded £567 from Henslowe, they settled for only £200 and further agreed that their debt to Henslowe amounted to £400. At some point; therefore, between presenting the Articles and finalising a settlement, the actors must have had to do a lot of back-pedalling.

Edward Alleyn was involved only on the fringes of his father-in-law's new theatrical venture at the Hope, giving advice after script readings but otherwise taking no active part. From 1613, his energies were tied up almost exclusively within the College of God's Gift.

EDWARD ALLEYN Esqr
Founder of Dulwich College

7.   Edward Alleyn in his role as the Founder of Dulwich College (Dulwich College. By permission of the Governors)

Philip Henslowe died in January 1616. From the position of apprentice dyer he had clawed his way up the social ladder and ended his life an extremely wealthy man. As well as a fortune, he had amassed a number of respectable offices. Starting as Groom of the Chamber to Elizabeth I in the 1590s, he continued his connection with the Court by an appointment in 1603 as Gentleman Sewer (presumably one who sews: a minor Court appointment) to King James. He collected tax subsidies on Bankside, was vestryman of St Saviour's, governor of the Grammar School and left enough money for forty poor men to mourn at his funeral, and for his disinherited nephew to institute a Court case over the disputed will.

In July 1616, the chapel of Alleyn's college was consecrated, but the death of his father-in-law forced Alleyn to take a more active part in the theatrical enterprises. And it was Alleyn who reached a final settlement with the disgruntled actors of Lady Elizabeth's Men. The Hope's fortunes had declined since the new Globe's rebuilding in 1614 but it continued to be used by a few minor touring companies until 1617. After that it permanently reverted to bear-baiting under its old name, the Bear Garden, and was finally demolished in or around 1682.

In 1625, Charles I acceded to the throne. The King's Men (formerly the Chamberlain's Men) continued to use the rebuilt Globe as their summer headquarters despite the fact that, since 1608, they benefited from James Burbage's investment in Blackfriars, which had become their winter headquarters. The Parliamentary Ordinance closed the Globe in 1642, although the theatre was not demolished until 1644. Edward Alleyn was long since dead. In 1626, he died aged 60, three years after his wife, Joan, his 'good swett harte & lovinge mouse'. He had not remained a widower long. Six months after Joan's death, the upwardly mobile Alleyn married Constance, the twenty-year-old daughter of the poet, John Donne, the Dean of St Paul's. Edward Alleyn, like Philip Henslowe, had travelled far but it was at the Rose Theatre that their journey had begun.

CHAPTER THREE

Significance of the archaeology
'. . . how many sides?'

Speculations and conjectures about Elizabethan playhouses form an industry in itself. Go into any library and shelves of books will say that Elizabethan playhouses had eight, twelve, twenty-four sides; that they were octagons, polygons, circles and polygons passing themselves off as circles. Each book will be solidly researched, fulsomely footnoted and each theory will be soundly presented. You will however find no book written before this one which claims that Elizabethan playhouses were wholly irregular, 13-sided polygons. But that at least is true for one of them – the Rose Theatre. The excavation of its foundations in 1989 literally unearthed incontrovertible hard evidence. Perhaps, one may think, that should now put an end to the whole matter, but those questions raised by past scholarship and now answered by the excavation, do not in themselves provide a full answer. Instead, they have been replaced by a fresh set of questions. It is unlikely that the Rose will cause mass redundancies from the coalface of Elizabethan theatre scholarship. On the contrary, the Rose has opened up a rich seam which should outlast the lifetime of at least the present generation of toiling workers, if not those yet to come.

The Rose was built at a midway point in the development of English theatre. In 1576, when James Burbage opened the Theatre, there was no established tradition of regular play-making or play-going in London. By 1599 when James's son, Richard, built the Globe, the position had changed. It had changed so much that the Rose Theatre, erected by Philip Henslowe in 1587, had to be rebuilt and enlarged just five years later to take account of those changes. Hard information about playhouse architecture, until the date of the Rose's excavation, was slight. It is doubtful if any of the timber-framed buildings would have survived much beyond the seventeenth century, but before they could be put to the test of time, Cromwell's soldiers made sure that all playhouses were dismantled under a Parliamentary Ordinance in 1642. Between 1576, when James Burbage built his Theatre, the first purpose-built theatre in England since Roman times, and the 1642 Ordinance, six other important playhouses were erected; the Curtain (1577), the Rose (1587), the Swan (1595), the Globe (1599), the Fortune (1600) and the Hope (1614).

The excavation of the Rose Theatre foundations brings scholarship one step nearer to completing the whole jigsaw puzzle of an Elizabethan playhouse. The archaeology is able to give an objective description of every detail and feature of a site. Each layer of mud or dumped deposit can be recorded as well as the more substantial items, a wall, a timber drain, a block of chalk. As a site is excavated, so it is recorded in chronological sequence, layer by layer. There is a limit on how much archaeology can prove and in the case of the Rose, as this is written in 1990, the excavation is by no means complete – nor is the analysis of its interim findings. The excavation of the Rose Theatre foundations, led by Julian Bowsher and Simon Blatherwick and their team from the Museum of London, and partially completed by the Central Excavation Unit from English Heritage, has so far only been able to dig up three-fifths of the site as the remaining two-fifths still lie buried on land not yet available for excavation. Much of the evidence comes from negative features – 'robbed out' foundations. As the term suggests, something that is 'robbed out' is the trace left behind by a feature which has long since disappeared or been destroyed; the footprint not the foot itself.

Nevertheless an examination of the archaeological findings has overturned many accepted notions – and confirmed others, equally well established. To start with, let us consider, as objectively as possible, the evidence that the Museum of London has unearthed. The site today on Bankside is bounded to the south by Park Street, to the west by Rose Alley, to the east by Southwark Bridge Road, and to the north by office development. In 1587, Park Street was Maid – or Maiden – Lane and, like Rose Alley, it followed much the same route and pattern as it does today. The Little Rose Estate, which Philip Henslowe bought, was then bounded to the south by a sewer and to the north by a ditch. The ditch was not a straight east/west divide but was broken by a gravelled surface in the

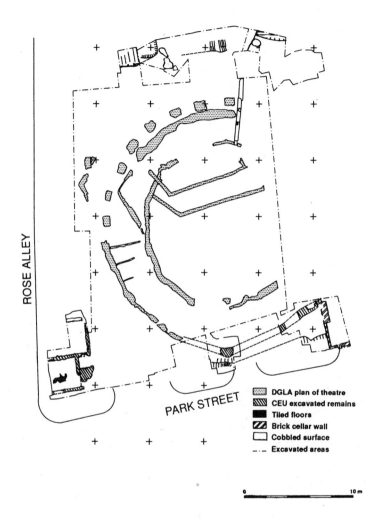

8. Combined layouts of Phase One and Phase Two buildings. (English Heritage)

middle indicating a footpath leading into the northern plot. Overall the Little Rose Estate measured 94 feet square and excavation indicates little substantial use of the site prior to the construction of the theatre.

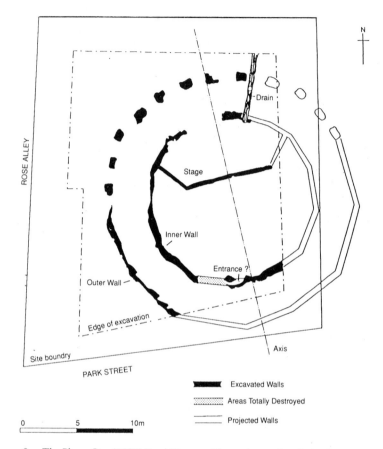

9. The Phase One (1587) Rose Theatre. The conjectured walls in the east
have been plotted by establishing a mirror image from an axis set
perpendicular to the centre of the stage's front wall. Note the asymmetrical
southern sections. (Museum of London)

The layout of the 1587 building (dubbed 'Phase One' by the
archaeologists) is a polygon of perhaps 13 sides whose 12- or
14-sided regularity is broken in the south by a wall measuring
some 33 feet, more than twice the length of each of the other 12
walls which, in themselves have irregular measurements of
between 15 and 15½ feet. The assumption is that the east/west
section of the building was symmetrical with the east mirroring
the west to provide 12 fairly regular sides. The long wall, in the
south, contains only the shallowest of angles, just a tiny kink, to
indicate the possibility that it might have been divided into two

bays to provide a more or less regular 14-sided polygon. The design was probably restricted by the wall's close proximity to the sewer in Maid Lane and, given that Maid Lane was the main thoroughfare, the wholly different configuration of this southern wall suggests that it might have been the main entrance. Some brick footings in its shallow angle would seem to support this notion.

The external diameter measures 72 feet. No definitive centre point has been found, thus the remains of the outer wall define the shape. It consists of chalk blocks laid on a series of foundation piles some of which have been strengthened by brick. The chalk blocks are about 2 feet square and set approximately 8 feet 2½ inches apart with five blocks to every two bays. Their close spacing indicates that they were intended to provide some stability in the marshy subsoil. The angle lengths have minor variations which appear to conform to the unit of a rod (16 feet 6 inches). The traditional Elizabethan building technique of setting chalk pile caps on top of timber piles seems not to have been used. Instead the chalk pile caps apparently sat on large stone blocks. In two cases, a brick plinth above the chalk pile cap remains. Traces of the chalk wall foundation which they supported have been found in the south west. Chalk was a common foundational material which only loses its durability when exposed to the elements.

The foundations were built at the level of the sixteenth-century topsoil so it is assumed that a low brick wall of about 13 inches in height was built on top of the chalk foundations to protect the chalk from exposure and provide a base for the timber sleeper beams which would have supported the load of the superstructure. Separated from the chalk and raised above the marshy ground level, the timber would be less liable to decay. None of this timber has survived. Given the cost of wood at the beginning of the seventeenth century, it is almost certain that the beams would have been re-deployed elsewhere after the Rose had ended its useful life.

Parallel to the outer wall, on the inside of the theatre at a distance of 11 feet 6 inches, is a trench-built structure of chalk and flint with some fragments of a brick superstructure. It includes three entire wall sections measuring about 11 feet. Into these trenches, the walls which supported the timber-framed galleries would have been slotted. The galleries would then have measured 11 feet 6 inches deep. Three small wooden blocks

10. The drain. (Andy Fulgoni)

survive in the south west set into the ground at points opposite the pile caps. It is probable that they supported the timber floor joists that would have taken the load of the gallery widths.

An erosion gulley around the edge of the yard approximately 2 feet from the internal foundation suggests that rainwater dripped from the gabled roof above. The absence of guttering indicates that the roof was almost certainly thatched. The floor of the yard was made of mortar whose present condition is patched and cracked. Its surface has been relaid at least once. The southern half of the yard is level but in the north the floor gently slopes towards the stage at a rake of 14 degrees. There is evidence of more erosion against the front of the stage although the line here is thinner and more confused. Elsewhere the floor laps around the perimeter of the yard and in the north west there is a dish-shaped depression. The yard measures 29 feet 6 inches north/south and 49 feet 2 ½ inches east/west and covers 1239 square feet.

Evidence of drainage is inconclusive despite the discovery at the back of the building of a prominent timber drain made of Baltic Pine and measuring 18 feet. It was built into the wall at

11. Both stages. (Andy Fulgoni) The concrete stamps are the remains of the old piles of Southbridge House.

the rear of the stage at the time of the building's construction. From here it sloped towards the north and probably ran into the ditch that marked the site's northern boundary. A small rectangular hole is placed about 5 feet from the southern end of the drain but it is not yet understood where it drained from and analysis of the sediments it contained, so far, provides no clues. It may have been connected to a vertical drainpipe in the roof.

The stage foundations are situated in the north-north-west and they indicate an elongated hexagonal shape projecting from the line of the inner wall and facing south-south-east. It is not entirely parallel to the straighter line of inner and outer walls. Its front foundation is built out of a solid line of brick tied with wooden beams which run across the yard from east to west. Examination of this wall is not complete and so it is not yet known whether it bonded with or butted the internal wall. The stage has a depth of 16 feet 5 inches with an approximate maximum width of 36 feet 9 inches tapering towards the front where the downstage area measures 26 feet 10 inches, in width. Only the west junction with the galleries has survived. A bit of timber with a mortice is embedded or crushed in the western side of the stage 'floor'. The 'floor' is of course the floor of the understage area and it is made of mortar and slopes to the south. There is no evidence for stage pillars or posts to support a roof above the stage although there is some disturbance to the mortar of the yard floor immediately in front of the stage. The tiring house (dressing room) appears to be part of the main frame of the building with the inner wall of the theatre serving as the stage wall at the back (*frons scenae*). The *frons scenae* was therefore angled but its precise line is difficult to determine owing to the disturbance caused by modern demolition.

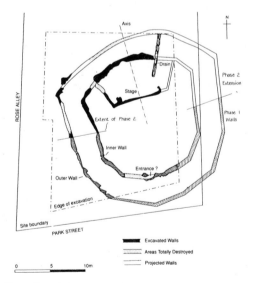
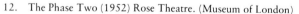

12.   The Phase Two (1952) Rose Theatre. (Museum of London)

In 1592, Philip Henslowe re-built his theatre. Phase Two resulted in an enlargement of the building towards the north, which also involved moving the stage. The south remained unchanged. The Phase Two foundations are less substantial than Phase One. The alteration would appear to have begun at the centre of the theatre, next to the northern cross wall. Here, the alignment of the mortar on the brick plinth has changed. A new brick wall was inserted across the galleries. Only one angled stretch of the new outer wall (measuring 8 feet 2 inches) has been recovered, west of the original. This wall is shallow and made entirely of brick. It has no chalk pile supports. The new inner wall is closer to the outer wall than in Phase One, indicating a narrower gallery depth. Two extra brick walls were inserted in between the southern gallery walls, parallel to one another and 5 feet 2½ inches apart but the notion of another main entrance is excluded by the presence of a pile cap in the middle. The two brick walls may be associated with an internal entrance from the yard (*ingressus*). Within the limits of the 1989 excavation, no evidence was found of the original outer wall other than the pile caps. It is assumed that it was re-erected further north, on new foundations and that adjoining lengths were inserted into the now longer sides. Building work in the seventeenth and eighteenth century has, however, obliterated the evidence. The new layout of the Rose is therefore speculative but almost certainly it was much more irregular with an increased diameter of about 79 feet.

The mortar floor was relaid as a more conventional, because flatter, arena by burying both the Phase One rake and stage 'floor' in a compound of ash, compacted earth, cinders, peagrit gravel and crushed hazelnut shells. The floor therefore is much higher than the original mortar surface and the slope toward the north is correspondingly, slighter. Its new covering is less friable, more durable and better drained, nevertheless there is still a trace of an erosion gulley in front of the stage. Overall, the yard's area was increased by thirty-nine per cent to 1719 square feet. Recent disturbance has destroyed any evidence of an entrance in the south. Debris found on site, possibly as a result of looting when the Rose fell into disuse, includes laths and wall plaster made up of animal hair, suggesting the probability of pargetted wall panels. The collapsed plasterwork possibly came from the internal face of the superstructure and large quantities of lath and plaster were found near the stage area, where most of the 1592 re-building concentrated. Wooden shingles and humic deposits were found in the same area.

The 1592 stage front, whose full length has not been established, is represented by a wall of chalk footings with traces of a mortar façade. The 'floor' beneath was made of compacted earth. It was similarly aligned to its 1587 predecessor, orientated east/west with a difference of only 2.5 degrees. It was built 6 feet 10½ inches further north of the original. It had a depth of 18 feet 4 inches and overall, the acting area measured 533.43 square feet. The Phase Two stage was more rectangular than Phase One but it still tapered to the front and only appears to have a greater 'thrust' because of the extension to the yard on either side. A new and wider wall replaced the old *frons scenae* just inside the line of the original outer wall. Its foundations were brick rubble and short and indeterminate stretches of the brick superstructure still survive. It would appear that the Phase Two *frons scenae* this time was curved, rather than angled.

There is evidence that the 1592 stage was roofed. Just inside the line of the stage front at either end, excavation revealed the remains of two pillar bases, represented by brick footings on a timber base plate. They were built over the new compacted hazelnut floor and are clearly part of the construction of the Phase Two stage. A thin erosion line about 3 feet 3 inches in front of, and parallel to the stage suggests both the extent of the roof's projection and its lack of guttering. The old pine drain was still in position and had not been cut through by the new foundations and was possibly still in use.

The excavation of the site also unearthed an array of small finds; orange pips, Tudor shoes, a human skull, a bear skull, the sternum of a turtle, sixteenth-century inn tokens, clay pipes, a spur, a sword scabbard and hilt, money boxes, quantities of animal bones, pins, shoes and old clothing. John Cholmley's house was also discovered in the south west on the junction with Rose Alley and present day Park Street.

These are hard, incontrovertible facts. Interpretation of them is a less objective exercise than description and depends on a number of variables. One of them is the extent and state of the excavation itself. The Museum of London excavation which worked against the clock, officially finished on 14 May 1989. In mid-June another team of archaeologists working for English Heritage resumed work until late October. Parts of the Rose Theatre will never be recovered because of damage by previous building work and there are the two-fifths yet to be excavated. Much of Phase One, the last part to be dug up, needs further archaeological investigation. Excavation has not recovered *any* of the superstructure, although many misguided supporters, during the Campaign to Save the Rose, believed that it had – much to the annoyance of the property developers, who then had to take the flak. In the unlikely event of an entire 35 feet high Elizabethan playhouse being unearthed on Bankside, the Campaign would have entered a wholly different ballgame. Indeed, the fact that it was only the foundations that were un-covered, was a material consideration behind the Department of the Environment's (DoE) reluctance to intervene. The only way to 'create' that 35-feet structure is from interpretation of its bald geometry. Raising the Rose from the dust is still an act of imagination.

Julian Bowsher, on the many occasions he interpreted the site, often had recourse to the maxim: 'absence of evidence is not evidence of absence'. From the items listed in Henslowe's Diary, many things were hoped for, and looked for, but not dis-covered. The archaeologists looked for but found no evidence of Henslowe's penthouse shed, a 'lean-to' which probably abutted the tiring house door. Nor has excavation found any evidence of external stair turrets. But even when excavation can conclusively show that no traces were found outside the theatre perimeter of erosion gulleys which supposedly would have been formed by rain dripping from projecting turrets, interpretation cannot necessarily equate lack of erosion gulleys with lack of external stair turrets. Rain dripping on a mortar floor will eventually leave its print, but rain dripping on ordinary London mud is not the same thing. Those who want to believe in external stair turrets – or indeed stage posts for Phase One – will not be deterred by the negative findings of the excavation so far.

The excavation of the Rose Theatre is a key piece in the whole jigsaw puzzle of an Elizabethan playhouse. An early interpretation of the site became necessary to meet the popular demand following in the wake of the Campaign. Curiosity among laymen was high, and academics, who normally take their time pondering such matters, were invited by the design firm, Pentagram ('the art of thinking by jumping'), to jump in feet first and pool ideas for a model reconstruction of the 1587 Rose Theatre. By September 1989, the model was on display in the nearby Bear Gardens Museum run by Sam Wanamaker's International Shakespeare Globe Centre (ISGC). The ISGC has successfully achieved consensus amongst academics, for its longstanding plans to reconstruct a full-scale replica of the Globe, whose new foundations were being dug that summer even as the old foundations of the Rose, next door, were being unearthed.

Pentagram's Jon Greenfield, the project architect on the Globe, therefore, had ready access to the ISGC's team of advisors: Professor Andrew Gurr from the University of Reading, Professor John Orrell from the University of Alberta, C. Walter Hodges, a veteran Shakespearean scholar and illustrator, and the theatre consultants, Iain Mackintosh and Michael Holden. Pooling ideas on the Rose focused minds but minds remained open and a subsequent conference held by the University of Georgia in February 1990, added more to a full understanding of the Rose's archaeology. 'I do believe,' said Andrew Gurr, 'that where it's largely a matter of interpreting an incomplete array of facts, that the old Quaker principle of arguing until you agree is the best policy.' Any interpretation of the site depends on both a pragmatic handling of the possibilities and recourse to the body of evidence previously established. After all, the failure to find a penthouse shed or an external stair turret presupposes the prior knowledge of such features from other sources. Analysis is only possible by slotting the new facts of the excavation into the more problematic parts of the whole puzzle. These parts can be divided into documentary evidence, graphic evidence and the architectural formulae which may have been known to the Elizabethan builder.

Important documents to do with these playhouses have survived – some only found in the last hundred years. Philip Henslowe's Diary has, however, been around a long time and is an invaluable testimony. Its circumstantial evidence can now be backed by archaeology to provide almost full documentation for at least one Elizabethan theatre. Before the excavation, scholars were puzzled about Henslowe's £105 expenditure on his five-year-old theatre. Why was he spending so much money on bricklayers and carpenters, thatchers and labourers? Now it seems blindingly obvious. He was re-building it. But why? Archaeological evidence alone cannot answer this question. To answer it, one has to go back to the Diary and look at Henslowe's record of box office figures, his inventories of stage properties, as well as his actual details of building expenditure.

The building contract for Henslowe's second theatre, the Fortune, plays a key part in the puzzle. It provides some specific measurements. Unfortunately and uniquely, the Fortune was a square building whereas all the other playhouses were, almost certainly, polygonal. Nevertheless, because of its detail, the Fortune contract is important evidence particularly when it can be compared to the few contemporary eyewitness reports which have survived. These are more subjective impressions, but in the main they do confirm interpretations of Henslowe's Diary and the Fortune contract. Thomas Platter's visit to the Globe in 1599, resulted in a letter home, which has become a much quoted document. A much later eyewitness, Hester Thrale (1742 – 1821), said she had the remains of the Globe in her back garden and 'which, though *hexagonal* in form without, was round within'. (My italics). She was a friend of Dr Johnson but her evidence is seldom cited. Hexagonals have never been a much favoured shape.

Graphic evidence, on the whole, is less reliable, more impressionistic and certainly more contradictory than documentary evidence. The important illustrations are two sketches and a handful of panoramas of London. Since the discovery in the 1880s of a sketch copied by Arendt van Buchell from a drawing made by Johannes de Witt in 1596, it is virtually impossible to publish any book on this subject without including this much discussed illustration of the Swan's interior. However, as the theatre historian, Professor Peter Thomson, points out, it is a bit like trying to reconstruct the glories of Sydney Opera House from the artistic recollection of an enthusiastic tourist. Henry Peacham's drawing in 1596 of a scene from *Titus Andronicus,* staged at the Rose, is not concerned with the physical features of either the stage or the theatre interior, although what it leaves out invites as much comment as what it puts in. The panoramas have similarly been pored over for clues. They (like the de Witt sketch and Thomas Platter's letter) were mainly undertaken by foreigners, some of whom never even visited London and instead worked from secondhand sources. In them, Bankside figures in the foreground mainly to focus the eye on the real subject of interest, which lies to the north of the Thames. The details are

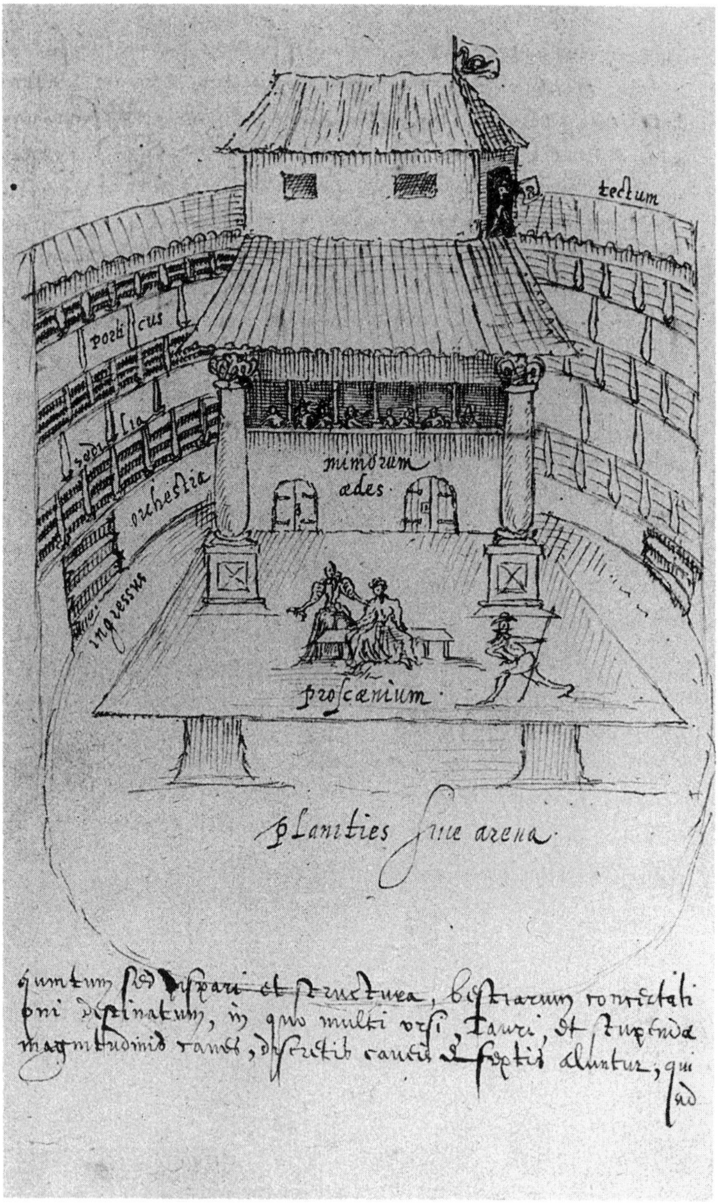

tectum

porticus

mimorum
aedes

orchestra

ingressus

proscenium

planities sive arena

13. The Swan Theatre copied by Arendt van Buchell from a sketch made
by Johannes de Witt in 1596 and discovered by the German scholar, K.T.
Gaedertz in 1886, from which date modern research may be said to begin.
(University Library, Utrecht)

very small. In the Norden panorama, the playhouses measure just 11mm across. Such features may be imaginary or symbolic, and, when put together, the evidence is contradictory.

All of the evidence has to be treated with caution, particularly when extrapolated to build theories about Shakespearean theatre in general. Because, in general, it was with Shakespeare's theatre that scholars were most concerned. And of all the Bankside playhouses, least now is known about the Globe's physical appearance. The excavation of the Rose foundations reveals the exact physical layout of an Elizabethan theatre, but it is only one. Incontrovertible though the archaeological facts are, the sifting of previous evidence by scholars continues in the hope that their former theories will either be further illuminated by what the Rose tells us, or, even, completely vindicated. C. Walter Hodges, for example, in a memorable phrase, cautioned Jon Greenfield against the hope of reconciling what has been found about the Rose with what has previously been conjectured about the Globe. Greenfield's initial thinking for the model Rose was based on a long-held theory about the Globe; the theory of *ad quadratum* layout (of that, more later). 'Here,' said Hodges, 'we are no longer considering *ad quadratum* but *ad hoc*.' He went on to say that the model 'ought not to look as though the Rose was a sort of prototype for the Globe'. 'Reading' the site is by no means straightforward. There is work a-plenty for those 'patient, dogged folk', as John Orrell calls them, 'who, loving the tumbling vitality of the Elizabethan drama, also admire the distant beauty of its theatres'.

Interpretation of the site relies on both an objective archaeological description and the much more subjective possibilities suggested by the panoramas. Four hundred years on, we are close to understanding the full layout of the theatre which gave the young William Shakespeare his first break. The question of 'how many sides' is one of the questions not fully satisfied by archaeology. Though there is clear evidence of a wholly irregular, thirteen-sided polygonal foundation, the eventual superstructure might well have enjoyed more regularity and even a different geometry. 'Foundation trenches,' said Jon Greenfield, 'are always dug inaccurately. In building work, every trade that follows on works more precisely than the ones that went before. Carpenters will be more precise than navvies and the plasterer will be even more precise than the

14. An engraving by Claes Jan Visscher, dated 1616, depicting Bankside with great elegance but possibly not much accuracy (Trustees of the British Museum)

carpenter.' The width of the foundations certainly allows for some degree of tolerance. Most probably the foundations were built before the superstructure was designed and any of its irregularities could be corrected in the eventual timber-framing. If the unexcavated eastern side of the Rose, mirrors the excavated west, then twelve equally-spaced bays can be assumed. In the south, the exceptionally long thirteenth foundation wall, with its shallow angle, may indicate that the superstructure was divided into two bays, making for a 14-sided polygonal playhouse, as Greenfield's eventual model suggests. Graphic evidence would seem to back such symmetry.

Until the Rose excavation, most of the panoramas, with the exception of one, had already in the main been discredited. The work of Wenceslas Hollar is, by general consensus, considered the most reliable but, unfortunately, it post-dates the Rose Theatre, which was probably demolished by then. So the need to find supplementary evidence as a key to interpreting the objective data, has led most scholars to go back to the less reliable panoramas and take them at face value. Four panoramas possibly depict the Rose: Claes Jan Visscher's, Jodocus Hondius's, and Francisco Delarem's, all three of which freely borrowed from the earlier work of John Norden, who himself provides us with no fewer than three different and conflicting images of Henslowe's theatre.

The most enduring, yet erroneous, image of Elizabethan theatres comes from the engraving of Claes Jan Visscher, who may never have visited London at all. Topographically, Visscher's panorama dates from 1594–1600 whilst the engraving itself was published in Amsterdam as late as 1616. By then, the Rose was no longer in existence, but on the basis of topography, Martin Clout believes that Visscher's Globe, which occupies the site of the Rose, may well be an illustration of the Rose Theatre. This playhouse does not have the external staircases which the Globe was known to have but which the Rose, after excavation, was probably found to lack. Visscher's preparatory work in the years after 1594 may have included a sketch of the Rose, which was then later incorporated into the panorama under the name of the Globe so as to reflect the position of theatres on Bankside at the time of the engraving in 1616. For centuries, Visscher's octagonal structures dominated the imaginations of generations of scholars. Victorian sensibility found the whole notion of outdoor playhouses so bizarre that they did not think to question the practicality of his tall, sloping buildings. The singular beauty of Visscher's panorama has had, as Andrew Gurr points out, unwarranted influence on the academic brain. Despite the championship of E.K. Chambers and John Cranford Adams, those heavyweight experts earlier in the century, any builder could have told them that Visscher's octagonal theatres would simply have fallen down.

The other two panoramas are just as removed from the original source. Jodocus Hondius lived in Southwark between 1583–4, before any theatres came to Bankside, and briefly was resident in 1593 by which time the Rose was a fixture of the local landscape. His small inset panorama appears in John Speed's atlas, *Theatre of the Empire of Great Britain,* dated 1610. It shows a polygonal Bear Garden and a circular, wedding cake-like Globe. Since Hondius had never seen the Globe for himself, this illustration has to be based on someone else's – perhaps John Norden's. The American scholar, Ernest Rhodes, thinks that Hondius's Globe is, in fact, the Rose, again because of its location. Francisco Delarem drew three Bankside playhouses underneath an illustration of James I mounted on a spirited horse. It is quite obvious that the playhouses are not his main concern. The drawing dates from 1615–1624 and is taken from Hondius. Once again, Delarem shows a wedding cake-like structure which once again, Rhodes thinks is the Rose.

The reliability of John Norden's graphic evidence is far less questionable than that of his three successors. Nevertheless, there are still problems regarding complete credibility. On the one hand, certain factors demonstrate Norden's accuracy. He was a qualified panoramist, geometer, surveyor and cartographer. He makes that plain by including a picture of himself, waving a pair of surveyor's compasses at us, as evidence of his professional credentials. Professionally, Norden was equipped for the task and had the undoubted advantage of being a Londoner, familiar with the view he committed to paper. On the other hand, his mathematical accuracy only pertains to the view north of the Thames, and his three versions of the Bankside playhouses display worrying inconsistencies. Subsequent excavation of the Rose Theatre foundations has, however, vindicated many of Norden's details.

Norden offers three versions of Bankside. His 1593 map (engraved by Pieter van den Keere) from *Speculum Britanniae*

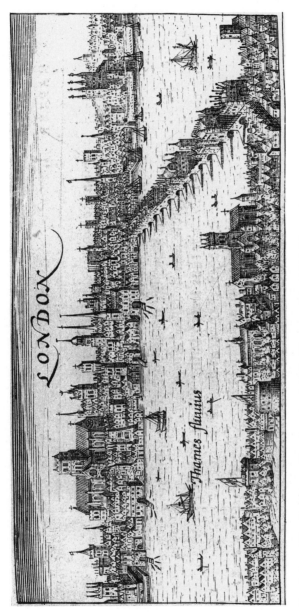

LONDON

Thames fluuius

15. Jodocus Hondius's view of London, dated 1610. (Trustees of the British Museum)

103

The
High and mighty
Prince. IAMES
KING of great
Britaine, Fraunce
and Ireland. &c.

16. A portrait of James I on a spirited steed by Francisco Delarem (dated 1615–1624). Beneath the prancing hooves, some details of Bankside can be discerned; clearly they are not the artist's main focus of interest. (Royal Library, Windsor Castle)

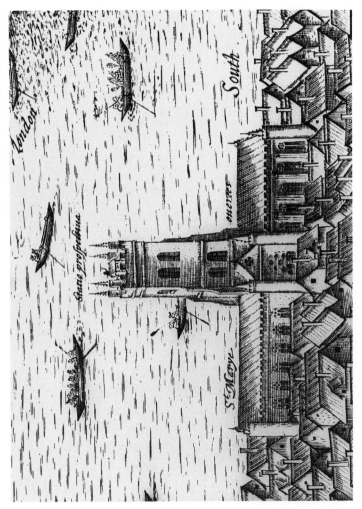

17. A detail from John Norden's *Civitas Londini* of 1600 showing the figure of Norden gesiculating at us with his surveyor's compasses, from the top of St. Saviour's Church tower (now Southwark Cathedral). (Royal Library, Stockholm)

shows *round* buildings for 'The Bear howse' and 'The Play-house', as Hondius and Delarem also suggest. 'The Playhouse' has to be the Rose as there were no other theatres on Bankside in that year, but it cannot be an illustration of the post-1592 Rose even though this was in business at the time of the engraving in 1593. Norden's theatre is not only unthatched, but also lacks a 'hut' (which formed part of the roof above the stage) and a flag flying from a mast above the hut: three features which Henslowe's Diary specifies were part of his 1592 rebuilding plans. This map therefore must be an illustration of the original 1587 structure which was certainly roofless over the stage and probably lacked a flag. Yet the evidence suggests that the 1587 Rose was thatched. The idea that it was thatched for the first time in 1592 is doubtful. Henslowe's payments then were for the thatcher, and not specifically for thatch. Furthermore, the 1587 erosion gulleys in the yard are indicative of a thatched roof at that time. Nevertheless, the roof of Norden's building in his 1593 map appears tiled. However Norden is right in one other respect. The land parcel on which his Rose stands, shows two smaller buildings, one in the south east and the other in the extreme south west; the latter was discovered during the excavation of the site, and its exact location conformed to Norden's layout.

Norden's engraving of 1600 from *Civitas Londini* is a full perspective drawing from the 'statio prospectiva' (station point) on the top of St Saviour's tower (now Southwark Cathedral). Here we can discern the little figure of Norden with his big hat and pair of compasses, indicating the point of view of the artist. From here, Norden would have been able to be wholly accurate in his depiction of the view to the north but would have had to use his imagination to re-create Bankside since he has incorporated the vantage point in the drawing. The only way Norden could have been as accurate about Bankside would be by drawing it from another high vantage point and there were no other towers in the vicinity, south of Bankside. *Civitas Londini* updates Norden's 1593 map. It shows both the Swan and the Globe, newly built additions to what was then a still heavily wooded Bankside.

The Globe can be seen behind some trees in the far right, the Swan towards the extreme left and the Bear Garden is the most discernible of the buildings, slightly towards the west of the Rose, which itself stands close by the Globe. None is named. All

18.   An extract from John Norden's *Speculum Britanniae* of 1593. The Rose Theatre is called 'The play howse'. (Guildhall Library, London)

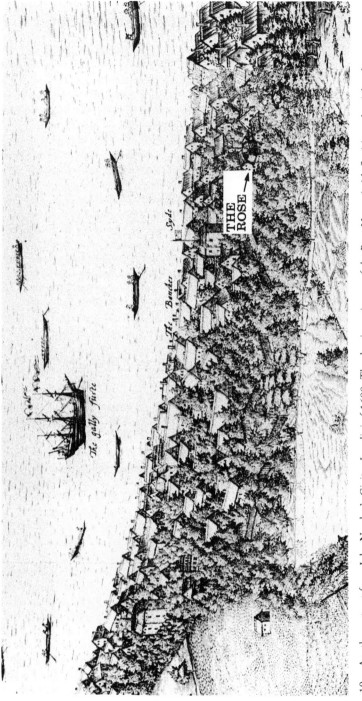

The gally fuste

The Bancke Syde

THE ROSE

19. Another extract from John Norden's *Civitas Londini* of 1600. The dominant image of the Bear House (with flag) is to the right of centre; further south and to the east is the Rose, and at the eastern extreme of the picture, the rooftop of the Globe peeps out above the trees. Further to the west and upriver, is the Swan.

four structures are *polygonal*. The Globe is hexagonal, as Mrs Thrale stated, but so too is the Rose, which the excavation now disproves. The Swan and the Bear Garden are octagonal, as Visscher suggested. The Rose is now thatched and has gained a 'hut' over the stage, revealing that the Rose's stage clearly lay in the *north,* where the archaeologists found it. All these post-1592 features are confirmed by excavation. Inset into *Civitas Londini* is a small map which revises Norden's 1593 map. It again includes the Swan and the Globe. All three theatres this time are *round*. The Rose is miscalled 'the Stare'. It is once again tiled, but has a 'hut' and at last sports a flag.

So within his three views, John Norden tells us that the Bankside playhouses were round, hexagonal and round again. This in itself does not inspire credibility despite Norden flaunting his expertise at us in *Civitas Londini*. This much more sophisticated illustration of the three was in fact only supervised by Norden. It is inscribed 'By the industry of John Norden' as opposed to the inscription of the 1593 map, which says, 'Johannes Norden Anglus descripsit'. The commemorative coat of arms, prominent in the foreground of *Civitas Londini*, suggests that this was not so much a cartographic project, as a commissioned artistic souvenir. Before the excavation, John Orrell's dismissal of Norden was based on a demonstration of the perspective which precisely and therefore, worryingly, matched the two-dimensional layout of his crude inset map. Furthermore, in the past, Martin Clout proved that Norden was not a good witness by demonstrating that the Maid Lane of Norden's map was topographically inaccurate. Given the scale of the maps, which reduce the theatres to 3.5 mm wide, Clout then concluded that Norden's circular buildings have to be judged as symbolic representations. Nevertheless, in the light of the excavation, Norden's revisions of his 1593 map show a sharp eye for detail which can be confirmed by items in Henslowe's Diary. In March 1592, Philip Henslowe, for example, did indeed buy a flagpole ('Itm pd for A maste xijs'). He also installed a roof over the stage. Some of Norden's apparent inconsistencies, as understood in the past, now seem clearly to reflect the architectural evolution of the Rose.

Most academics accept that Wenceslas Hollar's *Long View* of 1644 is the most reliable of all the panoramas. Andrew Gurr and John Orrell, the ISGC's principle advisors, have achieved

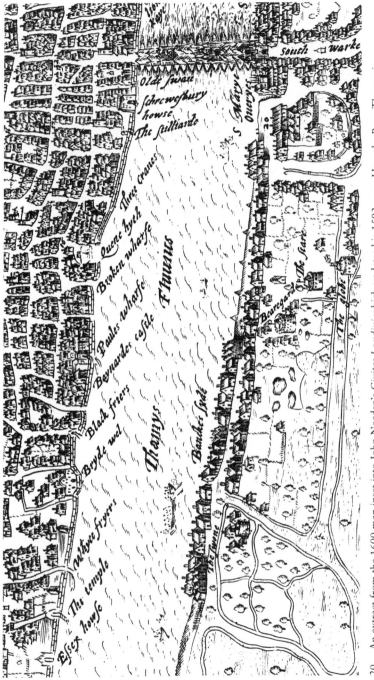

Old swane
Schrewsbury howse
The stilliarde
Three cranes
Quene hyth
Broken wharfe
Paules wharfe
Baynardes castle
Black friers
Bryde well
Whyte fryers
The temple
Essex house
Thamys Fluuius
Banke syde
The Tunne
south warke
S. Mary Ouerijs
Bearegarden Ye The Stare
The globe

20. An extract from the 1600 map inset into John Norden's *Civitas Londini* which updates his 1593 map. Here the Rose Theatre is erroneously called 'the Stare'. (Royal Library, Stockholm)

New Exchange

Convent garden

S. Clement

Savoy

Somerset h.

Arundel house

Bell house

Temple house

Temple

White fryars

The Globe

Beere bayting

21. Wenceslas Hollar's view of the Globe in 1647: wrongly described as Beere-bayting. (Guildhall Library, London)

111

international academic consensus based on their analysis of Hollar's illustration. Hollar's *Long View* is dated far too late to include the Rose, but it shows the Globe as a squat, perfectly circular building with an enormous twin-roofed hut, miscalled 'Beere bayting h'. The Bear Garden, erroneously called the Globe, is also depicted as perfectly circular. Hollar used a topographical glass to produce an accurate drawing. Analysis of both Hollar's drawing and de Witt's sketch of the Swan, suggests to them twenty-four bays, a twenty-four-sided polygon; a polygon that can pass itself off as a circle. For Gurr and Orrell, the question of 'how many sides' is of more than merely academic interest.

The theory of polygons that can pass themselves off as circles has much to commend it. Hester Thrale, after all, described the hexagonal foundations of a Globe that 'was round within'. The exterior, in its day, may have also looked round without. Prior to the Rose excavation, this view was the most widely accepted by a number of independent scholars. Peter Thomson, for one, agreed, and Richard Leacroft, an architect and theatre historian, opted for a sixteen-sided polygon as 'a reasonable approach to a circle'. Leacroft was of the opinion that the circular shape was taken from earlier bear-baiting rings whilst the interior arrangements were based on the experience of performing in inn yards. The polygon passing itself off as a circle is a practical means of reconciling Hollar's circular playhouses with Norden's circular and polygonal playhouses, and it accords with the literary evidence; 'this wooden O' etc. Perfectly circular timber-framed buildings, like Visscher's architectural chimeras, were, however, an impossibility. We know that the Rose was a timber-framed building because Philip Henslowe's 1587 Deed of Partnership with John Cholmley specifies that the Rose was then 'in framinge & shortly to be ereckted'. Prefabricated timber framed structures were a common Elizabethan building method. Timber, however, is not a circular medium. It can be forced into a circular shape but the resulting torsion would result in an unacceptably unstable building. Besides, Elizabethan carpenters did not possess the technology to bend timber. Only the Swan, being made of flint, could have been perfectly circular; a flint 'O'. There again, Ernest Rhodes has argued that, though expensive, it would not be impossible to fake a circular exterior with plasterwork.

The importance of proving the circle rather than the polygon rests on a third body of evidence. As well as the documents and the graphic illustrations, an understanding of Elizabethan playhouses has been reached in the past by those who have aimed to prove an architectural connection between Elizabethan playhouses and the well-documented neo-classical principles of theatrical architecture derived from Pollio Vitruvius, and widely disseminated in Renaissance Europe. Whilst some, like Richard Leacroft, suggest that English playhouses evolved organically out of practical experience, others, like Professor Richard C. Kohler, enthuse about the Vitruvian connection, with a degree of insistence that the unconverted find unacceptable. The assumptions that this theoretical basis 'has become a settled issue,' writes S.P. Cerasano, rebutting Kohler's recent paper on the subject, ' . . . (and) that Vitruvian theories are a primary text embraced by theatre historians everywhere' is certainly not acceptable to her as a basis for understanding the Rose.

Pollio Vitruvius' *Ten Books of Architecture* (40 BC) were well known in Europe. Described by the archaeologist Julian Bowsher as a minor provincial architect, his papers – like Henslowe's – are historical accidents which just happen to have survived. They were first translated into Italian in 1531. In them, he gives clear and simple rules for the construction of Roman theatres. He is as much concerned with matters of acoustics, the positioning and angling of steps in the arena, as with the stage and the area in front of the *frons scenae* (*proscenium*). His theatres are perfectly circular, within and without. The orchestra circle – the centre of the layout – is inscribed with four equilateral triangles at equal distances apart which touch the boundary line on the circle in twelve places, 'as the astrologers do in a figure of the twelve signs of the zodiac'. From this *ad triangulam* arrangement, all other architectural principles are derived leading to unity, symmetry and harmony. James Burbage's first playhouse was known under the classical name of the Theatre. A *theatron* in Greek was the 'seeing place'. The Latin term *auditorium* was the 'hearing place'. Eventually the term, 'theatre', was used for the whole building. The question is, how much would James Burbage have known of the classical world of theatre? Did Elizabethan theatre in its architecture knowingly look out to Europe and back to Ancient Rome?

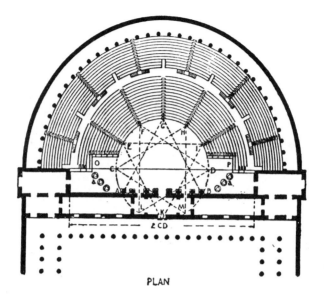

PLAN

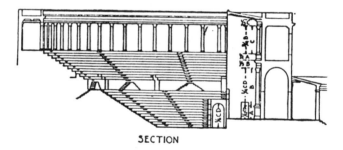

SECTION

22. The Roman Theatre, according to Vitruvius

114

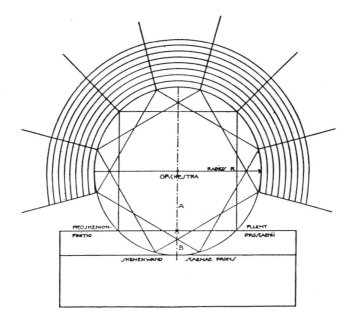

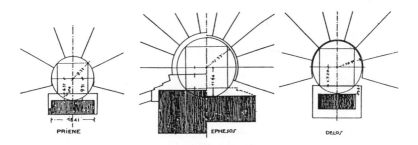

23. The Greek Theatre, according to Vitruvius

Attempts to prove Vitruvius' influence on Elizabethan playhouse architecture are tenuous in the extreme, although the Elizabethan theatre world was not entirely insular. It was relatively common for troupes of English actors to tour Europe and some may even have played at the Teatro Olimpico in Vicenza. But this outstanding neo-classical theatre, an adaptation of Vitruvius' theories by Andrea Palladio, was completed in 1585 – nearly a decade after Burbage built the Theatre. Richard Kohler, however, points out that previously, Palladio had built two temporary wooden theatres on the same classical principles and his interpretation of Roman design was published in a 1567 Italian edition of Vitruvius translated by Daniele Barbaro. Barbaro himself attended the English Court between 1548 and 1550 and Kohler suggests that Barbaro may have disseminated the ideas behind Vitruvian geometry during his stay in London, some twenty years before Burbage built the Theatre.

By 1570, Vitruvian concepts were certainly in circulation in Britain. John Dee, the mathematician, had referred to them in his preface to an English translation of Euclid that year. Martin Clout has also pointed out, that John Dee and James Burbage were possibly known to one another, as both men came under the patronage of the Earl of Leicester. Furthermore Dee had more than a mathematical interest in theatre design. In his student days, Dee had designed an early *deus ex machina* contraption and was to pass Vitruvius's principles directly on to Robert Fludd and Inigo Jones. Martin Clout, less convincingly, also goes on to point out a later connection between Elizabethan playhouse architecture and the Teatro Olimpico. William Shakespeare, he suggested, knew Emilia Bassano, indeed she is a possible candidate for the part of the Dark Lady of the Sonnets. Emilia hailed from Venice and lived with her family in London towards the end of the sixteenth century, and she would have travelled via Vicenza *en route* for visits back to Venice. She may have told Shakespeare about the glories of Palladio's theatre, who may in turn have told the Burbages, and so on and so forth.

The neo-classical connection between Elizabethan theatres and Renaissance Europe, for those who pursued it, was, until the excavation of the Rose foundations, further endorsed on the evidence of Johannes de Witt's sketch and backed up by the analysis of measurements provided in the Fortune contract and suggested in the Norden panorama. De Witt was inspired to make his drawing because of the similarities he perceived between the Swan and the theatres of ancient Rome and he underlined the connection by labelling certain features of the Swan with Latin names. Although Martin Clout has demonstrated a mathematical correspondence between Vitruvius and the Globe, and Richard Kohler has done the same research on the Fortune, faced with the evidence of the Rose, both should now take comfort from the fact that Vitruvius himself had written: '(The) architect ought to consider to what extent he must follow the principle of symmetry, and to what extent it may be modified to suit the nature of the site and the size of the work.'

Richard Kohler, whilst admitting that James Burbage, Philip Henslowe and their respective carpenters, Peter Street and John Griggs, were unlikely readers of Vitruvian theory, nevertheless is still convinced of the connection. The discovery of the Rose's stage in the north is the strongest evidence for a possible Vitruvian connection as Vitruvius had written that a stage should receive *maximum light* (there are no known Roman theatres in the southern hemisphere). Until its excavation, the common assumption had been that the stage of the Rose would be found in the south or south west of the site where it would have enjoyed an *even half light*. John Orrell, in preparation for the reconstruction of the Globe, has made extensive experiments with the fall of light on a southern stage. 'The Globe's stage,' he wrote categorically, 'was aligned precisely with its back to the midsummer solstice . . . The players evidently disliked sunlight.' However the stage of the Rose was found to be in the *north-north-west*, thus causing a great furore as it appeared to justify two men who until then had found little favour with the ISGC advisors, Pollio Vitruvius and John Norden.

Norden had located the stage of the Rose (and also the stage of the first Globe) with exactly the same orientation. 'On 11 June 1989,' wrote Richard Kohler, who visited the site on that date, 'the sun was shining strongly (as it seems seldom to do) at 2 p.m., when performances customarily began. At that time the altitude of the sun was close to the 53.7 degrees that it would be on the summer solstice. The stage may have been placed to receive the afternoon sun, especially on that longest day of the year, when it could act in the manner of a great spotlight, flooding the stage.' Since then, Kohler has published a paper suggesting a plausible series of correspondences between the dimensions of the Rose and Vitruvian design, if one is able to accept the consequent adjustments that Kohler makes to the Rose's known measurements. Kohler's analysis of the Rose's geometry admits both a Vitruvian and the later medieval *ad quadratum* solution (of which, more later). 'The methods are alike,' he says, 'in providing for the successive division of the theatre diameter by the square root of two.' If the thirteen sides of the Phase One Rose can be considered as *twelve sides,* then Kohler can demonstrate that the Rose is a scaled-down version of Orrell's conjectured twenty-four sided *ad quadratum* design for the ISGC's Globe.

The evidence of a northern stage is a strong claim for Vitruvian ancestry. Yet, John Griggs may have designed the Rose's layout on a much more pragmatic basis. Maid Lane was, after all, the main thoroughfare and it would therefore be a logical place to site the entrance into Henslowe's theatre. In turn, since no one would want an audience entering close to the acting area, the stage would be placed opposite. The Rose's northern stage may just be pure coincidence and any other Vitruvian connection may be the result of 'similar requirements and circumstances', producing, as Margarete Bieber, the classical theatre historian, says, 'similar forms'. The rebuttal of Vitruvius until the excavation, was based on both a pragmatic approach in considering the role played by the Elizabethan jobbing carpenter, as well as the scholarly evidence for the evolution of English drama itself. Certainly, no English edition of Vitruvius' works appeared until the eighteenth century. S.P. Cerasano points out that John Griggs or Peter Street literally used a rule of thumb when working out their measurements. 'A playhouse,' Cerasano writes, 'really cannot be calculated to have been "about 59.3 feet" in diameter or "70.6 feet, post centre to post centre" when the carpenters themselves were not operating within a framework that allowed for anything but the crudest approximations in measurement.'

Theorists, whether *ad triangulam* like Richard Kohler, or *ad quadratum* like John Orrell, tend to extend their findings based on one playhouse into statements covering all Elizabethan playhouses. Orrell, for example said, before the excavation that, 'it appears that there may have been a standard Elizabethan public theatre design, some 100 feet or so across and

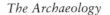

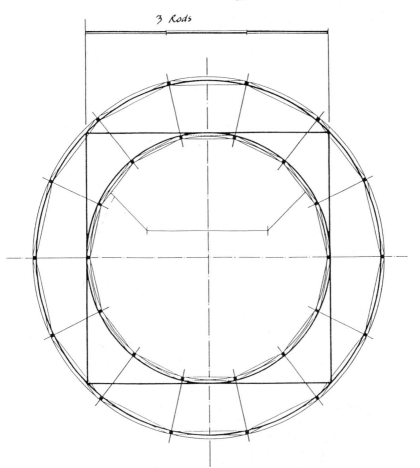

24.   A possible *ad quadratum* layout for the 1587 Rose, which was rejected
after further consideration – though later, the Museum of London accepted
this layout as providing an acceptable interpretation for all but the south
section. *Ad quadratum* is a surveyor's method of scribing two concentric
circles that are geometrically related by a square. In this case the square has
sides three rods long, or 43 feet 6 inches (one rod being 16 feet 6 inches) the
same dimension as the inner ring diameter; and the outer ring has a
dimension of 4.25 rods, or 70 feet. (Pentagram Design Ltd)

probably developed *ad quadratum*'. Kohler said, after the excavation, that: 'I assume that a comprehensive design for the Elizabethan theatre did exist, that it was not simply thrown together in random fashion.' Whilst it is tempting to imagine the English carpenter building a playhouse either in open defiance, or more likely in complete ignorance of Roman logic, in much the same way as Chesterton's 'rolling English drunkard made the rolling English road', Kohler's approach, if not his theories, has something to commend it. After all, Johannes de Witt said that the four theatres he saw (the Curtain, Theatre, Swan and Rose) were basically the same and only the Bear Garden was 'dissimilar in structure'.

Those who rebut Vitruvius advance other architectural theories. John Orrell, for example, is the main proponent of the *ad quadratum* approach; this method inscribes two concentric circles which are geometrically related to a square, or, as Julian Bowsher defines the formula, it is a method of doubling the area of a circle whereby circles are placed within squares within circles. The measuring instruments available to Peter Street and John Griggs would have included a surveyor's line divided into rods (16 feet 6 inches). Orrell's analysis of the Hollar panorama of the Globe has convincingly demonstrated *ad quadratum* proportions, based on these measurements so, not surprisingly, Orrell, at first, was happy to go along with Jon Greenfield's initial *ad quadratum* layout for the model of the 1587 Rose Theatre. Indeed, he urged him to go full out for total symmetry, 'The conjectured walls to the right of the diagram do not need to be so irregular; they are, after all, conjectures, and might as well be our conjectures as well as the Museum of London's'. Andrew Gurr admitted that an *ad quadratum* approach made it 'relatively easy to explain such a nicely symmetrical shape'.

However, the early application of the *ad quadratum* formula to the layout of the Rose caused other members of Jon Greenfield's team of advisors the most problems. C. Walter Hodges's reservations were grave; 'What we find does not fit in so neatly with an *ad quadratum* layout, and thus gives rise to the question, was carpenter Griggs working from any such principle?' Might not Greenfield be 'side-stepping the historical difficulty'? Iain Mackintosh, as befits a practical man of the theatre, was blunter still. 'Bugger your *ad quadratum,*' he wrote, 'the 1587 building was irregularly regular.' Michael Holden offered Jon Greenfield a wholly different approach.

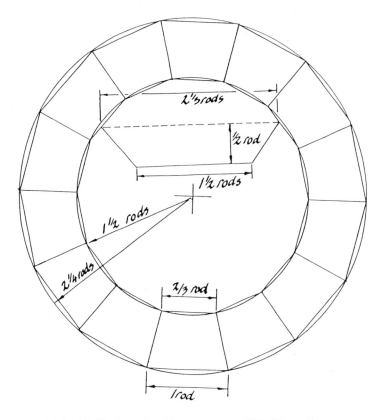

25. Michael Holden's suggested layout for the 1587 building, which Jon Greenfield adopted his model reconstruction, as he felt that *ad quadratum* does not explain how to divide a circle into 14 equal segments, which would have been problematic for surveyors in 1587. Holden worked out that segments of exactly one rod in length are obtained if the outer circle is enlarged to a diameter of 4½ rods, or 74 feet 3 inches.

'Take a 94 feet square plot, set up in the centre a 1½ rod radius circle, mark round it in cords and you come out with 14 sides. Extend radii until you come to a 2.25 rod circle on which the matching cord will be one rod. You set up the stage by striking a 2.33 rod cord and parallel to that, half a rod away construct a 1½ rod front to stage. The *ingressus* derived from the Swan drawing, fall on the outer edge of the junction of the stage to the inner ring.' In the end, Greenfield abandoned the *ad quadratum*

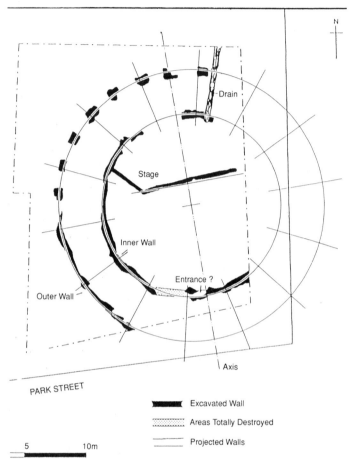

N

Drain

Stage

Inner Wall

Entrance ?

Outer Wall

Axis

PARK STREET

▰▰▰▰▰ Excavated Wall

⋯⋯⋯⋯ Areas Totally Destroyed

‒‒‒‒‒ Projected Walls

5   10m

26.   Jon Greenfield's 'best fit' geometry of the 1587 Rose Theatre. This gives a regular 14 sided polygon with an axial entrance. The fit is not perfect, especially for the southern-most wall segments and the stage alignment.

layout and went for Holden's. 'It offered an easier way,' he said, 'for the Elizabethan surveyor to mark out the site. This model is only an interpretation of Phase One. Clearly the issues are not resolved. The Museum of London archaeologists were as wary at first of *ad quadratum* as they were of *ad triangulum*. Notwithstanding their understandable caution, this workaday, commonplace medieval formula was subsequently shown to provide a basis for the 1587 Rose's layout, in the north at least.

27. Jon Greenfield's model of the 1587 Rose Theatre, a perfectly logical building which did not allow for subsidence. Today, Greenfield accepts that it was the lack of a stage roof, not problems over subsidence, which caused Henslowe to rebuild his theatre.

123

28. A model of the Rose Theatre made by Les Williams at Dulwich College. Scales is 1:30. (Photograph J.A. Bardell. By permission of the Governors of Dulwich College)

Two decades separate the building of the Theatre from the building of the Globe, with the Rose as a midway point. It is their possible differences which are as illuminating as their similarities. Whilst there is something to be said for both *ad quadratum* and Vitruvian theories in the light of the Rose excavation, there would seem to be more to be gained from focusing on an examination of the evidence in hand. As S.P. Cerasano cogently puts it, 'no theory can serve as a replacement for the physical evidence that will be contributed by the excavation of the Rose site'. From the excavation so far, it might seem that a completely irregular thirteen-sided building, which started life as basically 'circular' but ended it possibly as more of a 'closed horse-shoe' shape, would support the notion that John Griggs who built it, was, like the playwrights who wrote for it, inventing a distinctively English adaptation of the form as he went along. Subsequent interpretation of the Rose's archaeology has become almost as open as the roof above its yard.

When Philip Henslowe first built the Rose in 1587, employing John Griggs, he was embarking on a relatively unproven experiment. Playhouses were a recent phenomenon, and Henslowe, unlike James Burbage, lacked a theatrical background. Interpretation of the site involves not only reconstructing the Rose's physical appearance in 1587 and 1592, but also accounting for the reasons why Henslowe re-built his theatre. Although the opportunity to add a stage roof may seem an obvious reason to re-build, some scholars, like C. Walter Hodges, are reluctant to accept that Henslowe's original stage lacked a roof in the first place, and there are some archaeological clues, however slender, which do support this slight possibility. Of the many wooden shingles found in the Phase Two area on the stage which are associated with the 1592 roof, one tile at least has been found in Phase One. Furthermore, the mortar floor in front of the 1587 stage does show an erosion galley indicating, perhaps, that the remorseless drip-drip of London rain fell evenly from some sort of cover over the stage. Though there again, this gulley, thinner and more confused than the one around the gallery walls, may have resulted from five years of continual scuffling by groundlings, jostling for a better view. However, an unexplained fragment of timber embedded in the west end of the stage floor perhaps indicates the presence of a 1587 stage post. Without posts, it is as hard to support the argument for a 1587 stage roof as it would be to support the roof itself. Jon Greenfield included columns in his model but later changed his mind. 'I'm inclined now,' he says, 'to go for a totally bare stage with some kind of cantilevered covering. It was the lack of a stage roof that caused Henslowe to re-build'. As a practical architect, Greenfield's approach to interpretation prior to designing the model 1587 Rose, and afterwards – is remarkably open-ended. He has no axe to grind, and like the archaeologists, sought workable solutions.

If one accepts, as in all probability one must, that the 1587 Rose lacked a roof over its stage, then it is possible that the original building may have been intended for other uses than as a theatre: it would be typical of Henslowe, as a first-time speculator in this field, to attempt to hedge his bets and make his building suitable for activities such as bear-baiting. As theatre-going increased in popularity during the Rose's first five years, Henslowe may have been obliged to tinker around with the original flawed design until, finally, he was forced to tackle the root cause of the Rose's problems. The unexplained fragment of timber with the mortice, for example, could be an indication of a structure or it could be an indication of a much more advanced building. Is it evidence of a trapdoor (as the journalist, John Peter suggested) or a third stage pre-dating the Phase One stage (as the archaeologist, Martin Biddle suggested)? Julian Bowsher finds such elaborate interpretations hinder a true understanding of the findings, but, if one stays with them for a while, their implications could account for Henslowe's major rebuilding.

If this fragment of timber is evidence of a trapdoor, then it would be an indication of quite exceptionally sophisticated stage practices at the Rose as early as 1587. Glynne Wickham, however, has pointed out that there was virtually no use for a trapdoor in any theatre of this period. Most aspects of plays and play-making still harked back to the crude performance values of touring players. Almost certainly such players would not have had the use of trapdoors on tour and would have performed on a makeshift stage with limited possibilities for entrances from below. Richard Leacroft has argued that the stages of the Theatre and the Curtain had removable stages which would permit alternative uses of the buildings. And if their stages were temporary it is unlikely that they would have had any permanent cover.

Philip Henslowe may have originally modelled the Rose on this arrangement which would explain the lack of a 1587 roof over the stage and may even justify Martin Biddle's interpretation of the morticed timber as a third and earlier stage. Henslowe's Deed of Partnership with John Cholmley gives no indication that Henslowe, at that point, had much interest in, or knowledge of theatre and he may have been thinking, or hoping, that a simple building would suffice. The possibility for a third stage could indicate that in the Rose's very early days, the players may have used just a temporary wooden platform propped up on trestles, similar to those employed in the early inn yards, and in the later multi-purpose Hope Theatre. It is tempting to infer from the discovery of the bear skull and bone, that, like Henslowe's later Hope Theatre, the Rose was intended, at first, to provide a venue for both bear-baiting and theatre.

If the Rose started life with this kind of arrangement, it would seem then that Henslowe had not built his theatre with much of an eye to the future. Since the building of the Theatre in 1576, actors and audiences would undoubtedly have come to appreciate the advantages of a purpose-built venue with all the advances in stagecraft it afforded to the writer. Sometime after 1587 but prior to 1592, Philip Henslowe may then have come to see the advantages of providing the Phase One stage and catering only for a theatre-going audience. The Rose Theatre's architectural history of three stages would then neatly illustrate the gradual evolution of playhouses from their beginnings as places of entertainment to their transformation into places of drama. Unfortunately, at the Rose there is neither documentary nor archaeological evidence to support this attractive possibility other than the apparent lack of a stage roof in 1587. The bear bones found on site were not stratified so it is impossible to date them within the chronological sequence of the excavation. All that can be said is that they were found in an area associated with the demolition of the Rose, after it went out of use. As for the timber with the mortice, when all is said and done, it remains just an unexplained piece of wood with a hole in it, embedded into the mortar floor of the Phase One stage. To excavate beneath that floor in the hopes of finding more conclusive evidence of a third, temporary stage, would be to destroy the evidence of the stage that has indisputably been found.

The case for the original 1587 building being designed as a multi-purpose venue for animal-baiting and theatrical performance would be far stronger but for the presence of the raked floor of its yard. Nevertheless, this may not be an intentional design feature. Natural subsidence could be the explanation. Jon Greenfield's initial thinking behind his model reconstruction of the 1587 Rose relied heavily on this notion. The Thames embankment in Southwark was only reclaimed from the marshes in the Middle Ages and excavation does not indicate that the site had been used previously for substantial building. The depression in the north west of the yard may suggest that any heavy building set up on the unstable alluvial mud of Bankside would eventually start to sink. Many of the surviving panoramas show playhouse walls sloping at alarming angles and it may be that the structural integrity of the 1587 Rose was at risk.

At first when he was designing the model 1587 Rose, Jon Greenfield had imagined that Griggs had designed a logical edifice, perfect in every way, without making allowance for subsidence. This fatal flaw in the original Rose had, he said at the time, 'caused the stage to twist out of true'. Archaeological interpretation, however, does not support this idea. Subsidence on such a dramatic scale would have resulted in serious buckling of the yard's mortar floor and, besides, aerial photography of the site proves a straight edged stage. In all probability, Philip Henslowe and John Griggs did know what they were doing when they provided the rake. Actor Ian McKellen was only using his instincts when he wrote that, 'It took the Rose discovery for scholars to realise that 300 people need a raked auditorium to see over each other's heads.' In fact with a stage raised to shoulder height and with the primacy of the aural experience, a rake was not essential. Nevertheless in 1587, Henslowe seems to have been far-sighted enough to equip his theatre with a permanent stage and a raked yard, appropriate to theatrical performance only.

If so, then why did Philip Henslowe alter this sensible arrangement by providing less of a rake in 1592? Drainage, as often in Elizabethan matters, would appear to be the answer. Whilst audiences like to see over people's heads, they do not like to stand in puddles. The erosion gulleys around the perimeter clearly show that rain fell unguttered from the roof. We assume that the Rose was drained but we have no evidence of how it was drained, other than that it apparently was not quite adequate for the task. The raked mortar yard of 1587 would form a natural pond, with the gallery roof acting as a funnel for the rain. The large pine drain in the north is something of an enigma. Romantics like to cling to the idea that it provides evidence of unlikely ambitious aquatic stage effects. Quite what the reality of the drain was, what it did and how it worked is yet undetermined, although it may have been connected to a gutter similar to the one specified in the Fortune contract: '. . . a sufficient gutter of lead to Carrie & convey the water frome the Coveringe of the saide Stadge to fall *backwards* . . .' (my italics.). It would seem as if Henslowe, in 1592, concentrated on providing better drainage in the yard by changing its surface from hard mortar to a more osmotic compound of ashes, gravel, hazelnut shells etc. Romantics will go on clinging to the notion of hazelnuts as 'Elizabethan popcorn' (an enduring interpretation which snags in the memory), but their function was, literally, more down to earth.

The main advantage of rebuilding from the point of view of the owner, however, has to be that Henslowe was able to increase the capacity of his theatre. The popularity of theatre-going evidently justified Henslowe's £105 investment in the future. Thomas Dekker's allusion in *Fortunatus* (1599) provides literary evidence – 'this small Circumference' – which suggests that the Rose was always smaller than its competitors. The name 'little rose' is, however, misleading as it refers to the estate and not to the theatre erected upon it. In Henslowe's Deed of Partnership, the site is referred to as 'in lengthe and bredthe sqare every waye ffoorescore and fourteene foote of assize little more or lesse'. In other words, the estate was 94 feet square. The theatre on which it was erected has foundations which measure approximately 72 feet in diameter. The diameter of the square Fortune, according to its contract was 80 feet. John Orrell has calculated the diameter of the Globe at 102.35 feet. Compared with these other, albeit later theatres, the Rose was indeed small. Most people who were able to stand on the site in the summer of 1989, exclaimed at its intimacy.

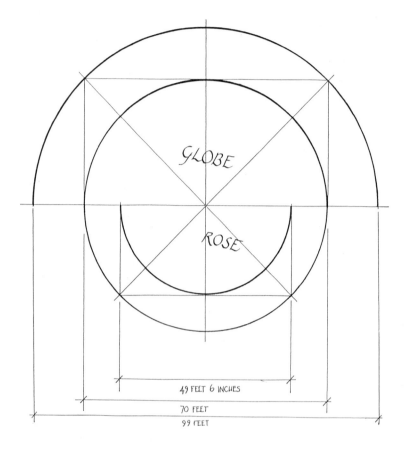

GLOBE

ROSE

49 FEET 6 INCHES

70 FEET

99 FEET

29. A comparison of sizes between the Rose and the Globe, although the extremely partial excavation of the Globe suggests a diameter of only 80 feet. (Pentagram Design Ltd)

Ralph Fiennes, an actor with the Royal Shakespeare Company (RSC), said, after being on site, that 'seeing how the Rose is only slighter bigger than the Pit convinces me that one would have been able to act at the Rose in a very real and intimate way. There isn't the huge amphitheatre feel of the RSC's main stages'. Ian McKellen, employing dead reckoning, estimated an audience of three hundred people standing in the yard. The site did indeed look small, about the size of a tennis court, but its capacity was generally under-estimated.

It is true that the Rose Theatre is intimate in that nobody is more than 40 feet away from its stage. It is no bigger than the Criterion, one of the West End's smallest theatres, and its galleries are no further away from the stage than in the National Theatre's smallest auditorium, the Cottesloe. Its scale is comparable to the 700-seater Royal Exchange in Manchester. The RSC's smallest London theatre, the Pit, holds 208 people, the Old Vic holds 878 in both its stalls and gallery and the enormous Theatre Royal in Drury Lane holds 883 people in all its vast acreage of stalls. Under modern safety regulations 600 would be the maximum number allowed into the Rose's entire space. Standing on the site of the Rose, actors used to playing in modern theatres would tend, therefore, to visualise small-ish audiences.

It is understandable why an actor like Ian McKellen, who excels in small-scale studio Shakespeare, would want to imagine no more than 300 people in the yard listening to Edward Alleyn, the principal player of the day and the Rose's star attraction. 'In the afternoon sunshine,' McKellen wrote, 'within the walls of lath and plaster, Shakespeare's audience could clearly catch every smile and frown, every blink of the eye.' The excavation of the Rose overturned many shibboleths of Elizabethan theatre scholarship, but, on the matter of capacity, it basically conformed to expectations. Playing to the admittedly intimate space of the Rose Theatre's yard, Edward Alleyn would have had to rely on more than just a pair of glittering eyes. By today's standards, his audience was huge.

Philip Henslowe has left a record of his box office income which in turn has, in the past, been interpreted to reveal something about the capacity of the Rose. These figures were then compared to the evidence of de Witt's sketch, the comments of contemporary eye witnesses and a petition organised by Thames watermen. De Witt, visiting London from Utrecht in

1596, said that the Swan, the largest of the four theatres then in the capital, held three thousand people. The watermen in 1614, petitioned the Privy Council to re-open the Bankside theatres, claiming that river taxis were losing trade at the rate of three to four thousand fares a day. At the time, only one playhouse, the Globe, was in business. In 1624, the Spanish ambassador claimed that twelve thousand people had seen the anti-Spanish play, Middleton's *A Game of Chess*. All these accounts suggest a capacity of three thousand people in the audience, but one should bear in mind that they all come from people with a vested interest in boosting audience numbers. De Witt was an easily impressed tourist from a comparatively small home town. The watermen would want to inflate the enormity of their lost fares whilst the Spanish Ambassador, like all who pursue a libel charge, would gain more from exaggerating the circumstances of the libel. One thing is certain, Henslowe's figures, admittedly for the smaller Rose, rarely tally with such crowds.

It was Henslowe's practice at first to take half of the income generated by admission to the galleries. It can be assumed that perhaps the Rose's galleries conformed to the arrangement at the later Fortune. Its height can be deduced from both this contract and the graphic evidence provided by Johannes de Witt for the Swan. De Witt clearly shows three storeys of galleries and the Fortune contract also specifies three storeys, with a ceiling height of 12 feet, 11 feet and 9 feet respectively. At a total of 35 feet in all, such a theatre would have been an impressive sight for a secular building, and more to the point, acoustically perfect. With a rapt audience, the three wooden-framed galleries would have added to the resonance of any nuance of speech or whisper of sound carried from the stage. As a smaller polygonal building, the Rose may not have had so much gallery height as the Fortune. Iain Mackintosh, advising Jon Greenfield on his model, recommended that he lowered them on two grounds: one being that the Rose was 20% smaller than the Fortune and the other, that it was circular and not square. He proposed measurements taken from domestic buildings, whose tiers are spaced only 8 feet apart. Greenfield subsequently modified his design to allow for Rose gallery heights of 11 feet 6 inches, 9 feet and 8 feet.

Either way, Henslowe probably benefited from the customary three galleries of patrons paying admission. Thomas Platter, visiting the Globe in 1599, explains that at the Globe, a three- tier pricing policy was in operation. It cost a penny to get into the yard, another penny to get into the galleries and a further penny to sit on a cushioned seat. It is reasonable to suppose that the new Globe was emulating the box office practice at the nearby Rose. In addition, there was a Lord's Room where admission might be sixpence each.

In 1592, Henslowe's most successful show, *Henry VI,* earned him £3. 16s. 8d. as his half share of the gallery income. It must have been the nearest thing to a sell out, so maximum capacity at the Rose can be deduced from its mathematics. The sum of £3. 16s. 8d. can be broken down into 920 pennies. How much of that came from gallery patrons paying a penny, or gallery patrons paying an added penny for a cushion, or lords paying sixpence to lord it over everyone else, is unknown. If one takes just the bare sum of 920 pence as representing Henslowe's half of the money paid by patrons paying one penny only, then simple arithmetic gives an overall yield of 1840 pennies. Thus, on that basis, it could be said that a maximum of 1840 people packed Henslowe's galleries.

The frame of an average Elizabethan, according to the size of burial plots for plague victims, was 5 feet 5¾ inches. Inigo Jones, designing indoor theatres for a fashionable seventeenth-century audience, allowed an 18-inch square per person, compared to the 17½ inch × 21 inch allowance at the twentieth-century Olivier Theatre which has to seat larger and bulkier people. Using Inigo Jones's measurement together with the figure of 1½ square feet for each groundling standing in the yard, Richard Leacroft calculated a maximum audience of 2726 for the larger Swan. Alfred Harbage, working from a more generous allowance of 3.73 square feet in the galleries and 2.25 square feet in the yard, calculated a maximum of 2344 people for the Fortune, 'although,' as he writes, 'I realise that the human frame appears to be compressible and wonder what might be accomplished by packing them in'.

In considering the Rose's known dimensions, Andrew Gurr reverted back to Inigo Jones and divided the galleries of the 1587 Rose into nine usable bays (allowing for the unusable stage walls which housed the tiring house) and has come up with a figure of 156 people per bay, totalling a maximum of 1404 customers in all three galleries. This figure would allow for two pence variations amongst the clientele. Alfred Harbage, who was writing long before the excavation of the Rose, calculated maximum capacity in the galleries by breaking down Henslowe's figure in 1592 of 920 pennies, according to his interpretation of what would constitute the best seats, and concluded that 216 people paid two pence whilst another 1408 paid one pence, making 1624 people in all, not so far off Andrew Gurr's more objective findings. But the galleries are only half the story. Until the excavation, Harbage's analysis of Henslowe's records was the only way of comparing eyewitness accounts of 3000 people in the audience at an Elizabethan playhouse, against any objective data. Whilst aspects of the Rose's galleries still remain speculative, analysis of its yard yields more reliable figures. All income from the yard went direct to the players, so Henslowe has left us no record in his Diary, nevertheless it is reasonable to assume that, if the galleries were playing to capacity, then the yard was similarly full. The diameter of the open yard of the 1587 Rose is now known to be 29 feet 6 inches north / south and 49 feet 2½ inches east / west. It covered 1239.3 square feet. How many groundlings might it then have held?

Thomas Dekker described the situation graphically when he wrote of the audience as 'pasted', 'glewed' and 'per boylde' (parboiled). In an informal practical experiment conducted (suitably) at Alleyn's School by the author, under the supervision of the archaeologist, Julian Bowsher, students during their lunch hour were invited to cram into a marked out rectangle representing the 1587 yard. The body shape of young people aged twelve to sixteen probably averages out at the Elizabethan adult norm, and, apart from all other results, the experiment proved that Alleyn's students most certainly needed more than just a pair of glittering eyes to hold their attention. After 480 students, in batches of twenty, had been counted into the space, the numbers of volunteers ran out before Dekker's description could be verified. The students were only very loosely packed. Later, in the same experiment, the same number of students were asked to cram themselves into an L-shaped extension which represented the 39% enlargement of 1592. This time, it was like asking a group of teenagers to find out how many could squeeze into a telephone box. Enthusiasm was high and they ended up, as Dekker had described, 'pasted' to one another. If one extrapolates figures from that on a percentage basis, then the 1587 yard, on a House Full Day, could hold 533 groundlings. Taken with Andrew Gurr's figure

30. 480 students from Alleyn's School taking part in an experiment to determine the capacity of the Rose Theatre's yard. (Gina Glover, Wandsworth Photo Co-op)

of 1404 for maximum capacity in the gallery, the Rose in 1587 held 1937 people, or well over twice as many as present-day London's largest non-musical theatres. As far as Philip Henslowe was concerned, by 1592 this simply was not enough. Edward Alleyn was poised to make a career-move south, and his popularity amongst theatre-goers almost certainly would have guaranteed larger audiences for the Rose on a regular basis.

By moving back the northern walls of the Rose Theatre by 8 feet 2 inches (and re-siting the stage accordingly), Henslowe increased the Rose's capacity overall by 39%. Andrew Gurr estimates that the galleries could now hold another 250 people; a total of 1654. The Alleyn students had demonstrated that the human frame, as Alfred Harbage had surmised, is almost infinitely compressible. Extrapolating the figures who crammed into the L-shaped extension, it can be said that either 567 loosely packed or 741 somewhat 'per boyld' groundlings would have filled Henslowe's rebuilt yard. Taken with Gurr's figures for the rebuilt gallery, this provided Henslowe with a maximum capacity of 2395 customers, an extra 458 people. It is hard to understand why some people fail to accept this significant increase as good reason for embarking on the rebuilding. If there is still any puzzle about Henslowe's enlargement, it lies with the fact that a sell-out like *Henry VI* was something of a rarity. However, Iain Mackintosh dismissed such qualms as laymen's qualms. 'Theatre managers,' he said, 'are always surprised when capital expenditure fails to be amortised as increased takings.'

In the course of a week or an entire season, bookings in any theatre, then and now, will peak and trough. Low returns on a Monday will be compensated by high returns on a Saturday. The Royal Court, for example, budgeted its production of Farquhar's *The Recruiting Officer* (a critical and popular success in 1988) at 55% cash. In the event, it played to 59% cash and 71% attendance with most business being made at weekends. The important thing for any theatre is to have a house sufficiently big to accommodate the likely maximum audience. Unlike indoor theatres with fixed seating, the Rose, when less than full, would never produce the dismal effect of rows of empty seats in a theatre today. Iain Mackintosh suggested to Jon Greenfield that, after his model was complete, all the advisors should meet 'and play Henslowe and decide how we change (the theatre) to increase take. We may even "invent" the second Rose, i.e. the second theatre that the Museum of London dug up.' Henslowe's 1587 theatre possibly failed to accommodate the crowds that flocked in on holidays or for new plays. His maximum capacity in 1592 still fell short of the numbers estimated by contemporary witnesses but only by about 500, and other than total rebuilding, perhaps on a larger site, Philip Henslowe would have had to make do as best he could with the original Rose.

Dismantling the northern section of the Rose and moving it back in this manner would have been relatively easy. It was a speedy operation which took place in little over a month. Despite the decline in timber-frame building towards the end of the sixteenth century, we know that the Rose was made of timber as were all the early theatres. The influence of the Renaissance, and the impact of the Armada had not yet resulted in plaster and brick buildings, although by 1587 most of the historic oak forests had been plundered towards building up a fleet for the British navy. John Orrell links the discovery of large quantities of nails found on the site with the probability that the exterior of the Rose was covered in plaster panels, although C. Walter Hodges opposed any such rendering to the walls. Whether exposed or not, the timber-framed techniques were standardised and allowed for certain flexibility. The component timbers were pre-fabricated in advance and could come down as easily as they could go up. Peter Street, when interrupted in his task of dismantling the timbers of the Theatre, claimed that he was just taking them down in order to set them up in a different way, much as Philip Henslowe had done. In reality, the timbers from the Theatre were taken down to be transported across London and re-erected south of the river as the new Globe Theatre. This was a normal way of treating timber-framed buildings and Shakespeare's mother's cottage near Stratford is built the same way. The thinking behind them has more in common with a tent. A playhouse was something that could be lifted up and carted away.

Having enlarged the exterior to increase capacity, Henslowe then addressed himself to the task of installing the new stage technology, so as to keep the Rose competitive with its rivals and perhaps to satisfy Edward Alleyn's wishes for modern stage technology. Still later (in 1595), at a time when he must have been aware of the building plans for the nearby Swan, Henslowe invested more money in the Rose's interior décor. The evidence for the interior of an Elizabethan playhouse, until the excavation, rested entirely with de Witt's sketch which, despite being both of imperfect perspective and in black and white, still carries authority. The monochrome graphics lack the exuberant painted details which made these theatres such cheerful places to visit, particularly in comparison with the scarred post-Reformation churches, whose stained glass and statuary had been systematically ripped out by determined iconoclasts. The full force of classical architecture had not yet hit England, and the major influence in vernacular design was the strap work and mannerist detail of Holland.

Excavation will never recover any of the interior although there is a wealth of evidence to suggest how the Rose may have looked. 'If you look at buildings of the period,' says Theo Crosby, architect for the reconstruction of the Globe, 'the popular ones are extremely wild and vulgar, a riot of crude plaster modelling and all brightly coloured.' John Orrell's imagination, at first, went into overdrive. He conjectured that the Rose would have been more brash than the later Globe and advised Jon Greenfield to include 'painted grotesque decoration after de Vries, perhaps lion's heads among the strapwork. Masks on the arch keystones, and plump, recumbent figures in the spandrels. Larger, especially wider, uncanonical Ionic capitals in the subordinate order; a more florid Corinthian in the giant columns. The style of Robert Smythson, but all done in paint'. C. Walter Hodges was more restrained and did not favour 'fully formed classical columns, capitals and all'. Andrew Gurr tended to agree with him, 'colourful paint, yes, but major carvings, no'. Later, Orrell modified his exuberance and suggested, 'paint rather than carving and nothing canonical,' whilst adding, 'not a barn either'. Opportunity for further display would have also been provided by emblazoning the underneath of the stage roof with motifs and emblematic signs.

A strong sense of decorative detail is illustrated in the de Witt drawing by the stage pillars which de Witt said were tricked out to resemble marble. Later, the contract for the Fortune took the trouble to spell out that specialised craftsmen should fashion satyrs' heads on top of its stage columns. The Fortune and Swan posts were anything but unobtrusive. The Swan's two bulky Corinthian columns had massive bases which seem to be the same height as the actors on stage (although allowance for inaccurate perspective should be made). Any sightline problems at the Swan would have been exacerbated at the 1592 Rose whose posts were close to the front of the stage and supported a 'carport' style roof above the stage. Problems with sightlines in general have been suggested as a reason for Philip Henslowe to have rebuilt his theatre once he had decided to install this kind of roofing, but it is difficult to tell how much sightlines would have mattered in an era when watching a play was only one aspect of an exceedingly complicated cultural experience in which the aural impact dominated over the pictorial, and the social pleasures mattered as much as the artistic. The Henry Peacham sketch of *Titus Andronicus* (1594) omits stage posts entirely. Perhaps, Peacham had simply failed to register them. In themselves, stage posts were aesthetically pleasing and added to the visual impact of a play by defining the stage space and the three-dimensional nature of the relationships within it. They came in useful in the course of the play's action and could imaginatively double up as trees and the like. It is only a modern audience at a venue like the Almeida, the Soho Theatre or the Theatre Upstairs, who, sitting in the dark, eyes focused on a well-lit stage, will object to obtrusive posts between them and the actors.

Posts alone were not Henslowe's sole objective. With posts he could hold up a stage roof. The Rose's new stage roof may have been tiled with wooden shingles. The columns in de Witt's sketch of the Swan also show a tiled roof, jutting out above the gallery roof. The roof offered the actors shelter from either rain or the glare of the sun. Pleasant though such considerations are, Henslowe possibly had something more practical in mind: provision for a 'hut'. In the de Witt sketch, the 'hut' above the roof appears as a looming superstructure, large enough to incorporate the very latest technology – the 'heavens'. The 'heavens' were a hoisting device, which could 'fly' in thrones, gods and anything else: possibly Alleyn insisted on this technology. The Swan 'hut' would have enough space to store costumes, props and other machinery. The Hollar depiction of the still later Globe, illustrates a huge twin-roofed structure of imposing dimensions, topped with an ogee-shaped Tudor turret, suggesting extra accommodation for all the further advances in technical stagecraft. Yet the Rose would appear to be significantly different from both illustrations indicating, perhaps, that uniformity was far from the norm in Elizabethan playhouse architecture. The Rose differs from the de Witt sketch in three important areas.

Firstly the Swan's 'hut', in the de Witt sketch, appears to be constructed independently of the main playhouse, whereas Norden's Rose depicts a 'hut' which is integral to the playhouse design. The stage roof in the Norden panorama, appears to extend right over the stage, another detail that the excavation can confirm, and which sent scholars back to his maps and panorama. C. Walter Hodges discounted the reproduction of de Witt's overstage structure for the Swan at the smaller Rose. 'It looked oppressively large and burdensome, aesthetically offensive,' he said, advising Jon Greenfield to adopt the 'hut' featured in the Norden panorama and locate it level with the ring of galleries; 'it is precisely the structural logicality of this feature, in an otherwise questionable engraving, that makes it so attractive.' Norden depicts a narrow half-gabled 'hut' on top of a roof pitched steep and low but sufficiently wide to account for the erosion gulley. Its stage posts are positioned right at the front of the stage.

Secondly, de Witt's sketch of the Swan Theatre appears to show an old-fashioned rectangular platform stage (such as would have been erected on trestles outside an inn). Archaeology at the Rose shows that Henslowe wanted a fixed stage. The 1587 stage was an elongated hexagon which Henslowe substantially retained when the stage was moved back as part of the 1592 rebuilding. Thirdly, the Rose seems to have had a much shallower stage. The 1587 stage was 16 feet 5 inches deep, with a maximum width of 36 feet 9 inches, tapering to 26 feet 10 inches at the front. Overall, the acting area was 490.05 square feet. In 1592, the stage depth was 18 feet 4 inches and its complete area increased to 533.43 square feet. It was slightly more rectangular but kept the tapering arrangement and gave the appearance of a greater thrust, despite being only 18 inches deeper, because of the extension of the yard. Compared to the Rose's stage measurements, the Fortune contract called for a stage 43 feet wide and 22 feet 9 inches deep, with an overall area of 978 square feet, almost twice that of both Rose stages. Unlike the Swan, whose stage seems to project half way into the yard, it is the extreme shallowness of these two stages of the Rose which accounts for its small acting area. Interestingly, the Henry Peacham sketch of *Titus Andronicus,* with its straight horizontal line-up of actors, indicates how this wide, but shallow stage must have been used; there would have been little scope for much more imaginative groupings. The shallowness of Henslowe's stage is understandable, given Henslowe's concern with the theatre's capacity and his undoubted wish to squeeze in as many groundlings as the Rose's inner circumference allowed.

By contrast, in 1990, Shakespeare, as performed by the RSC in London, is played on the Barbican main stage in an area measuring about 3504 square feet (73 feet wide by 48 feet deep). Its adaptable studio space, the Pit, has an acting area, when the audience is on three sides, which measures about 858 square feet (26 feet wide by 33 feet deep), and when played in the round, about 676 square feet (26 feet wide by 26 feet deep). The RSC in Stratford has a main stage with an acting area of about 2420 square feet (44 feet 6 inches deep by 54 feet 5 inches wide), plus an additional apron with an area of about 488 square feet (16 feet 6 inches deep and 29 feet 7 inches wide). This apron extends further to both sides, and is generally used to place musicians. Coincidentally, the area of Stratford's forestage is not only roughly the same as the Rose, but it is also roughly the same shape. The RSC's recently opened Swan Theatre in Stratford has a total acting area of about 817 square feet (19 feet wide, 42 feet deep). Furthermore, this studio space built inside the shell of the old Memorial Theatre, offers some surprising correspondences with the Rose.

The Swan was established to present the neglected repertoire written by Shakespeare's contemporaries – many of these plays, having originally been written for the Rose. Michael Reardon, the Swan's architect, has caught the atmosphere of a theatre like the Rose with its galleries, and, until the excavation, its assumed thrust stage. Influenced, perhaps by de Witt, but also by the 'in the round' experience of the RSC's former Stratford studio, the Other Place, Reardon and Trevor Nunn favoured a long narrow apron, creating an almost 'in the round' environment. Since the excavation of the Rose, Roger Howells, Stratford's production manager, has experimented with groundplans of both layouts and found correspondences between the circle of the Swan's and Rose's galleries and, also, the Swan's 'inner stage' and the Rose's 'tiring house'. Since the Swan opened, certain actors and directors have had difficulties with its acting area. Some are tempted to use, to the hilt, the 'inner stage' at the back which, as far as Howells is concerned, is like re-inventing the proscenium. He thinks a solution could be found by shortening the Swan's apron, along the lines of the layout of the Rose's tapering stage. However, other actors and directors have succeeded in this space by instinctively deploying techniques which would have been familiar to Edward Alleyn. The director, Danny Boyle, for example, often makes allowance for an actor to make two entrances – one, to get him on to the stage, and the other into the acting area. Actor and director, Gerard Murphy, finds that vocal control is the solution to playing a multi-focused auditorium with a pit and three tiers of galleries. Both commend the space for its honesty. Nothing can be cheated on the stage of the RSC's Swan.

The stage of the RSC's Swan is only 21 inches above the ground, which is fine for its seated audience. Henslowe's groundlings would have demanded a much higher stage. Richard Leacroft estimates from the de Witt sketch that the Swan's stage was 4 feet above ground level (Ernest Rhodes says 5 feet 6 inches or more, Andrew Gurr says about 4 feet 8 inches). Excavation of the Rose foundations can add little to the discussion of an Elizabethan stage's height. Whatever its exact measurements, it would appear to be about level with the groundlings' shoulders, and compatible with the notion of an actor crouched beneath it, waiting to make an entrance via a trapdoor. Ernest Rhodes has offered 32 instances in 14 plays of the Rose's repertoire where a trapdoor would have come in useful. They range from a character falling into a hole to the ceremonial arrival of Pluto's wagon drawn by a pair of devils.

In between the stage and the 'heavens', de Witt's sketch of the Swan shows the façade of the tiring house (the dressing room). Both the 1587 and the 1592 stage appear to back straight on to the polygonal walls of the playhouse, suggesting that the wall of the tiring house, the *frons scenae* was angled, unlike the assumed flat surface derived from Tudor hall screens as depicted in de Witt. The new stage wall of 1592 suggests a curved, rather than an angled *frons scenae*. 'As usual,' said Andrew Gurr, 'there is uncertainty. Was it a planar surface taking a chord across the gallery walls or did it follow the inner gallery walls? A planar surface, respecting Vitruvian principles, is unlikely as it would reduce the depth of the Rose's already shallow stage. The de Witt drawing showed two pairs of doors, in the *frons scenae* and a partitioned gallery containing a number of people – spectators, players or musicians?

142

One of the problems in 'reading' de Witt (apart from his perspective) is that it is hard to tell whether he has sketched a rehearsal or a performance or an entirely imaginary moment. The empty theatre and the man with the trumpet are indicating that a performance is about to begin, yet the players on stage are clearly acting away like mad. Perhaps de Witt has sketched the interior and peopled it in a way to indicate the various functions of its features rather than capturing a real scene. Everything that de Witt shows on the stage could be incorporated into the action of the play. The position of the man with a trumpet, so close to the roof, could have been used at the Rose in *Henry VI,* as 'This Turrets top', from which point the English look down on the city of Orleans. From the same vantage point, Joan might have entered 'on the top, thrusting out a torch burning'.

The gallery above de Witt's stage may, as Andrew Gurr says, be the Lord's Room at the Swan. It is impossible to tell from the illustration who the people are inside it. Certainly, the gallery is the best position for anyone wanting to be seen, and there is ample evidence that many patrons attended the theatre with personal display in mind. In the indoor playhouses, young blades hired stools and sat on the stage itself. At the outdoor playhouses, where the social mix was far more diverse, this custom was not encouraged. Any ostentatious behaviour was restricted to the privacy of the six-penny Lord's Room. Henslowe when he refurbished the Rose made sure that his Lord's Room was suitably attractive ('pd for sellinges my lords Rome xiiijs' – fifteen shillings). It was finished with a plastered and painted ceiling but where exactly it was located is much contested. The argument for placing it above the stage was that it completed the full circle of audience and players. On the other hand, if the Lord was actually interested in the play, from that position, he would have to be content with a view of the actors' backs. The stage arrangement shown by de Witt is not 'theatre in the round' and, neither too is the gently tapering arrangement of the Rose. The cast, no matter a lordly presence in the room, would have to position themselves democratically so the majority could see. In the case of the Rose, Andrew Gurr, who normally holds out for an above stage position for the Lord's Room, concedes that at Henslowe's theatre this location is unlikely.

The people in the de Witt sketch could, therefore, be part of the performance. They could be musicians, although integral music was a feature more characteristic of the later indoor theatres. At the Rose, music was an interruption to the action and often performed by the actors themselves – 'Exeunt omnes, playing on their Instrumentes' (*Alphonsus of Aragon*). Edward Alleyn first entered the records as a 'musician' before he achieved fame as an actor. The Swan's stage gallery could almost certainly, if reproduced at the Rose, have been used for the action scenes in *Henry VI* which calls for walls to be scaled – 'Enter Talbot, Burgundy and Bedford, with scaling ladders'. This gallery, which probably was on a level with the audience's first-storey gallery, would only have involved a small climb. The Fortune contract asks for a 12 feet high ground-floor gallery and an 11 feet high first-floor gallery. With balustrade, this first-floor gallery would provide access (via ladder) at about 15 feet above the yard. Allowing for the stage's probable height, the climb for Talbot & Co would be about 10 feet. Later in the same scene, the actors playing the French army would have been able to leap over the balustrade, in their shirts, to a 10-feet drop; a reasonable requirement for an athletic actor – Olivier would have enjoyed doing it. The more familiar Shakespeare plays point to obvious gallery usage at the Globe; the balcony scene from *Romeo and Juliet,* the monument scene in *Antony and Cleopatra* etc.

Apart from leaping out of balconies, actors at the Rose would be able to make less dramatic entrances from the doors on stage. De Witt shows two such doors for the Swan although two doors would not allow much scope for movement and the position they hold is not very commanding unless the actor made two different sorts of entrances; the first entrance which got him through the door and the other one which announced his arrival, in character, into the acting area. Brecht, and Brechtian productions, frequently make this distinction. On the Rose's shallow stage, entrances via these doors would not provide the same problems of command as at the Swan. They may also have been used as a 'discovery' space. Ernest Rhodes tells us of the Rose play, *David and Bathsheba,* which contains the stage direction: 'He draws a curtain, and discovers Bathsheba with her maid bathing over a spring'. This tableau would be revealed by drawing back the curtain which covered the open doorway and there was sufficient area behind the *frons scenae* at the Rose to have allowed for that.

De Witt shows two entrances from the yard (*ingressus*) on

either side of the stage. They provide access from the yard into the galleries and it would appear from the excavation of the Rose that the *ingressus* at the Rose occupied the same position. Neither Norden, de Witt, nor the excavation can give proof of external stairs. In the absence of evidence, this is unresolved. Andrew Gurr thinks it unlikely that Henslowe would have wasted valuable space inside his theatre by providing internal stairs and the Hollar panorama shows the Globe at least to have two projecting turrets. De Witt marks the top gallery of the Swan as a *porticus,* suggesting a promenade area. Hindered by the roof over the stage, the *porticus* would not be a very good position for anyone wanting to concentrate on the play. De Witt's middle section, the *sedilia,* is distinctly meant for sitting and offers a good view. The bottom gallery at the Rose, what de Witt calls the *orchestra,* was raised above the level of the yard by deposits of alluvial mud, and in a Roman theatre would be left empty unless occupied by VIPs. It is here that Jon Greenfield finally sited the Lord's Room in his model reconstruction of the 1587 Rose. However, the sixpenny patrons would have had a barrier of groundlings between their seats and the stage which makes the *orchestra* of the Rose not necessarily the best location for the Lord's Room. Instead, the *orchestra* seats adjacent to the stage, on either side, would have suffered fewer impediments, as well as providing a choice position for being on display. The Fortune contract calls for 'two boxes' to be made 'in the lowermost storie', and it may be that this was their position at the Rose.

De Witt does not show any outside doors. His point of view is facing the Swan's stage and it may be that that was the position of the Swan's entrance, in which case it seems likely that the Rose was the same. The actual entrance into the Rose probably came from Maid Lane, a long-established main thoroughfare. Brick footings in the shallower, south eastern angle might suggest an entrance. It would seem natural for audiences travelling by river to arrive separately from another entrance in Rose Alley; one entrance on its own for maybe nearly 2500 people would, in any case, cause a severe backlog of disgruntled customers either trying to enter or to leave. The Globe certainly had two entrances because, as we are told, when it caught fire, the audience made an orderly exit through two narrow doors. The excavation, however, provides no conclusive proof about any entrance at all. As the archaeologist,

Julian Bowsher, has said about other matters, this has to be a case when 'absence of evidence does not prove evidence of absence'. Clearly the Rose had to have some sort of entrance, so why not two?

'Progressive correctionism' is how C. Walter Hodges describes the series of illustrations of the Rose that he has undertaken since its excavation; 'I've been making pictures to meet specific requirements – as well as to try things out for myself – each time before there was enough material to work with. Actually, the Rose has thrown all our established working premises and assumptions into disarray. It hasn't made them necessarily wrong in themselves, but they've all had to shove over to make room for another piece in the game. The balance of evidences has been altered.' In the name of the Rose, analysis continues and "progressive correctionism" is the name of the game.

CHAPTER FOUR

The Excavation of the Rose Theatre
'... not a green field site'.

'London archaeology has had an exhilarating year. Two of the capital's most exciting post-war sites have been unearthed, both a surprise.' Simon Jenkins, the deputy chairman of English Heritage, wrote that in *The Times* on 12 May 1989, three days before a massive public outcry protested at the plans endorsed by English Heritage which would, effectively, have destroyed one of the two great archaeological surprises of the year. Later that summer, Jenkins was to write, in a letter to the same newspaper, that England was 'awash' – not with a sea of sewage, as the term suggests – but with 'sites in need of excavation'. Like many people in power who played a part in the great drama of the Rose, Jenkins will not be in the same position when, and if, the Rose makes its expected comeback in 1992. Since then, he has moved on to become editor of *The Times*, and in the process has resigned his position at English Heritage. Ironically, it was *The Times* which played a leading role in reporting the outcry of support in defence of the Rose during the summer of 1989. Indeed Jenkins' own article for that paper cogently and passionately put the case for the preservation and display of the Rose because, even more ironically, it was as a young campaigning journalist on the *Evening Standard* that Jenkins raised everyone's heritage consciousness in the first place. After all, back in 1957, when the site of the Rose, in theory, was made available to modern archaeology, there was no public outcry then, and no journalist to orchestrate it.

Back in his days of the *Evening Standard* in the early 1970s, a typical Simon Jenkins' article on urban archaeology might have read: 'Developers, both public and private just hate the idea of having to postpone the rate and rent revenue from a new building for a day longer than they have to – and there are no powers, other than publicity, to force them to wait.' And, indeed, that was a typical Jenkins' article on urban archaeology for the *Standard*. Then, he was writing about the uncovering of a fifteenth-century fishing vessel near Blackfriars in the seventies, but his words might equally have applied to the uncovering of the Rose Theatre in 1989. Jenkins' conclusion that, 'Certain things about a city are more important than a developer's profit', was a sentiment close to the heart of the Rose Campaign. He outlined proposals which would ensure that such a fiasco should never happen again: 'What is needed is simple. It is a regulation requiring the inspection by experts of the demolition and excavation of any London construction site which might be of archaeological importance. There should then be a compulsory delay in further building operations if anything of significance is found. Such a delay will obviously cost the developer money. But I cannot see why he should be spared this cost – any more than a man who inhabits a historic building must forego the profit he could get by pulling it down.' It is worth quoting this *in extenso*, to show what little progress has been made over nearly two decades. It took another near fiasco – it took the Rose – to really bring home the weaknesses not just in law, but in the political will to use the law.

Since the opening of Tutankhamen's tomb, never can archaeology have enjoyed so much publicity than the street jamboree surrounding the Rose Theatre. Before the summer of 1989 was out, the Rose had polarised two hitherto entrenchedly conservative institutions, English Heritage and the Museum of London. The High Court had been asked to litigate the 1979 Ancient Monuments and Archaeological Areas Act (AMAA). Questions had been raised in both Houses of Westminster. And an army of international mega-stars had posed for a posse of paparazzi outside an undistinguished building site in North Southwark. The central issue, as George Dennis, the Museum of London's archaeological planner, said at a conference organised by RESCUE, the British Archaeological Trust, on 17 February 1990, was simple. "Is the nation's cultural heritage sometimes important enough to require permanent preservation *in situ* for public display and enjoyment, and if so who pays for that, the government or the developer, and how is conservation reconciled with development?' Many excavations since the discovery of a fishing vessel in the early 1970s could have prompted this debate, but only the Rose could have provoked so much passion and posed so many questions about the legislation designed to protect our heritage. Most people simply could not understand why the site did not automatically come under public ownership. Legislation though, as well as archaeological expectation, was, until the Rose, largely about excavation and not about preservation and display. There are many strands in the heritage debate but it took the Rose to complete the tapestry. To understand the political complexity of the Campaign, one has to go right back in time.

Southwark or 'Suth-UCK', as it was helpfully phoneticised by an American reporter, is, indeed, awash with history: the Hop Market, Southwark Cathedral, Clink Street, St Mary Overie's Dock are still there to be seen and enjoyed. Living history continues through the quaint anomalies of the past – the Borough Market with its specially uniformed police, the election of the Alderman of Bridge Ward Without, the rituals of Founder's Day at Dulwich College, and, until 1932, the existence of a Coroner's Court in Guildhall: the last tangible link from the days when the City attempted to govern the borough. Walk down the Old Kent Road and you are walking down what the Romans knew as Watling Street, the main road to Dover and a passage home. Chaucer's pilgrims travelled the same route on their way to Canterbury, after stopping a night at one of the many inns in Borough High Street:

It happened in that season that one day
In Southwark at the Tabard as I lay . . .

The Tabard was destroyed in 1676 but the George has survived, one of the few galleried inns left in London, a forerunner for a playhouse like the Rose.

Philip Henslowe would find many of today's street names familiar: Cardinal's Cap Alley, Rose Alley, Bear Gardens, Skinmarket Place. In *Henry VI* Shakespeare had written:

Soldiers, I thank you all, disperse yourselves.
Meet me tomorrow at St George's Fields.

In *Twelfth Night*, his recommendation that, 'In the south suburbs at the Elephant is best to lodge,' proves, that although some place names have stayed the same, other aspects to life in Southwark have moved on. However, Henslowe would not have been surprised at the tragic sinking of *The Marchioness* near Southwark Bridge. The tides on this part of the Thames were always dangerous. His audiences preferred to alight down river of London Bridge and walk the few yards before re-joining their boats, rather than risk the river's swirling currents.

Henslowe would not have known Southwark Bridge, although he would most certainly have welcomed a bridge so close to his own theatre. Southwark Bridge, in terms of Southwark's history, is a relative newcomer. It was first built in 1819 and known as the Iron Bridge in Charles Dickens' *Little Dorrit*. For, Southwark is Dickens country too. The site of Marshalsea is still there, where Dickens' father was imprisoned. The White Hart Inn, another pilgrims' watering hole in Borough High Street, was the place where Mr Pickwick met Sam Weller. London Bridge Station was the capital's first terminus and made North Southwark important to the development of Victorian London.

Southwark, like most historic parts of London, was built upon layer and layer of the past. On the foundations of Roman Southwark, Chaucer's Southwark was built. On Chaucer's Southwark, Philip Henslowe's Southwark was built. On Henslowe's Southwark, Dr Johnson's Southwark was built. Indeed, Shakespeare's Globe was partially excavated underneath a listed Georgian terrace. Most Georgian buildings were demolished to make way for the Victorian warehouses of Dickens' Southwark. North Southwark has been constantly dug up, but never more so than in post-war times. The voracious demand for offices close to the City has led to unprecedented redevelopment, which accelerated in the late 1980s following the 'Big Bang'. Every movement of every spade unearths some fragment of Southwark's rich past. 'What is known,' says Martin Myers, the developer who acquired the site of the Rose, 'is that in that broad brush sweep of London, there are relics on almost every site. Over the years it's been demolish and build. The most beautiful Georgian building replaces something equally unique.'

Until the last century, for the most part, Southwark got on with the business of living in the present and was not overly concerned with its ghosts. Indeed, Philip Henslowe would have been taken considerably aback if told he could not have planning permission for the Rose Theatre because it might disturb some Roman revetments beneath. The nostalgia expressed by his contemporary, John Stow, for a pre-Reformation London was at odds with the national mood. The urge to preserve the past is a relatively modern phenomenon. By the early nineteenth century, Bankside parishioners so much resented the expensive maintenance of the thirteenth-century St Saviour's, that, in 1839, they had their ancient church razed to the ground. Either an antiquarian zeal, or just plain avarice, then inspired many enthusiastic laymen. The *Gentlemen's Magazine* reported that, 'it was surprising how greedily every bit of moulding was purchased by the hosts of collectors who gathered around the falling ruins.' Whilst the portable bits of Southwark's heritage were removed, its more permanent historical record came under scrutiny. The mid-nineteenth century saw the beginning of Southwark's fight for self-government, and there was plenty in its history to justify the political autonomy from the City that it sought.

By the end of the century, the misguided plundering of historic places on a national scale led to the 1882 Act for the Better Protection of Ancient Monuments, which in turn gave birth to the Ancient Monument and Historic Buildings Inspectorate headed by General A.H.L.F Pitt-Rivers, 'the father of scientific archaeology'; this was the start of the systematic preservation of our heritage. In 1908, the Royal Commission on Historical Monuments was set up with the brief to make a complete inventory of 'Ancient and Historical monuments and constructions connected with or illustrative of the contemporary culture, civilisation and conditions of life of the people of England'. By the 1920s, archaeology was still, however, largely the preserve of the amateur. Sir Mortimer Wheeler relied on such enthusiasts for his description of Roman Southwark when writing his survey of Roman London in 1928.

Professional excavation of North Southwark only really began in 1944 when the Surrey Archaeological Society set up the Southwark Excavations Committee under the leadership of Dr Kathleen Kenyon. In general, British archaeology at that time was dependent on random finds. Contractors working on a Walbrook site in 1954, for example, accidentally came across the Roman Temple of Mithras and it took a major public outcry, then, to secure its proper excavation. Its *display*, however, out of context, was to be another matter, and one to which the Campaign to Save the Rose often referred. In Southwark, Kenyon investigated five major sites over a ten-year period before the limited funding ran out. (It was after this period that Southwark Council gave planning permission for the 1957 Southbridge House to be built on the site of the Rose.)

It was in the early 1960s that the public became aware that its buried history was in danger of being destroyed without record. The Roman palace at Fishbourne, in Sussex, was, once again, found only by accident. A workman, digging a water-main in 1960, sliced through some Roman tiles and the subsequent six-year excavation laid bare the most spectacular Roman palace in Britain and the largest Roman palace outside Rome. It gave a tremendous fillip to a profession which at last found not only its voice, but also, started to find the sort of funds which could take archaeology out of the hands of the wealthy amateur. In 1962, at a time when only one or two professional archaeologists were working in Greater London, the Southwark Archaeological Excavation Committee (SAEC) was formed out of various local societies and London museums. Ten years later, it had achieved sufficient funding from the DoE (Department of the Environment) and Southwark Council, to employ four full-time staff. Led by Harvey Sheldon, they worked from office space, with storage facilities provided by Hay's Wharf. SAEC's first long-term excavation was at Topping's Wharf where Roman and medieval buildings were uncovered, together with a thirteenth-century river wall erosion.

That same year, 1972, the Ancient Monument and Historic Buildings Inspectorate merged with an Inspectorate formed in 1947 by the former Ministry of Town and Country Planning (to carry out a post-war survey of historic buildings, which led to the establishment of the principle of listing important buildings). Together, the two organisations formed the Directorate of Ancient Monuments and Historic Buildings within the newly created DoE. (The DoE had been established in 1970 to reconcile the conflicting interests of three former Ministries: Housing and Local Government, Public Building and Works, Transport and Planning.) During the 1970s, as the Simon Jenkins' *Evening Standard* article indicates, increasingly more excavations became *causes célèbres*, and the need for fresh legislation was pressing. In the dying days of the Callaghan government, a Labour majority passed the 1979 Act (AMAA). Under this act, individual monuments could be placed on the Secretary of State's schedule for their continuing protection.

Scheduling is a heavy measure designed to give heavy protection to heavy monuments, and it was this measure that the Campaign sought to save the Rose. Once scheduled, a monument needs government consent for banging just one nail into its structure. 'Monument', however, is a somewhat misleading term, suggesting, as it does, something that is, well, monumental. 'It's not Stonehenge' was one of the more frequent and fatuously self-evident remarks made about the Rose Theatre's foundations. An ancient monument can embrace anything from earthworks to castles to factories dating from the Industrial Revolution.

By 1983, SAEC, now called SLAEC (to acknowledge the Lambeth element) had expanded to a dozen full-time professionals and the entire team was taken under the wing of the Museum of London's Department of Greater London Archaeology, one of its two archaeology departments, (the other being the City Archaeological Department). In the same year, the National Heritage Act gave birth to the new Historic Buildings and Monuments Commission. Michael Heseltine, the new and high-flying Secretary of State for the Environment, aimed to turn around this dusty corner of his Department and brought in as English Heritage's Chairman, Lord Montagu of Beaulieu (author of *How to Live in a Stately Home and Make Money*). The department was relaunched as English Heritage, with a brief to realise the economic potential of the country's glorious past. Today English Heritage works from the somewhat unfortunately named Fortress House and like the Arts Council of Great Britain, it is a 'quango' (quasi autonomous non-government organisation). The government provides ninety per cent of its funds, approves its annual corporate plan and vetoes the appointments to its governing body. English Heritage is the government's official advisor on conservation law concerning the built environment. It has a permanent staff of about 1500 and is responsible for some 400 properties in its care.

The Museum of London's Department of Greater London Archaeology in 1989 employed 160 archaeologists working in 23 of the 33 Greater London Boroughs. In the days of the Greater London Council (GLC), GLC funding via the Greater London Archaeological Service, went directly to the Museum of London and the Passmore Edwards Museum (in East London) as they were the two most experienced bodies able to give coherence to archaeology throughout the London region. Following the GLC's abolition in 1986, this funding responsibility passed to English Heritage along with the GLC's own Historic Buildings Division (now the London Division). Because of their increased responsibilities towards London archaeology, English Heritage was given an additional amount of £455,000 from the government, to continue overall grant-aiding the Museum of

London. In 1988/9 (the financial year in which the Rose excavation took place), the overall grant-in-aid from the DoE to English Heritage accounted for £66.2 million out of a total income of £75.4 million. Whilst 'earned income' had risen by thirty per cent, government money had only increased by one per cent; thus the cost implications of the Rose were fated to loom heavily over all other considerations. In all, during that year, English Heritage received over 60 applications from archaeology in London, and made 32 grants totalling £723,000 – of which, 85% was towards the publication of past excavations.

The Museum of London's Department of Greater London Archaeology, headed by Harvey Sheldon, had an income of £2.3 million in 1988/9 of which nearly £400,000 was provided by English Heritage for establishment purposes, and £300,000 for projects; the remainder being made up from the private sector (of which, more later). During the year 1989/90, Sheldon's department investigated more than 70 sites of all periods, including the Rose, the Globe, and the royal riverside houses of both Edward II and Edward III. Because of the seemingly incessant redevelopment in the capital, Museum of London excavations are on the increase. The Museum of London sees its work as the definition and review of archaeological priorities, the provision of advice to local authorities and other bodies, the identification of threatened sites, fieldwork projects, preparation of site and research archives and reports for publication. They also advise English Heritage on scheduling and area designation.

The Rose Theatre was not the only ancient monument not to be scheduled in 1989. The previous year, English Heritage had been able to process only 871 applications. It is argued that there are 600,000 important archaeological sites in the whole country, ten per cent of which English Heritage aim to schedule at some point before the end of the millennium, whilst at present, just 12,674 ancient monuments receive the government protection of scheduling. Those privileged few have not, however, received eternal immunity. Ninety-three cases of criminal damage were reported in 1988/9, of which only five led to prosecution and of this handful of prosecutions, only two succeeded. Scheduling is not much of a deterrent to the law-breaker. Even to the law-abider, a legal remedy is possible to remove a monument from the schedule if it happens to be in the way of building plans. Application can be made – and often is – to demolish or disturb ancient monuments, and such applications are on the increase. In 1987/8, English Heritage advised the government to waive scheduling by granting Scheduled Monument Consent (SMC) in 798 cases (slightly less than all the cases which were put on the schedule the following year). Originally SMC was granted to the Roman baths at Huggin Hill – the second of the two exhilarating finds of 1989 referred to by Simon Jenkins in his *Times* article.

Huggin Hill was partially excavated in 1964, before re-burial and redevelopment. It was scheduled at that time. When the site once again became available, due to the obsolescence of the 1960s office block by the end of the 1980s, Hammersons, the property company, gave the Museum of London five months plus a £500,000 grant in return for advice which would lead to the DoE granting SMC. The remains turned out to be more substantial than prior excavation had indicated, so the SMC was rescinded at a cost to Hammersons of £3-4 million after much public outcry. However, SMCs are often given quietly, and behind closed doors. Tim Schadla-Hall, vice chairman of RESCUE, has said that 'Government decisions to give developers permission to destroy or damage scheduled archaeological sites should be open to public scrutiny and not be shrouded in excessive secrecy'.

Despite the growth in its professional standards, archaeology is bedevilled by the lack of political will and muscle. When Virginia Bottomley, the Under Secretary of State for the Environment in 1989, said in the House of Commons during one of the debates on the Rose's future, that in London a choice has to be made between 'a modern living city' and 'a square mile of archaeological remains', it was clear, given such a black and white alternative, where the government's choice would lie. The legislation which should protect archaeology has, unfortunately, proved to be such a deterrent that the wily developer is persuaded to seek stealthy ways around it. Yet it is the developer, churning up London's history, who alone is responsible for the growth in archaeology. Last year, in the capital, more than 22 million square feet of office space was under development whilst a further 39 million square feet were in the pipeline. Reluctant to use the muscle of the 1979 Act, the government has increasingly relied upon voluntary co-operation between archaeologists and the private sector. For some years prior to the Rose, their interests were not irreconcilable.

In 1986 a Voluntary Code of Practice was drawn up by the British Archaeological Trust and the Developers Liaison Group, sponsored by the British Property Federation and the Standing Conference of Archaeological Unit Managers. Brian Hobley, representing the Museum of London, was a key figure in drafting this document. The Code forms the basis for financial agreements between developer and archaeologist, the omission of which from the 1979 Act was always one of its weaknesses. In effect, the Code is a *de facto* tax on archaeology. In 1978/9, a survey indicated that financial contributions from the private sector totalled £58,000, but by 1988/9, such contributions had leapt to £14 million – more than twice English Heritage's entire budget for rescue work. The Museum of London last year relied on the private sector for almost £1½ million, which would not have been provided by any other source. In return for their money, developers expect archaeologists to give early notice of the need for investigation and to work to an agreed timetable. The archaeologist is expected to inform the developer of discoveries and to acknowledge the developer's support in all publications and documents.

Should the discovery warrant preservation, then advice must be sought from English Heritage who will take account of the development's timetable and the cost to both the developer and the public purse. 'While under contract,' the Code states, that the archaeologist should not, 'publicly campaign for *in situ* preservation ... or, through the media bring pressure on developers to alter the conditions of the contract, e.g., to gain further time'. In return, the developer is asked to be aware of 'the community and political benefits of full co-operation'. Professional evaluation should be sought and financial support offered. The Code reminds the developer that the preservation of *in situ* heritage features results in 'both a more visually attractive scheme and an investment'. Tony Banks, MP for Newham North-West has called the Code, 'an agreement struck between unequals. It places archaeologists in the position of supplicants, relying almost entirely on the goodwill of property developers – a group not noted for their altruism and selflessness.'

One further strand has to be woven into the tapestry of the Rose's background. It is the local authority. They are responsible for planning decisions and, in the case of the Rose, it was

Southwark Council who twice granted the developers permission to go ahead. A local authority's statutory powers do not include archaeological provision, although a 1985 DoE circular to all local authorities states that archaeological conditions *can* be imposed before permission is granted. One of these minimal conditions is that 'access must be afforded to archaeologists' who 'shall be allowed to observe' but that '*conditions should not require work to be held up*' (DoE italics). Southwark's own conditions are more satisfactory for archaeology. In Southwark, the developer is '*required* to provide access to allow any remains to be excavated' (My italics). Furthermore, 'no works of construction shall be carried out until reasonable opportunity has been afforded'. On both occasions, when it granted planning permission, Southwark utilised its conditions, despite a previous Public Inquiry's objections to Southwark's interpretation of the 1985 DoE circular.

Under the 1979 Act, it is also possible for the Secretary of State to designate an entire locality as an Area of Archaeological Importance (AAI). So far, the historic town centres of Canterbury, Chester, Exeter, Hereford and York have been thus designated. The advantage of designation is that it allows archaeological investigation to take place for a four and a half month period without compensation and *before* building can take place. As early as 1988, a year before the discovery of the Rose Theatre, Simon Hughes, the local MP for Bermondsey and North Southwark, asked Colin Moynihan, then Secretary of State for the Environment, to designate North Southwark as an AAI. Had Colin Moynihan done so back in 1988, Simon Jenkins might have found London archaeology a lot less exhilarating in 1989. 'AAIs are a breathing space which put developers on even more notice,' said Simon Hughes, speaking in the House of Commons debate about North Southwark's designation. Although AAI designation would have bought the Museum of London the time they needed to explore fully the site of the Rose, the problem of its eventual preservation and display would still have remained unresolved. At best, AAI designation is more appropriate for what is, these days, rather euphemistically called 'rescue archaeology'. The euphemism resides in the nature of such archaeology. Essentially, although controlled, it is a destructive exercise, a 'get in, grab it and get out with it' operation. At the end of the day, all that has been rescued is the record. Of the 350 sites excavated and investigated by the Museum of London in the past 15 years, 344 have subsequently been destroyed, 'mucked away' and dumped in out of town gravel pits. Only *six* sites have been saved for posterity.

'Official', said the *Evening Standard* in 1988, 'Bermondsey, until now something of a mystery, really is pre-historic.' The newspaper was referring to the site of the former Bricklayers Arms' goods depot, which after excavation offered proof of a permanent habitation where man had settled at a time when hippos still roamed over what is now Trafalgar Square. 'I do not think,' said Simon Hughes in the adjournment debate of 24 June 1988 about North Southwark's AAI designation, 'that the area has been a mystery to many of us, but archaeologically that has been the case.' In that year, the Museum of London also investigated three other major sites in Hughes' constituency; Bermondsey Abbey (an eleventh-century Clunaic priory), Hay's Wharf (the Rosary Palace of Edward II) and Courage Brewery (Roman timber revetments). 'There are various exciting discoveries on Southwark's streets,' Hughes said. In reply, Colin Moynihan talked about the absence of a 'bottomless pot of gold' and the 'hard facts of life'. The House of Commons debate, in fact, was but a rehearsal for the arguments which were to rage outside its chamber a year later. Simon Hughes was right about the exciting discoveries on Southwark's streets. In the summer of 1989, there was huge excitement on one street in particular. The Rose Theatre was excavated on a site of land bounded to the south by Park Street, and to the west by Rose Alley, 'Rosse Alleye leadinge from the Ryver of thames', on a site originally leased by Philip Henslowe over four hundred years ago.

The location of the Rose has always been well documented. The *Survey of London*, a 1950 publication by the London County Council (LCC), available in any reference library, reprinted an Ordnance Survey map of 1875 which clearly marked the spot. So far as is known, the Rose Theatre was the first substantial building to have been erected on the site and after its disuse, the low-lying Rose messuage seems to have lain relatively undeveloped. Rocque's map of 1746 shows an open site, with some housing bordering what was still known as Maid Lane. Housing may have continued along Smiths Rents, an alleyway that, at that time, occupied the eastern section of the Rose foundations. Today, Smiths Rents is the site of a depot owned by the City of London. In the late eighteenth century,

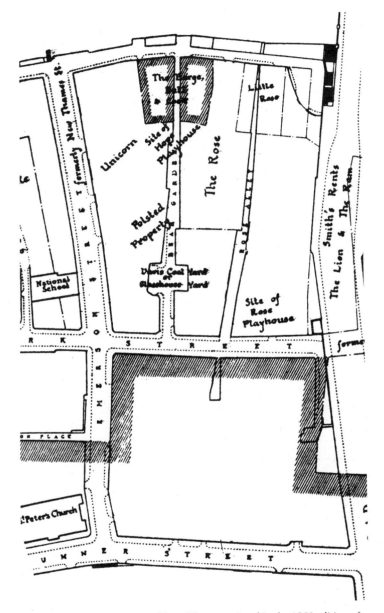

31. Map showing position of Rose Theatre, printed in the 1950 edition of *Bankside* (LCC).

domestic houses were built on the site, followed in the mid-nineteenth century by warehousing. The excavation uncovered evidence of all this later use. Indeed the imprint of a Victorian sewer in the eastern section of the dig is plain to see. In 1946, aerial photography indicated that the site suffered bomb damage and lay derelict.

On 15 July 1956, an application was made to the LCC for a six to seven storey building with 10,470 square metres of office space, followed by a second application, asking for extra warehouse provision in the basement. On 6 May 1957, application was granted and building went ahead on South-bridge House, which became home to the Property Services Agency, later a department of the DoE. Thirty-six piles had to be driven straight through the heart of the Rose to support this building, which despite the LCC's concern over 'colour, type and texture of materials to be used in external finishes', was something of an eyesore. Riverside House, standing to the north, is a similar building from that period. In 1971, Richard Hughes, the consultant archaeologist for Ove Arup, spent just two days in a library researching the site, realised it was the location of the Rose, and advised them that, 'Since the water table is relatively near the ground surface and since the area before the initial occupation was marshy, structural timbers are likely to be preserved'. With great prescience he forecast that, 'this should be considered one of those areas where public action could make excavation and preservation a national issue'. What nobody could have foretold was that anything would have survived the onslaught of 36 piles driven into the site in 1957, let alone the foundations of an insubstantial timber playhouse, easily dismantled and removed.

By 1987, Southbridge House was obsolete. Nineteen-fifties buildings simply do not have the ceiling height for air conditioning and all the other essential features of office life in the 1990s. Furthermore, the land was, by now, extremely valuable. Interland Estates Ltd, a part of the Heron group, bought the site. On 20 November 1987, they applied for planning permission from Southwark Council for a nine-storey block with 10,712 square metres of office space. Southwark Council liaised with the Museum of London and on 12 January 1988, George Dennis, the Museum of London's archaeological planning officer, wrote the standard, non-specific Museum of London letter to Heron's architects, Michael Lyell Associates,

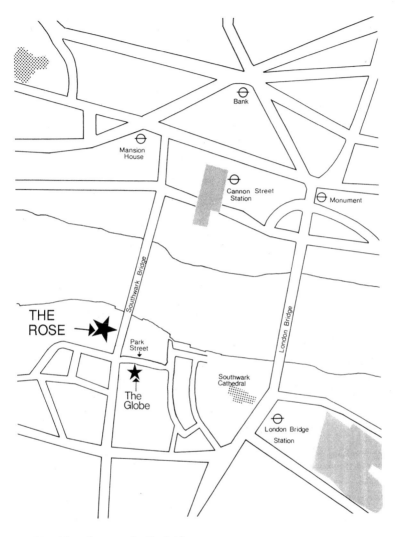

32.   Map of present day Bankside.

asking for permission to evaluate the site for excavation prior to any development. The letter spoke of 'an area of historical importance' but, at that stage, the Museum of London made no mention of the Rose Theatre. Museum of London archae-ologists were equally concerned about Roman and medieval waterfronts since similar evidence had been destroyed, unrecorded, on the land to the south (currently occupied by Unisys office block). What they hoped to do was to evaluate the site *inside* Southbridge House, and assess any of its buried remains. Engineers vetoed this scheme for fear that any trench large enough to achieve a representative sample, might destabilise the whole block, so any evaluation had to await demolition.

On 1 February 1988, Southwark granted Heron planning permission, subject to their archaeological conditions. On 26 February, a meeting took place between representatives from the Museum of London, Heron and Michael Lyell Associates, to establish procedures and a programme for site investigation, according to the Voluntary Code. The Museum of London asked for a three to four month excavation in which they hoped to determine lines of medieval river frontages, as well as 'the possibility of establishing the site of the Shakespearean "Rose Theatre" which lay at the NW corner of the site'. It was also minuted that 'a further period of excavation could be requested for more detailed inspection but this would be programmed into any construction contract to avoid disruption'. In April 1988, Heron went back to Southwark Council for permission for a larger scheme. Meanwhile on 5 July 1988, agreement was reached over a timetable for excavation, with the appropriate costs. It was Heron's intention to enter into a contract with the Museum of London for:

Phase 1 – 8 week period site evaluation commencing 17 October 1988, at a total price of £25,979 and (we) *are prepared to enter into a similar contract for Phase II (excavation), at a time period and price to be negotiated.*

The latter part of this agreement has been italicised to indicate the essentially open-ended agreement reached by the Museum of London with Heron.

Before either the new Heron scheme could be approved by Southwark Council or the contract signed by the Museum of London, the site unexpectedly changed hands. CMD, the development wing of Imry Merchant, had acquired the land on behalf of PosTel, the pension fund of the Post Office. Imry Merchant submitted new plans which involved a ten-storey office block. Subject to the same archaeological conditions, Southwark granted permission in December 1988 (although permission was not actually signed until May 1989). The Museum of London, naturally hoped for the same arrangement they had secured with Heron. Instead, Imry Merchant offered them only Phase I of the Heron agreement. It was to be a case of two months on site, 'take it or leave it'. The Museum of London stuck out for 17 weeks, and eventually ended up with ten. Archaeologist, Julian Bowsher was interviewed on 15 December 1988 for the position of site director. He already knew something about subterranean North Southwark having excavated post-medieval river walls on the land where the *Financial Times* building now stands, and he was interested in theatres, having dug up a Roman theatre in the Middle East. 'Dare I say it,' he says in lectures, 'it was a real one.' Bowsher got the job and the quest for the Rose was now truly underway.

The Museum of London's Lambeth and Southwark team are housed just off Borough High Street, in a decrepit building possibly in need of excavation itself. A scrawled notice on its red door says: 'Leave muddy boots outside'. Not only was the site of the Rose not a 'green field site', as observed on many occasions by Victor Belcher from English Heritage's London Division, it wasn't even a vacant site. Demolition of Southbridge House went on at the same time as excavation. The entire plot on which Southbridge House stood, has to be considered as divided into north and south. The north soon established itself as lacking significant archaeological remains, so once the deafening sound of demolition was over, the shuddering noise of piling in the north began. Meanwhile, thundering lorries used the entire south east for access. Amidst this constant turmoil, excavation began in the south west. The Museum of London team, who on average numbered 20, moved in at 8 a.m. on 19 December. Thereafter, they were left with many muddy boots to park outside the door in Cole Street. The cradle of Western civilisation was nothing better than a swamp.

By 23 January a sump needed to be dug to prevent the archaeologists from becoming completely bogged down. They had excavated the seventeenth, eighteenth and nineteenth-century levels. 'Some areas of the site had been used for dumping horse dung,' said Julian Bowsher, 'it still looked and

33. Julian Bowsher (centre, with beard) and the team from the Museum of London's Department of Greater London archaeology. (Andy Fulgoni)

smelled like it – the exhaust fumes, if you like, of yesteryear'. So far, the dig had turned up some former cesspits, post-Tudor bricks, the odd barrel and a few remains of Victorian flooring – but not Philip Henslowe's theatre. Then, on 31 January, whilst working in the west of a trench dug in the south west, Bowsher came across what he described as 'funny white stuff' and this proved to be the foundation walls of the Rose. A few days later, on 2 February, two test slots were dug and the exploration revealed an external wall at an angle junction built out of chalk and brick. Theodolite bearings confirmed that these would not comprise a regular polygon, but that it *was* a polygon; the first incontrovertible fact of an Elizabethan playhouse had been established. Sixteen sides, at that time, seemed the most likely. No stage was found yet, but the remains of a mortared floor were there, covered in a quantity of lath and plaster. The Rose – if indeed it was the Rose; some said it was just a bearpit – consisted of inner and outer foundation walls with angles of 160 degrees. It took a great deal of imagination to visualise the theatre from this slender evidence but the real problem was that the excavation was due to end on 19 February, before much more would be discovered.

According to the Voluntary Code of Practice, the Museum of London alerted English Heritage to the significance of the find. On 10 February, Harvey Sheldon wrote to them saying that either the Rose or a bear-baiting arena had been discovered (from an archaeologist's point of view, both are equally fascinating). He asked for better security on site and a public expression of English Heritage's interest. Irrespective of the Code's ban on publicity, the Museum of London also took the case of the Rose to the media for the first time. The persuasive significance of its slender but tangible evidence converted most people to the Rose's defence, but it was not yet a front page story. Simon Tait of *The Times* broke the news on 15 February, and was the first to carry the 'Elizabethan popcorn' interpretation. On 18 February, Ian McKellen came down to the fenced-off site and posed for cameras, standing on the duckboards over the Rose's fragile chalk foundations. Great mechanical diggers were scooping up mountains of mud in the north, whilst in the south, archaeologists were painstakingly trowelling handfuls of earth.

On 23 February, Ian McKellen was back. Julian Bowsher's diary, recorded on disk, noted that on that day, the site got a general clean up, bunting was hung, and 'hordes of actors' descended, clutching unseasonal roses as a tribute. His entry that day noted that 'it was clear the site was a theatre'. The day's events got some attention in the press. Meanwhile, under pressure from Imry Merchant, Bowsher got on with the excavation of the clay on top of the ash deposits. Sam Wanamaker, around this time, proposed an ingenious scheme, which involved re-burial of the Rose in a 7 feet high basement and its partial display, by way of mirrors, with access from Bear Gardens Museum. Dame Peggy Ashcroft and James Fox, working on the award-winning film *She's Been Away* with Sir Peter Hall, wrote to David Davies, the Chairman of Imry Merchant. 'I was told,' she later said, 'that it made a difference.'

Imry Merchant agreed to a nine-day period to allow for full evaluation, which would end on 28 February. On 25 February, Julian Bowsher organised an academic conference on the site: a brainstorming on the position of the stage. The stage was a 'whole can of worms', as he put it. Was it likely to be in the north or in the south? Torn between the Vitruvian thinking of Martin Clout, which said the stage would be in the north, and the received wisdom of the John Orrell consensus, which said the stage would be in the south, Bowsher looked everywhere. 'Archaeology,' he said, 'has to be as objective as any other scientific discipline. It doesn't bother us if what we find fails to fit in with previous conjectures.' Before the stage could be unearthed, yet more time had to be negotiated. On 1 March, Simon Jenkins and Lord Montagu of Beaulieu, from English Heritage, visited the site and following their visit, on 3 March, the developers offered another ten weeks. The final day of the dig would be 14 May. It was to be brinkmanship all the way as the race for the Rose was on.

It was on 8 March, that Julian Bowsher found what had to be the stage. It was in the north, facing south-south-east. Things were still far from clear because there were so many apparent structural anomalies. The shallow projection of the stage was too shallow to indicate with any certainty that what had been found was the stage at all. It had none of the projection indicated by de Witt's sketch. Further digging came across a *second* projecting wall. It was all fairly baffling. If the site proved difficult to 'read' after excavation, during excavation it was a nightmare. No one was expecting to find two stages with

166

evidence of a completely re-built exterior. Public interest was growing. By now English Heritage had put up £30,000 for a protective canopy, viewing platform and presentation material. After Easter, Simon Blatherwick joined in as site co-ordinator, so that Bowsher could spend more time on PR and analysing the findings. On 22 April, the ISGC hosted a symposium at the Bear Gardens Museum which brought together all the experts for an attempt at interpretation. The discoveries had been far more extensive than anyone had anticipated, yet clear interpretation was only made possible after the much later removal of the protective canopy. Aerial photography of the Rose's whitened chalk foundations lying in the dark earth made immediate sense to the layman, although the scale detail plans of the archaeologist eventually gave better results to the expert. At the symposium, a member of the audience asked Julian Bowsher if there was a future for the Rose. Bowsher laconically replied, 'Well, our last day is 14 May.' Was this to be the end of the road for the Rose?

Acting by the Voluntary Code English Heritage had accepted that the discovery of the Rose warranted preservation, but, again according to the Code, they had taken into account the timetable for development – and the cost, both to the developer and the public purse. The plan they endorsed was to 'preserve' the remains under a protective carpet, backfilled with sand, hardcore and rubble. Up and until now, such measures had been a normal practice for safeguarding much more substantial remains than the Rose Theatre, such as the Roman stone and brickwork at Huggin Hill. In theory, this measure would 'preserve' the Rose, against the day when further excavation would be possible, following the certain obsolescence of the Imry Merchant office block. Had this plan gone ahead, the Rose would almost certainly have been irretrievably damaged, if not by the insensitive backfill, then almost certainly by the nature of the piling then proposed by Pell Frischmann, the structural engineers.

To build the Imry Merchant office block, 20 piles were to be driven through the site – one pile would have been zapped straight through Edward Alleyn's stage, the very heart of the Rose – yet English Heritage maintained that only 'localised damage' would ensue. As well as the piles, damage to the Rose Theatre was threatened by the planned lift shaft and diaphragm wall. At the symposium in late April, Julian Bowsher had

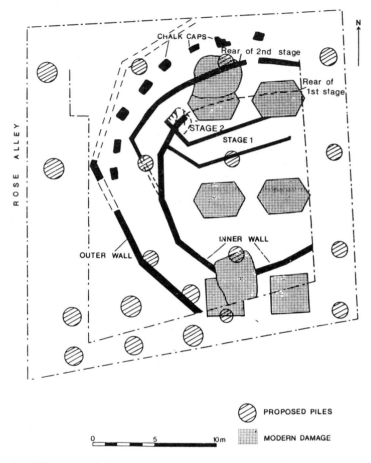

34. The proposed piling positions on 14 May 1989. Note that one pile is placed right through the Phase One stage. (Museum of London)

expressed the archaeologist's perennial dilemma. He was tempted to do a total rescue excavation, to find out as much as possible, even though 'No one would ever see the Rose again, except on paper.' Not everything that an archaeologist digs up is worth preserving, but the Rose had prompted a quantum jump forward in archaeological thinking. The stand that the Museum of London were prepared to make over the Rose, related to the perceived importance of the remains. As a member of the audience at the symposium had said, 'It seems to me to be the most important archaeological event in British theatre history.'

But there was no early, let alone a co-ordinated, campaign to save it. 'Perhaps, there should have been,' admitted Simon Hughes, who was briefed of events throughout the excavation of the Rose. In its last weeks, however, individuals rallying around the Rose built up an unstoppable momentum which led inexorably to the much publicised 'final' weekend of 13/14 May 1989. Philip Ormond, a theatre publicist, who was later to play an active part in the Campaign, for example, visited the site on 5 May, and described the experience as 'a patch of damp mud with some stones sticking out: an archaeologist's plan stapled to the hoarding, some cold minutes of cross-referencing the plan to the stones – an intellectual exercise, then suddenly, the site of the theatre clicked into place and I was standing where the best seats had been, looking down on the stage where Shakespeare had probably acted – a unique emotional experience.' He decided there and then to commit his company, Theatre Despatch, to help save the Rose. Peggy Ashcroft went direct to RSC actor, Ralph Fiennes. 'She visited me in my dressing room to ask if I would help save the Rose, because I was playing Henry VI in *The Plantagenets*, an adaptation of the Rose Trilogy,' he said. 'Everyone knew about the Rose, but nobody really appreciated that it was just going to disappear'. Martin Clout had been pressing the Museum of London for some time to make a stand over the Rose's preservation and display, and, on 9 May, he had the dispiriting experience of watching Hughes stand up at ten minutes to midnight, in a deserted House of Commons, to ask Virginia Bottomley for the remains of the Rose to be scheduled.

In a set reply, Virginia Bottomley said, 'I commit myself to working with all parties to find an effective outcome that will achieve the goal we are all pursuing.' Despite Bottomley's hint of backstage negotiations, Simon Hughes described her statement as a 'nothing reply'. Martin Clout was despondent and took his concerns about the Rose to a colleague, the historian, Dr Ruth Richardson. 'I realised,' she said, 'that it was up to us to do something.' The following day, they drafted a letter to *The Times*, and telephoned a long list of eminent actors persuading them to add their signatures. As a hot story, the Rose started to be picked up in earnest by the media. That same day, on Thursday, 11 May, the Prime Minister, the Right Hon. Margaret Thatcher, was asked by Hughes during Question Time to join with him 'in rejoicing at the discovery on Bankside in Southwark, in my constituency, of the ruins of the Rose Theatre'. In reply, Thatcher said that 'everything must be done to preserve those remàins so that one day they may be on public display'. 'It was then,' said Andrew Gurr, 'that the Rose became national news.'

35. Dame Peggy Ashcroft sitting on her camp stool by the site of the excavated Rose Theatre. (Andy Fulgoni)

On the same afternoon, Dames Peggy Ashcroft and Judi Dench were photographed on the site of the Rose. Dench removed her shoes to stand on the stage. 'I just had to get as close as I could,' she was reported as saying, 'because we'll never have the opportunity again'. Sir Peter Hall interrupted rehearsals of *The Merchant of Venice* to bring most of his cast down to Park Street – including its international star, Dustin Hoffman. Hoffman declined to play at archaeology by posing with a trowel for the assembled photographers, but he happily grinned at the cameras alongside Ashcroft, who was sitting on her sturdy camp stool just inside the site perimeter. 'It was then,' said Councillor Geoff Williams, Chairman of Southwark's Planning Committee, 'that the whole thing took off.'

Imry Merchant denied that bulldozers would move in on Monday, 15 May. Their press statement said that, 'The remains are going to be wrapped as carefully as a porcelain doll. There must be a building over it and to protect the Rose Theatre there has to be a protective covering for it, and that is being done under the guidance of English Heritage.' Privately, Martin Landau, Imry Merchant's Deputy Chairman, was asking Simon Jenkins, 'What can we do?' On Friday, 12 May, *The Times* carried three letters about the Rose in its letters column, including the one drafted by Ruth Richardson and Martin Clout and signed by a list of prominent thespians. It also carried the article by Simon Jenkins, the Deputy Chairman of English Heritage, who made a last minute plea to; 'beg the firm to make a last effort'. Eileen Chivers, Head of Drama at Alleyn's School, visited the site with a party of students. In the school magazine, she later described the Costain's pile-driving equipment: 'waiting vulture-like to the north of the site'. Meanwhile, the press office at the RSC's Barbican headquarters had been commandeered by Ralph Fiennes and Nick Woodeson who were organising the first public demonstration to save the Rose. Imry Merchant in their press statement added that they 'were absolutely committed to ensuring that the remains are preserved under the new building with minimal damage'.

On Saturday, 13 May, Simon Hughes, met with his assistant Amanda Kenyon, Ralph Fiennes, Philip Ormond and Maureen Tomison, a political lobbyist, to co-ordinate activities for the weekend. That day, the protective canopy which had spanned the site of the Rose excavation was removed and sent on its way to Glasgow. The photographer, Andy Fulgoni, then photographed

36. Drawing by June Everett, who has illustrated many of the key moments in the reconstruction of the Globe. It shows the excavation of the south site, whilst building work was underway in the north site. Note the pile-driving equipment looming 'vulture-like' behind the perimeter fence. (By courtesy of the artist)

37. A bird's eye view of the excavated foundations of the Rose Theatre, which made the site more easily 'read' by the layman. (Andy Fulgoni)

the site of the Rose from on top of the Unisys office block. Julian
Bowsher, the archaeologist who had been there from the first,
was on another professional engagement, so it was Simon
Blatherwick who supervised the Museum of London's last
weekend of excavation. The wooden drain which had been
found on 28 April, was carefully removed and sent for
treatment to Portsmouth, where laboratories had gained
experience of timber preservation, following work on the *Mary
Rose*. Seeing the drain removed, convinced many reporters that
this was an amazing last-minute discovery. Not that the story of
the Rose needed much heightened drama. There was quite
enough excitement in Park Street as it was.

On Sunday, 14 May, the road was closed and a makeshift
stage with crude sound system set up. Ian McKellen, Tim
Pigott-Smith, James Fox, Rosemary Harris, Peter Hall, Peggy
Ashcroft, a crowd of hopefuls and extras, were about to present
a star-studded extravaganza of street theatre, held together by
Simon Hughes and Ralph Fiennes as joint compères. Hundreds
gathered in the course of the afternoon. A highlight of the
occasion was the message from Lord Olivier delivered by Ruth
Richardson. 'I realise that the advent of so-called progress rings
the death knell on this magnificent find. But it seems to me
terrible that one's heritage can be swept under the concrete, as
though it had never existed. It is a vitally important part of our
theatrical history, a very great shame.' Choristers from
Southwark Cathedral sang. Musicians from *The Plantagenets*
played a fanfare. Students from Alleyn's School read extracts
from *Dr Faustus* (with Eileen Chivers fearlessly playing the part
of Lechery). Circus clown and street entertainer Robbie Barnett
walked the street on his giant stilts. People gravely inspected the
broken circle of weathered stone. Children clutched placards.
One of them said 'Don't Doze the Rose'. James Fox asked, 'Shall
time's best jewel from time's chest be hid?'; Rosemary Harris
reminded the crowds that, 'The quality of mercy is not strained';
Peggy Ashcroft pointedly intoned, 'Nor marble nor the gilded
monuments/Of princes shall outlive this powerful rhyme.' It
was the start of open season on the Bard. At 8 p.m. Simon
Jenkins spoke to the massed crowds, many of whom were
staying the night as part of a candlelit vigil.

It had become abundantly clear to Simon Jenkins that Sunday
morning, that English Heritage had a crisis on its hands and he
went down to the site. But trying to persuade people that

English Heritage had booked emergency discussions for Monday morning between Imry Merchant and the DoE, did not get him very far with the crowd in Park Street. He was booed; an unnerving experience for one who had grown up with the conservation movement. 'I had a lot of sympathy with the demonstrators,' he said, reading from a diary which he too had kept of the events. 'The piling positions were insensitively placed. The nature of the backfill might be destructive. The remains of the Rose were not rocks or stone but pathetic hunks of highly fragile chalk and fragments of wood. Tipping hardcore over that lot could have proved fatal.' Simon Jenkins was in telephone negotiations with Imry Merchant throughout Sunday night. 'They said that their instruction to the foreman on Monday morning was to take delivery of the sand which would be distributed round the site with wheelbarrows and by hand. Had I been a part of the mob, I would have been somewhat sceptical but I believed them. I'd been talking to them the previous week and they had clearly indicated a willingness to be flexible and a desire to do the right thing. I was pushing at an open door.'

'What we were trying to do,' recalled Martin Myers, Imry Merchant's Chief Executive, 'was to preserve the Rose by covering it in sand, as advised. Then we planned to start negotiations with the DoE to work out the best solution for everyone. It was our intention at that time to re-design the building. The crowds down on the site that Sunday afternoon were being whipped into a frenzy with the emotive use of words like bulldozers, concrete, destruction and vandalism.' As Sunday wore on, unconvinced and desperate Campaigners made threatening telephone calls to Myers, other members of his board and their families. 'Despite this provocation,' said Simon Jenkins, 'Imry Merchant felt they had given an undertaking and intended to stick by it and they have stuck to it ever since.'

Nobody in Park Street believed in any of these promises and good intentions. As midnight approached, and the Museum of London's tenure of the site came to an end, the atmosphere grew tense. At 11.30 p.m., the outer perimeter of the site was ringed by those still in Park Street. As midnight chimed, Simon Jenkins returned to observe the official handing over of the site to the security firm, Reliance. Padlocks were changed in his presence. 'The night was fortunately warm,' wrote Sarah Gregory in Alleyn's School magazine, 'and our spirits were kept high by donations of chocolate, bagels and other provisions.' Monday, 15 May, was to be the first day of what turned out to be an exceptionally hot summer. A few people attempted to bed down for the night on the pavement. Anne Matthews, the Leader of Southwark Council, got out her sleeping bag. Coral Stringfellow dozed in her car and, from time to time, phoned through the news of events to the DJs working the late shift at Stringfellow's, her nightclub in London's West End. Nobody really got much sleep. At 4.30 a.m., the demonstrators invaded the site and ringed its inner perimeter. 'This enraged Imry's,' said Jenkins, 'who claimed the agreement had broken down. They said they were now entitled to proceed exactly how they wished, even though they had no intention of doing so.'

Shortly before dawn broke, the BBC News camera crew arrived and despite the transport strike which paralysed the City throughout Monday, many of Sunday's demonstrators returned. Peggy Ashcroft took up her position on the camp stool inside the fence, by the northern boundary. Obstructing a public highway would have been an immediate matter for police intervention but invading the site of the Rose was different. As Iain Mackintosh said, 'We stood on the developer's land because it would take a court order to evict us.' There were many famous faces amongst the trespassers, but the majority in the crowd were anonymous Londoners. Shortly after 6 a.m., lorries started to mass at one end of Park Street. A line of people, arms linked, moved in front of them. There was a lot of intense, but short-lived, excitement. Someone decorated a lorry with a rose. The driver of another signed a petition form. Simon Hughes went off to telephone the developers at a home number. On his return, he said that if the demonstrators left the site, Imry Merchant would continue negotiations. The crowd rejected this offer. Hughes went back to the telephone, taking Ashcroft with him. She had threatened to throw herself in front of the bulldozers. 'Look around the site,' Martin Myers suggested to her, 'Tell me if you can see any bulldozers. There are no bulldozers. All that is there, are wheelbarrows, to distribute the sand. Throwing yourself in front of a wheelbarrow is not going to have the same impact.'

'He told me we were trespassing,' said Peggy Ashcroft, 'and I said it might be illegal, but it's not a crime.' The demonstration had reached an *impasse*. The crowd refused to leave unless Museum of London archaeologists were allowed back on site.

By now it was 7 a.m., and the pile drivers in the north had started up their deafening dawn chorus. For no clear reason, the lorries reversed and left. The sun was already strong in the sky, glaring down at the exposed foundations of the Rose. Simon Jenkins was worried about the lack of protection for the remains of the Rose Theatre. 'Imry Merchant were so furious about the invasion that they were refusing to allow any archaeologists back on site to water the remains. I was concerned that they might go back on their informal agreement to delay work in the south, pending the planned negotiations on piling positions.' A proposal from the crowd that Peggy Ashcroft be left behind as hostage and the site vacated, was voted against. 'Amidst the mud and rubble and flying cranes,' recalled theatre director Richard Williams, 'I expect she was relieved.' Eventually, after more telephone calls, deadlock was broken. Imry Merchant agreed to allow two archaeologists back on site with their hosepipes. Ashcroft assured the crowd that this was an honest deal. The crowd left the site which once again was made secure. People stayed in Park Street to await the outcome of the day's proceedings. Simon Hughes intended to persuade the Speaker to take a private notice question in the House of Commons which would initiate an emergency debate. Imry Merchant, English Heritage and Nicholas Ridley, the Secretary of State for the Environment were due to meet at 10 a.m. Was it possible that this public outcry might save the Rose?

Described variously as the Rosetta stone of theatre architecture, the Wailing Wall of European culture and the cradle of Western civilisation, the Rose now had a lot to live up to. To scholars the significance of the Rose's vestigial foundations warranted no justification. But scholars accounted for only a handful of people. Overnight, the debate had moved from preservation to display, and the problem of display, to the unconverted, was that all that could be seen was a 'hole in the ground' (Bernard Levin), 'a disused mine' (Anthony Beaumont Dark, MP), a 'sweet smelling pile of bricks and rubble' (Terry Dicks, MP), or a 'patch of mud scattered with a few theatrical mementoes' (columnist Julie Birchill). The Rose was 'not the Parthenon; it is not Tower Bridge; it's not even a building' (arts journalist, Joan Bakewell); it offered only 'a passing gawp' (Lynda Henderson from the University of Ulster). Lord Howie of Troon put the question that was on many minds. 'Are we preserving a footprint rather than an artifact?' Lord Hesketh gave the only reply possible; 'It depends slightly on whose footprint it was.' The Rose's future could not rest on objective data. It was tied in with a sense of place and the emotions aroused by that sense of place. Privately unconvinced by the argument that displaying the Rose was worth a huge proportion of the national archaeological budget, Simon Jenkins, as a democrat, said he believed that if that was the majority wish, then he, representing English Heritage, would continue negotiations.

For the rest of the morning of 15 May, Simon Jenkins, Martin Myers, Martin Landau, the architect Richard Seifert, engineers from Pell Frischmann, officers from the DoE and Nicholas Ridley were locked into a meeting, hammering out ways which could stay the execution. Ridley, to the dismay of Treasury civil servants, suddenly offered Imry Merchant an unspecified amount of compensation for any delay. Following an emergency phone call to Downing Street, this was prudently re-phrased as a million pounds. Martin Landau, in return, agreed to a further month's delay in construction whilst Seifert re-thought the piling positions. Simon Jenkins returned to Park Street with the news that Ridley had galloped to the rescue of the Rose in the final reel. Imry Merchant would be re-designing the piling positions of the office block so that preservation and display could become a reality. This time Jenkins got ecstatic cheers.

The crowds from the previous night were still milling around. Fresh people were arriving. Gradually, all those who eventually joined the committee to campaign for the Rose were making themselves known to one another. There was a lot of confusion. Cement on the north site started to leak on to the south site. Lorries arrived with sand to plug the leak. Lorries once more were turned away. Lorries trying to get down Park Street to completely different building sites were blocked. A carnival atmosphere grew. Brian Cox and Patrick Stewart did an impromptu reading of the Mechanicals' scene from *A Midsummer Night's Dream*. 'The sort of thing I was hoping for on Sunday, started to happen on Monday,' said Ralph Fiennes who had already missed several trains to the Lake District, where he was due for a short holiday. At 2.30 p.m., Simon Hughes left Park Street to grab a tie and at 3.31 p.m. he stood up in a packed House of Commons and asked the Secretary of State for the Environment if he would make a statement on the future of the Rose Theatre site. In reply, Nicholas Ridley said, 'I am very glad to tell the House that Imry has agreed to delay work on the theatre site for one month. This is to enable it and its architects to work with English Heritage and with us on various options. The roof will go back over the site immediately so that the excavated remains are fully protected while these discussions continue.'

The debate that followed was spirited and good-humoured. Sir Bernard Braine said that a month was not long enough. Mark Fisher invited Nicholas Ridley to join him on a visit to the site. John Fraser asked Nicholas Ridley if he agreed with Oscar Wilde that where archaeology begins, art ends. Eric Heffer said that Nicholas Ridley's answer was the best statement that he'd ever heard Ridley make. Clive Soley, however, said that basically, Ridley's answer still amounted to two of sand and one of cement. In summing up, Nicholas Ridley said that a month would concentrate the mind, that he would visit the site but choose his own company, that Eric Heffer had obviously not been in the House very much, and that he would never take on Clive Soley as a builder's mate since 'one of cement and two of sand . . . would be wasting cement on a unprecedented scale.' And finally, Ridley said that he claimed dissimilarity from Oscar Wilde in more than one respect. 'No genius to declare?' suggested Neil Kinnock. At that 'several Hon. Members rose', but it being 3.52 p.m. it was time for them to consider Kurdish refugees.

Ralph Fiennes heard the news in a taxi on his way to Euston. At the site the crowd had swelled. Dozens of camera crews from all over the world had descended. The British media were covering the story as if it was a major public event, a Royal wedding or military invasion. Simon Hughes went back to the site and set up a campaigning committee based on guidelines suggested by Ian McKellen. This included representatives of different groups, an archaeologist, a historian, an actor, a schoolteacher and so on. Hughes asked for volunteers from the crowd thronging Park Street. Names were put forward and a popular cheer from the street confirmed election.

From now on, references to the Committee mean that body of people who met privately, whilst references to the Campaign mean its public manifestations. A brief meeting of those elected from the street, on the afternoon of 15 May, was held straight-away at the Bear Gardens Museum. In the time-honoured fashion of all committees, its main business was to set a date for the next Committee meeting, which would include those people nominated for membership who were absent from Park Street. Later in the Campaign, Martin Myers referred to this Committee as a 'load of agitators that Simon Hughes couldn't control'. There was often doubt amongst the Committee, as to who, strictly speaking, was a Committee member. Some people were members of sub-committees with no voting rights at main Committee, other people had declined Committee status and a few individuals who started out representing someone else, ended up representing themselves. Prominent celebrities like Vanessa Redgrave and Timothy Dalton often spoke on behalf and at the request of the Campaign whilst not being members of its Committee. At one tense point in its affairs, the Committee asked non-members to wait outside the meeting room, whilst it voted to exclude them from the proceedings. A trio of expensive actors, Ian McKellen, Sam Wanamaker and Tim Pigott-Smith, (plus a woman who had wandered in off the street) obediently trooped out and awaited the verdict. Finally, all were allowed to return (with the exception of the woman who had wandered in off the street).

At various times, the Committee consisted of the following people: Dr Anthony Grayling, a philosophy don at Oxford, Dr Ruth Richardson, a historian at London University, Dr Urmilla Khan from the University of Delhi, Professor Martin Biddle, an archaeologist at Oxford, Professor Stanley Welles from the University of Birmingham, Martin Clout, a Shakespearean 'gentleman scholar', and John Burns, studying for his PhD in fifth-century Athenian White Grand Lekythoi vases. The Museum of London fielded a number of archaeologists with a watching brief, George Dennis, Derek Seeley, Harvey Sheldon, Julian Bowsher, and Simon Blatherwick. Solicitors, Martin Kramer and Nicholas Armstrong from the legal firm, Theodore Goddard, offered legal services. The architect, Jon Greenfield from Pentagram, offered architectural advice, Martin Village, a building restorer, offered advice on the property market, Iain Mackintosh on behalf of Theatres Trust, submitted an alternative architectural scheme. ISGC publicist Jennifer Jones, PR consultant Elizabeth Day, nightclub owner Coral Stringfellow and Philip Ormond from Theatre Despatch, volunteered PR expertise. Schoolteacher Eileen Chivers, local councillor Hilary Wines, and Heather Pickering from

Southwark Heritage, represented the local community. Lauryn Beer, Pat McDonnell and Alex Wilbraham were the young enthusiasts. Dame Peggy Ashcroft was the main spokesperson for the theatrical profession, backed up by James Fox, Rosemary Harris, Ian McKellen, Tim Pigott-Smith, Irene Worth, Sam Wanamaker, Barbara Todd (from RADA), Walter Gotell (the KGB 'heavy' in the '007' films), Coral Stringfellow, fringe director Michael Batz and ex-actress Fiona Carton. Simon Hughes, Gerry Bowden, (Dulwich's Tory MP), and, in theory, Harriet Harman, (Peckham's Labour MP), served as an all-Party alliance.

For the first real Committee meeting a few days dater, on 18 May, this large and unwieldy group came together under the chairmanship of Simon Hughes, with Gerry Bowden deputising. It considered its options. There were three. Option One was to take over the entire site, north and south, and preserve the Rose without any office development; the 'blue skies option'. Option Two was to develop the north site whilst leaving the south site for a Rose museum. Option Three was to negotiate with Imry Merchant for the best possible re-design within the planned development. It was a crowded and confused meeting, which voted firmly against Option Three and committed itself irrevocably to an expensive solution. Iain Mackintosh, on behalf of the Theatres Trust (established by an Act of Parliament 'to provide the better protection of theatres for the benefit of the nation'), volunteered a feasibility study of Option Three, commissioned from Ove Arup & Partners, but was essentially on his own. The Campaign which the Committee represented had many public faces but Simon Hughes' was the most familiar and it was he who took on the task of negotiating with Imry Merchant.

Born on 17 May 1951 Simon Hughes is the third of four brothers. During the 1966 General Election, the young Hughes discovered Liberalism and subsequently all his family have converted from left-wing Toryism and followed him into the Liberal Democrats. Two brothers are local councillors and his mother is chairwoman of the parish council. 'Although Liberalism is a Welsh tradition – indeed members of my family not only knew Lloyd George, some of them even worked for him – being a Liberal at school was enough for me to be branded a Communist.' Hughes was educated at Llandaff Cathedral School and Christ College, Brecon. He read law at

Selwyn College, Cambridge and was admitted to the Inner Temple in 1974. Meanwhile, he had settled in Southwark and become involved with both voluntary youth work and community politics. 'This was the experience which allowed me to become an MP. It taught me so much about inner London. I knew how South London worked and how the people of South London worked. I could speak their language and live on the street with them. I feel I can honestly say I know what they want.'

In 1981 he stood for the GLC and, although he lost, Simon Hughes comforted himself with the knowledge that he had overtaken the Tories and increased the Liberal vote from 3% to 15%. In September 1982 the MP for Bermondsey, Bob Mellish, resigned. If the Labour Party nationally at this time was in disarray under the leadership of Michael Foot, then locally it was a disaster. As the February 1983 by-election approached, factions surrounding Mellish's resignation split the Labour vote between its official candidate, Peter Tatchell, and a number of independent Labour alternatives. When the Tory candidate pulled out at the last minute, Hughes was the only candidate left with unequivocal backing from a national party. It was one of the ugliest campaigns on record with Peter Tatchell pilloried in the press for his militant advocacy of homosexual rights. 'It was unacceptable,' says Hughes with hindsight, 'and it shouldn't have happened. Sometimes I remained silent when I should have spoken up but I was never regarded by the media as a likely winner and it wasn't until the last week that they reported me at all.' Simon Hughes' eventual win turned a Labour majority of 12,000 into a Liberal majority of 9000. It was the biggest swing in British parliamentary history. The following autumn, Hughes' election was vindicated in the general election when he went on to defeat the less controversial Labour candidate, John Tilley, former MP for Brixton.

Simon Hughes, who lists his recreations in *Who's Who* as 'music, discotheques and good parties, history, sport, theatre, the countryside and open air, travel', is adept at handling the media and has the reputation of a strong constituency MP. Almost one of the first people to lobby him after his election was Harvey Sheldon and it was a Bankside issue – the redevelopment of St Mary Overie's Dock – that engaged him. For all his involvement in local affairs, Hughes lacks a power base in the borough. Southwark Council has 15 Democrat councillors amongst its 62 elected members but a clear Labour majority runs the borough and many councillors remember the Tatchell election. To bolster the Rose as an all-Party issue, Hughes offered the position of deputy chairman to the Tory MP Gerry Bowden, whose leafy constituency includes Margaret Thatcher's neo-Georgian Barratt home. The third Southwark MP, Labour's Harriet Harman, who represents Peckham, was nominally a committee member but it was always very much Simon Hughes' show. The Campaign Committee, in the main, were as suspicious of Tories as they were hostile to the Labour Party. At a fraught moment in its deliberations one of its members denounced another Committee member, in tones of high moral outrage as 'a card-carrying member of the Labour Party': so much for Martin Myers' perceptions.

Simon Hughes enjoys a somewhat lightweight reputation in the House of Commons itself. Matthew Parris, of *The Times* is a merciless critic of the MP whom he perceives as a typical third party politician in search of the protest vote; 'Hughes has a speech for every occasion – and frequently two. It is just that they never quite add up to a philosophy. No sparrow falls in Bermondsey without a Hughes' eulogy; and should the cheeping have disturbed a constituent, there will be a Hughes' diatribe against sparrows too.' In negotiation with English Heritage and Imry Merchant, Hughes' ability to see both sides of the question led to difficulties. 'When I went to see Simon Hughes and some of his people at the House of Commons,' says Simon Jenkins, 'he accepted that blue skies was never an option. My impression was that Simon Hughes found himself in an impossible predicament. He had been offered the site for display and the total co-operation of, by this stage, a sympathetic developer but the anti-developer militants on his committee were clearly hamstringing him. I felt he was saying different things to different people at different times.' As Martin Myers recalls, 'I can remember Simon Hughes sitting in my office, enthusiastic about our re-design proposals. And then I'd hear him on the news saying how awful they were. Talk about business ethics.'

Imry Merchant Developers plc, London's most reluctant theatre proprietor, was formed as a result of a merger in March 1988 between Imry International led by Martin Myers, and City Merchant Developers led by Martin Landau. On 2 June 1989, the day the company unveiled the re-designed 'office on stilts', it also unveiled exceptionally high profits, a 72% increase on its net asset value. Even in a sector grown accustomed to buoyancy, this was considered good. In the annual report, Martin Myers wrote that the benefits of the merger 'have exceeded my most optimistic forecasts'. Pre-tax profits stood at £22.81 million against £11.73 million of the previous year. Partly this was attributable to the sale of its remaining 50% interest in the St George's Hospital site on Hyde Park Corner to investment tycoon, Alan Bond. It was a growth in profit that meant the Remunerations Committee could comfortably afford to pay its highest paid director a salary of £191,026 – excluding pension rights. Whilst Myers, Managing Director and Chief Executive of Imry Merchant, was fending off media attention that focused on the Rose during the summer of 1989, he was also trying to keep a low profile in the face of rumours about an imminent takeover. Before July was out, his company would be in the hands of another.

Nearly three quarters of the group's portfolio was in London although with property values in the City of London on the wane, it was Imry Merchant's intention to steer clear of London altogether, balance its portfolio and diversify. Since the end of 1988, property had been purchased in Birmingham, Manchester and Sutton Coldfield and planning permission sought from Kent County Council for an enormous 2000-acre development in the wake of the Channel Tunnel. The development of the Rose site was relatively unimportant to Imry Merchant's long term commercial prospects. The £60 million 130,000 square foot building was prefunded by PosTel, the Post Office workers' pension fund and City analysts estimated that profits from the venture would not exceed £10 million. Imry Merchant's future in the summer of 1989, to some extent hung on its ability to bring its £860 million programme to a successful fruition against an immediate background of high interest rates and the medium term prospect of a slower market.

Imry Merchant was never a darling of the market. The merger of the original two companies left doubts about its inner cohesiveness. It was called a 'marriage of convenience rather than one made in heaven'. Martin Myers and Martin Landau, who have three year contracts dating from 8 February 1989, were seen as two forceful characters whose strength of personality could stunt the growth of the company, despite the plethora of talent on its board. During the summer of 1989, the jump in Imry Merchant's share prices, led to a £314 million cash takeover on 11 July by Marketchief, a consortium headed by Stephan Wingate. The Rose Campaign dominated the coverage of Imry Merchant's successful year. 'Currently enveloped in controversy over London's Rose Theatre,' wrote *The Times*, 'Imry is out of the City except for its unfortunate Rose Theatre development.' Like many property developers these days, Imry Merchant was sensitive to the twin charges of vandalism and philistinism. The sign at the site of the Rose proudly proclaimed 'Revealing today's heritage – building tomorrow's'. Although speculators have only themselves to blame for the long-held public perception of them as cigar-toting, wheeler-dealers on the make, property developers nowadays prefer to act as patrons of the arts. They take care to court the environmental and heritage lobby. After all, who isn't Green at heart today?

Imry Merchant is housed on the third floor of an anonymously discreet mansion cornering St James's Square. Its tables in the foyer are piled with expensive cultural glossies. Hanging on the wall is an award. At the time of writing, it is the only one on display, so clearly Imry Merchant are proud of it. Given to them by the Reigate Society in appreciation of Weston House, it reads:

'To be watchful of our heritage of beauty in fine buildings, open spaces and natural landscape, to influence future changes and developments so that the destruction or disfigurement of things of beauty and character may be avoided and so that the contribution of our time to the development of this district may be a worthy one.'

This award was made at the height of both the Rose Campaign and the rumoured takeover, and it must have been some sort of a consolation. 'It always makes me laugh,' says Martin Myers, 'to hear that property developers are all philistines and vandals and capitalist pigs and so on. I go to the theatre. People on my board are involved with theatre trusts. (Martin Landau used to be on the board of the Institute of Contemporary Arts.) Our board is made up of ordinary people who are as interested in the remains of the Rose as anyone else.'

38. Martin Myers (right), Managing Director of Imry Merchant, with two members of the management board.

Martin Myers was born in 1941, the son of a socialist property developer. He was educated at Arnold House and Latymer School, and went on to obtain a BSc at London University and is a Fellow of the Royal Institute of Chartered Surveyors. Following a partnership with a firm of chartered surveyors, he set up Arbuthnot Properties, merging it with Imry Property Holdings in 1987. The following year this was merged with Martin Landau's City Merchant Developers. He is married to Nicole and they have two children; Clementine and Kim. Shortly after the Rose demonstration of 15 May he hosted a lavish fancy dress party at their Berkshire home to celebrate Nicole's fortieth birthday. The theme was Legendary Lovers. Myers and his wife attended as Lord Byron and Lady Caroline Lamb. Clementine and Kim were togged out as Colombine and Harlequin. The guest list included a number of personalities from the racing world; William and Miriam Francome, trainer Kim Brassey and jockey, Dermot Brown. Myers lists riding as one of his recreations in *Who's Who* and displays watercolours of the sport on his office walls.

He can be an abrasive man. Perhaps a Philip Henslowe *de nos jours*. He is certainly able to turn around Proudhon ('Who said property is theft? What the Campaign proposed really is taking things away from you. All we wanted was to be paid for what we had put into it.') to his own advantage. Imry Merchant's public relations consultant advised him not to go on television to put Imry Merchant's case throughout the summer. The Rose was an issue which he took personally, particularly as he received well over a thousand letters. At least one supporter of the Rose Campaign was considerably startled to find the Chief Executive on the phone, putting his point of view to her direct. On another occasion, he wrote to a Rose supporter pointing out that as she owned a house, 'What would happen, if you were pottering around in your garden and you came across something interesting in the earth which the local antiquarian society said was part of King Charles's trysting house and so you therefore had to go. No compensation. Just go.' Most of the time Martin Myers contented himself with a standard letter: 'I have been inundated and preoccupied with finding a way . . . Rest assured that as an Englishman, lover of our heritage and tradition I will do everything within my power to find a solution.' Nevertheless, Myers is deeply ambivalent about the worth of the Rose. 'It's not like Stonehenge', he says, 'believe me, nobody will want to come and see it.' Yet, there is no mistaking the passion when he also declares, 'Imry Merchant saved the Rose. One day my children will see it and say, Dad did that.'

'He's an unexpected man,' says Simon Hughes, 'prepared to give the impression that as a Londoner he was concerned about our heritage. Yet one was never convinced that he was enthusiastic or committed. He always argued defensively and took it very personally. He spent a lot of time on the morning of 15 May when we spoke on the telephone, concentrating on what he called the 'hooligan element.' He said that my reputation would be ruined. He had a naïve perception that the demonstrators were all left-wing activists. In some ways I had to hide my thoughts. I felt that building any sort of office block over the remains of the Rose was a ridiculous idea but I could not have negotiated with him if I had said that. I would never choose him as a negotiator.'

CHAPTER FIVE

The Campaign to Save the Rose Theatre
'. . . never a blue skies option'.

The Campaign Committee planned its first public event and statement on 26 May, ten days into the four-week moratorium. Following the events of 15 May, it was in a strong position, tacitly accepted by both English Heritage and Imry Merchant as the central player in the cliff-hanging drama of the Rose. Having decided at the first meeting, on 18 May, to go for broke on Option One, the Committee asked Pentagram's Jon Greenfield to design an appropriate architectural plan, whilst they organised a public appeal to be launched at Stringfellow's nightclub on 26 May. It was coy about naming a specific figure in this appeal, partly because of the difficulty in guessing the asking price of the site. Simon Tait of *The Times* had said the site was worth £20 million. Privately the Committee thought it was more like £50 million. Imry Merchant was quoted as asking for £100 million to include compensation. Whether £20 million or £100 million, the sum was daunting. The ISGC's Jennifer Jones knew that, over a twenty year period, Sam Wanamaker had only managed to raise £3 million of his £20 million target for the ISGC. Committee members who daily rubbed shoulders with millionaires were more confident that the sum could be raised – perhaps from a single individual. Much more insurmountable was the problem that Imry Merchant had said that they had no intention of selling. If they sold for less than the speculative value of the land, Imry Merchant could be accused of betraying their shareholders. If they sold at the speculative value, Imry Merchant would be accused of fleecing the Campaign. In any event, Martin Myers said later he had no wish to encourage any number of crackpots.

On 24 May, Theatres Trust showed Imry Merchant a draft of the Ove Arup feasibility study. Imry Merchant responded the next day, Thursday, 25 May, by announcing that they would be making a comprehensive statement about their own re-design within the week. Friday, 26 May, the day of the Campaign launch, turned out to be an afternoon of sunshine early on in the season, before Londoners came to curse the prolonged heatwave. The glare of the West End streets provided stark contrast with the cavernous gloom of Stringfellow's nightclub. It was a strangely raffish exercise. Distinguished actors, many who had made their names in Shakespeare, sat uneasily together around a table normally propped up by the likes of Rod Stewart or George Best. White wine and nibbles did the rounds. Simon Hughes and Ruth Richardson took the microphone, whilst simultaneously appearing on a giant video screen. Everyone wore tee-shirts with the slogan, 'Be a Thorn in their Site'. Richard Coe from the *Washington Post* reminded the crowd that 'culture costs cash'. Two waitresses were sufficiently moved to donate a tenner each.

At the Finance and Fund-raising sub-committee the following day, ideas about raising money to buy the site were aired; the United Nations, the EEC, compulsory purchase, the government (on a pound for pound basis) and a bank loan. A realistic scheme, at this stage, seemed to be the 'Bard Bond': a scheme similar in intent to Mappa Mundi plc, which had hoped to raise at least £2.8 million towards saving Hereford Cathedral's thirteenth-century map of the world, by selling shares at £1000 a time. With seed-core capital raised from public appeal, Jeremy Greenwood from Goldman Sachs, the American investment bank, advised the Sub-committee that he could then go to the City for loans in the form of 'Bard Bonds' to save the Rose. In the end this scheme, which the *Financial Times* wrote about in a mixture of enthusiasm and mockery ('building hope upon hope . . .'), was quietly dropped after fewer than a thousand of the minimum 2800 shares in Mappa Mundi plc had been sold within the time allowed under the Companies Act. Mappa Mundi plc had failed to convince the City that the prestige of saving the map outweighed a return on capital of the more traditional kind. Meanwhile on the same Friday, Imry Merchant filed a new application with Southwark Council to alter the building under construction. Their plans were not yet ready but were due within the week.

The first weekend since the moratorium was the Spring Bank Holiday, celebrated by a small 'Elizabethan Fayre' held on site. The next day, the Roman baths at Huggin Hill were back-filled.

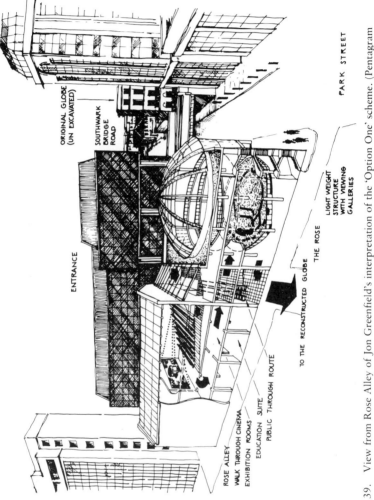

ORIGINAL GLOBE
(UN EXCAVATED)

SOUTHWARK
BRIDGE
ROAD

ENTRANCE

PARK STREET

LIGHT WEIGHT
STRUCTURE
WITH VIEWING
GALLERIES

THE ROSE

TO THE RECONSTRUCTED GLOBE

ROSE ALLEY
WALK THROUGH CINEMA
EXHIBITION ROOMS
EDUCATION SUITE
PUBLIC THROUGH ROUTE

39. View from Rose Alley of Jon Greenfield's interpretation of the 'Option One' scheme. (Pentagram Design Ltd)

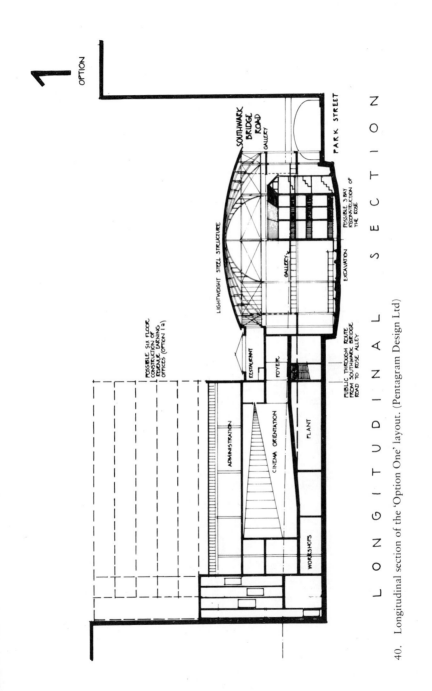

1 OPTION

SOUTHWARK BRIDGE ROAD

GALLERY

PARK STREET

LIGHTWEIGHT STEEL STRUCTURE

GALLERY

POSSIBLE 3 BAY RECONSTRUCTION OF THE ROSE

EXCAVATION

POSSIBLE SIX FLOOR CONSTRUCTION OF REVENUE EARNING OFFICES (OPTION 1a)

RESTAURANT

FOYER

ADMINISTRATION

CINEMA ORIENTATION

PLANT

PUBLIC THROUGH ROUTE FROM SOUTHWARK BRIDGE ROAD TO ROSE ALLEY

WORKSHOPS

L O N G I T U D I N A L   S E C T I O N

40. Longitudinal section of the 'Option One' layout. (Pentagram Design Ltd)

193

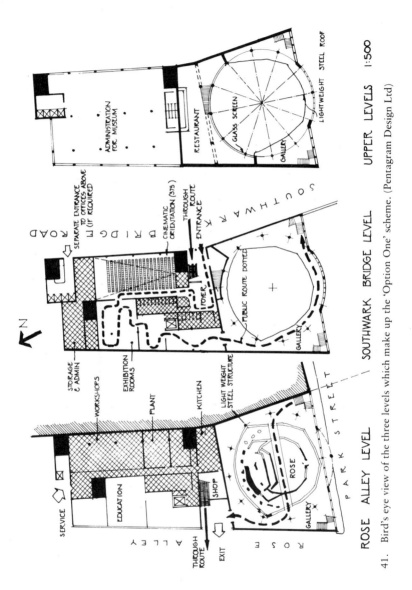

41. Bird's eye view of the three levels which make up the 'Option One' scheme. (Pentagram Design Ltd)

ROSE ALLEY LEVEL   SOUTHWARK BRIDGE LEVEL   UPPER LEVELS   1:500

194

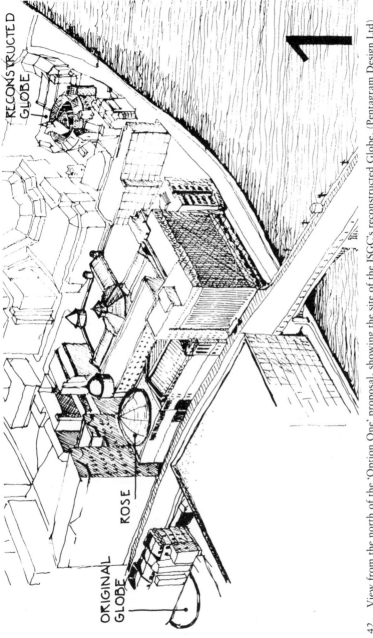

RECONSTRUCTED GLOBE

ORIGINAL GLOBE

ROSE

42. View from the north of the 'Option One' proposal, showing the site of the ISGC's reconstructed Globe. (Pentagram Design Ltd)

That evening, 30 May, the main Committee met. It was a fortnight into the moratorium and this meeting proved crucial to the outcome of the Campaign. Jon Greenfield presented his designs for the two options. Excluding such matters as compensation or the price of the land, Option One (the whole site given over to a Rose museum) was costed at £14.35 million. Option Two (office development in the north, a Rose museum in the south) was costed at £25.1 million. This option was supposed to recoup some of the costs of displaying the Rose by allowing for commercial use, but Fletcher King, the chartered surveyors, discredited it because it yielded too little office space to justify costs.

Simon Hughes then asked the Committee to re-consider its allegiance to Option One. Clearly he was dismayed at the prospect of launching an appeal for vast sums to save the remains of an Elizabethan theatre, whilst representing a deprived constituency in inner London. Ian McKellen, for one, expressed the belief that a change of mind would not be a loss of face, but Coral Stringfellow held the day when she reminded the meeting that she and her husband originally started off with one record player and two speakers in a church hall. As midnight approached, the Committee solemnly voted on its options and once again, Option One was the clear favourite with the majority. The Campaign's main strategy to secure the whole site was now going to rest with the Secretary of State's powers of scheduling. Martin Kramer was asked to make this request in writing and a press conference on 2 June would set a target of £500,000, to 'prime' the eventual appeal.

The next day, 31 May, Simon Hughes and some Committee members met Simon Jenkins at the House of Commons. Jenkins revealed details about the re-design that Seiferts had been working on during the last fortnight and felt he and Hughes were in agreement about what was to become known as the 'office on stilts'. 'The Campaign accepted at that meeting that blue skies was not an option,' says Jenkins, although Ruth Richardson remembers that 'There wasn't much room for manoeuvre.' Peggy Ashcroft's appearance later that night with James Fox on *Wogan*, the TV chat show, indicated that the Campaign was still fighting on. Watched by millions, Ashcroft handed over to Terry Wogan the gold medal that she had won with the young Laurence Olivier, when they were students at the Central School of Speech Training and Dramatic Art. Wogan agreed to put the medal up for auction.

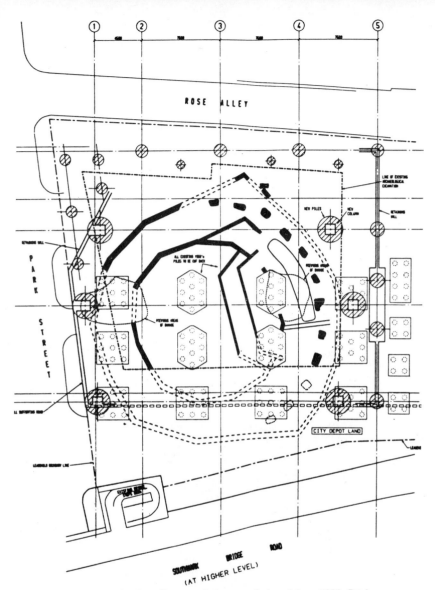

43.   The layout for the 'office on stilts' as unveiled on 2 June 1989. During the weeks and months that followed, the piling positions were constantly modified (Imry Merchant plc)

Imry Merchant stole the Campaign's thunder by unveiling its re-design to the world's press at 9 a.m. on Friday 2 June, just two hours before the press conference already scheduled by the Campaign to launch its appeal. Seiferts, the architects, and Pell Frischmann, the structural engineers, had been working solid overtime for a fortnight. This was the 'office on stilts', whose

197

structure cleared the site of the Rose. They had come up with a taller eleven-storey block. Overhead, the site would be spanned with 650 tonnes of three steel girders, whilst 120,000 square feet of office space stood on six steel columns, 22 feet above the Rose remains, at an extra cost of £10 million, bringing the final bill on the office block to £70 million. The six piles were a metre thick and would go 55 metres deep, avoiding the *perceived* perimeter of the excavation, although the precise definition of the perceived perimeter was to develop into a much more contested issue than Simon Jenkins or anyone else realised. Leaving aside the argument for 'blue skies', the 'office on stilts' was regarded by the Campaign as failing to take into account the three basic concerns which it had expressed: the need for further excavation, particularly in the east, the proximity of the piles to the remains, the inadequate ceiling height and the clutter of lift shafts and service ducts which interfered with the clear display of the Rose Theatre remains. The Theatre Trust/Ove Arup feasibility study of this option had made more generous allowances than the Seifert proposal (of which, more later).

At 11 a.m. on 2 June, two and a half weeks into the

44.   The Campaign's press conference. Simon Hughes is addressing the media. From left, Simon Hughes, Anthony Grayling, and Martin Clout.

moratorium, the Committee formally presented its alternative plans at a press conference. Media interest was intense but focused mainly on the famous faces. Timothy Dalton modestly lurked well behind the row of arc lights trained on the Campaign spokespersons, but he got a laugh later on by suggesting that out of their recently announced record profits, Imry Merchant could afford to make a donation to the costs of saving the Rose. The following day, in the main, the press quoted Campaign spokespersons using aesthetic or emotional grounds for their attack on the Imry re-design. 'It will look horrendous' said Dalton, quoted in *Today*. 'This is like building an office block on the Forum in Rome or a Hilton Hotel on Stonehenge,' said Anthony Grayling, quoted in *The Guardian*. Although Grayling was to go on to say in *The Times* that, 'Putting piles down like this so close to the perceived remains is like pinning the tail on the donkey', the archaeological argument against the 'office on stilts' was scarcely covered. The intense media interest in the Rose, which fed off the public outcry of so many famous actors, was directly instrumental in winning the moratorium, but by the end of the four weeks' coverage of the Rose was consumed with trivialities.

Competing for attention in the media throughout the Campaign were such once-in-a-generation volcanic political earthquakes as the unfolding events in China and the death of Khomeini. Closer to home, headlines were made by the EEC elections and the perennial stock items of Ascot, Henley and Wimbledon ('Strawberries 40p Each!'). The build-up of excitement over the Rose in the weekend of 14 May, at first resulted in a number of serious articles, which in the main were pro-Rose. As John Peter argued in the *Sunday Times*, 'These dead stones hold the secrets of a living art'. There were some writers, however, who refused to subscribe to the element of hysteria, engendered by the events. *The Independent*, in a typical piece by Alex Renton, asked some experts the exact value of these secrets, and concluded from their cautious responses that Nicholas Ridley's £1 million might be put to better use by theatres forced to go dark, like the Royal Court's Theatre Upstairs. Simon Tait of *The Times*, who had followed the story since early February, summed up the situation on 2 June; 'the most likely solution will be a mix-and-match one: that Imry adopt something similar to the Manning (Theatres Trust/Ove Arup) plan.' Thereafter serious feature writing on the subject ceased.

Reporting itself though did not cease. Everyone from *China Daily*, *Worker's Weekly* (the Organ of the Central Committee of the Revolutionary Communist Party of Britain (Marxist Leninist)), *Southwark Sparrow*, *Chartered Surveyor's Weekly*, *Private Eye*, *Antiquity*, *Christian Science Monitor* to *Hello!* the gossip magazine, had something to say about the Rose, and it was usually said in the language of theatre itself. The favourite sport of all was quoting or paraphrasing the Bard. As Jonathan Bate observes in his book *Shakespeare Constitutions*, it is an important characteristic of Bardolatry that 'the perennial significance of Shakespeare is enacted by praising him in his own words'. Since this was a story which affected correspondents covering not only the arts, but archaeology, property, law, architecture, finance and local government, the sport continued long after the game had palled for the original contestants. Towards the end of the moratorium, Southwark's chief planning officer, Robin Thompson, promised, to everyone's relief, that not a single Shakespearean quotation would pass his lips in the course of the planning meeting.

The tabloids in general loved the story, particularly when Leslie Grantham donned doublet and hose for a Tom Stoppard spoof in aid of the Rose – 'Dirty Dane Blimey! Old Den knocks off *Hamlet* in 15 minutes flat'. Band-wagoneering was an accusation never far from the surface. Julie Birchill in the *Mail on Sunday* had, predictably, been the first journalist to put the boot in. Writing on 21 May, she accused the theatrical profession of 'moral incontinence' in the way it had rallied around the Rose. In the face of NHS cuts, she said, the over reaction would make even doctors and nurses 'blush at such mock heroics'. Ian McKellen, the actor who had largely set the ball rolling, was incensed at the suggestion that actors had got the issue out of proportion. 'I belong to the Rose,' he said at a public discussion held at the National Theatre, 'and that's where my voice should be heard.' Only Peggy Ashcroft was absolved. On one occasion during the Campaign, she was photographed next to a placard that said 'Prime National Treasure' and it would be hard to say whether the placard referred to Peggy Ashcroft or to the Rose Theatre that she was committed to save. Even *The Independent* found itself resorting to untypical novelettish prose to describe her: 'A frail elderly lady sitting quietly in the late afternoon sun, clutching a pink silk rose on her lap, grey hair blowing in the breeze, her stick resting against the arm of her chair and the light of battle shining brightly in her eyes'. In some subtle way in the course of the Campaign, Ashcroft was transformed into Britain's alternative Queen Mum.

Actors were out in force for the Rally for 4 June compèred by Ian McKellen. Speeches and readings from celebrities as assorted as Steven Berkoff and Leslie Grantham ('If I started to recite Shakespeare, the bulldozers would move in straightaway'), culminated with the RSC production of *Dr Faustus*. Gerard Murphy, on top a flat bed-truck with an all male company gave life to Edward Alleyn's most famous role and for the first time in 400 years, a Park Street audience thrilled to Marlowe's mighty line. This Rally was the occasion which caused the Campaign's main political emphasis to switch from buying the site, to call on Nicholas Ridley to schedule the Rose. Admittedly 'Schedule the Rose' wasn't as snappy a slogan as 'Don't Doze the Rose' but Susan Tully ('Chelle from *EastEnders*) did her best to put heart into it.

On 6 June, the Committee received from Nicholas Ridley, a 'holding reply'. The next day, Martin Kramer sought counsel's opinion about the probable success of a judicial review overturning Ridley's likely decision not to schedule. Irene Worth marched down Downing Street with her petition of 150 American stars (among them, Lauren Bacall, Johnny Carson, Robert de Niro, Katherine Hepburn, Liza Minnelli, Paul Simon and Meryl Streep). The moratorium of four weeks was ticking by and very little, other than publicity, had been achieved. As a result of the publicity, thousands of people clutching A-Z's, visited Park Street, SE1, to see the Rose Theatre once again open to blue skies. Academics flew in from all corners of the globe. Celebrities dropped by. Autograph-hunters followed on. Great numbers of unknown faces in Equity paid their dues. Parties of schoolchildren arrived in crocodile. Office workers spent their lunch break on site and local residents called in on their way home.

To the untrained eye there wasn't a lot to see. Nothing much was happening. A rudimentary viewing gallery allowed people to look at the site but it was hard to conjure up the former glory of the Rose Theatre from the abandoned polygon, marked out in chalk lying in the baked clay of Southwark. The brute reality of construction work was far more evident. Commerce forged ahead to the north of the Rose throughout the day, ferrying cement and driving piles. The noise practically drowned out the informal explanations offered by the archaeologists from the Museum of London. Under the terms of their agreement with Imry Merchant, only two archaeologists were allowed on site and then only for the purposes of maintenance, not excavation. The protective canopy had returned from Glasgow and was replaced over the site but hot sun blazed down remorselessly every day during the moratorium, causing the clay to break and crack. Eventually the temperamental sprinklers were replaced by a more sophisticated watering system loaned from Chelsea Flower Show. The enforced idleness of the Museum of London team and the profound inactivity on the site of the Rose, was in marked contrast to the turmoil of building work which surrounded it.

Onlookers peered through the wire mesh of the viewing gallery. An archaeologist might move a sprinkler. Perhaps another might sit on one of the 1957 concrete stumps and finish recording his notes for the day. It was like visiting a patient in coma. There the remains lay, intravenously fed on a permanent drip. Like the medical staff in intensive care, the archaeologists took regular soundings, consulted their notes and one another. Alarmed visitors arrived in a state of panic but soon sunk into boredom. Their concern was expressed by gifts of roses or cards embellished with the aphoristic sayings of the Bard and left behind to decorate the fence. Despite the seeming hopelessness of the case, many people returned again and again. The prognosis never changed. The patient was stable. Things were always much the same.

Pat McDonnell, a Committee member, spent 24 hours a day on site from 14 May to the end of July. For visitors to the site of the Rose, this young actor from County Kerry, dubbed 'my hero' by Timothy Dalton, was the public face of the Campaign. Local councillor, Hilary Wines, had persuaded Southwark Council to provide a Portacabin for him and the other volunteers who manned the permanent vigil. Inside, the walls displayed messages reminding everyone to 'view everything as if being watched by the press . . . keep a clean image, watch the booze . . .'. It was a home from home for everyone; the workmen contracted by Costains, the security guards working for Reliance and the local police. Andy from Reliance, popped in for tea. Gerry from Costains, borrowed McDonnell's copy of the Imry Merchant design plans. Sean, an Irish navvy, would arrive in his filthy work clothes splattered with mud, and his aggressive cynicism would invariably manage to provoke rage from one of the more impassioned Rose supporters. Another Irish builder from an adjacent site sought out an archaeologist for advice on a coin he'd unearthed. ('It could be Celtic. It's very heavy. Don't clean it because the information will come off the corrosion points.') Armed with radio phones and walkie talkies, McDonnell and his team patrolled the site at night like the heroes of a *Boy's Own* story. Bearing mounds of food from an Indian takeaway, Vanessa Redgrave would arrive after her show had finished at the Lyric, Hammersmith, or Coral Stringfellow would turn up with champagne from her club. Under the strong arc lights on those hot summer nights many a party sprang up.

Politically, the Museum of London's position grew more sensitive. Everyone had read that the site needed further excavation. Martin Biddle had written to *The Independent* on 31 May, and said that for archaeologists, 'to do nothing as the days slip by, ignores the needs of scholarship.' The site needed a minimum of five weeks full excavation which, at first, Imry Merchant were not prepared to allow. After 2 June, the situation changed. Once Imry Merchant had unveiled its re-design, the Museum of London was given the go-ahead – but only to excavate in the new piling positions. This is a method of excavation known as 'keyhole' excavation and the Museum of London refused to do it. With 'keyhole' excavation it is difficult for an archaeologist to observe, let alone understand, what is being uncovered in a confined space. Furthermore, anything excavated in this manner is destroyed, which would leave only the areas between the piles for future archaeologists to observe. To dig the pile positions would prejudge the issue of scheduling and pre-empt the Campaign's battle to preserve the entire site *in situ*.

On Friday, 9 June, with the end of the moratorium in sight, the Museum of London team, in an unexpected move, was sacked. English Heritage prepared to move their own archaeological unit on site, backfill the remains and carry out 'keyhole' excavation. 'This was quite an extraordinary step,' said Martin Biddle, 'unprecedented in British archaeology.' Despite a second letter from Martin Kramer, on 8 June, Nicholas Ridley had still not yet made any pronouncement about scheduling the Rose. On that evening, following the sacking of the Museum of London, *Time Out* hosted a debate about the Rose Theatre at the National Theatre. Only Ian McKellen came close to raising the emotional temperature despite the fact that the clock that had been ticking away for the last four weeks had now wound down. McKellen asked Dr Geoffrey Wainwright from English Heritage: 'Can you say that the remains won't be damaged?' And Wainwright simply answered, 'No'. Time for the Rose was up.

Another candlelit vigil was organised for Sunday 11 June, following a big Rally planned by the Campaign Committee. No one, however, seriously expected a repeat of the events of 15 May. The makeshift impromptu performances of 14 May gave way, on 11 June, to a blockbuster marathon extravaganza, organised by Cubby's daughter, Barbara Brocolli. An unlikely company of artistes trouped across a stage erected in Unisys car park. Peter Brook jostled with Steve Martin ('I just came to get free publicity for my film – Ho! Ho!'), Sir Anthony Quayle jostled with Helen Lederer. It was worse than the BAFTA awards. Nigel Planer in his *alter ego* of Nicholas Craig wondered, 'What is it that makes actors so special?' Speeches from specialists and Tom Stoppard spoofs were enjoyed by the thousands of people who stood in the road, 'glewed', 'pasted' and 'per boyld' to one another during that long, hot afternoon. 'I hear the second half is due to begin next Wednesday,' quipped Gary Wilmot. Peggy Ashcroft introduced an emotional message from Lord Olivier, whose voice, she reminded the crowd, once rang out around those other theatres along the Thames. Quaveringly, a disembodied Olivier launched into 'O for a muse of fire'. Though it lacked the fiery attack of his famous 1944 film rendition, it was all the more moving, bringing to mind that terrific extended crane shot that Olivier had used in the film, which swooped down Bankside, past the site of the Rose, before homing in through the 'wooden O' of the Globe stage. Olivier ended by asking if a 'muse of fire can exist under a ceiling of commerce'. Only the morning of 12 June could tell.

It was a sultry night and the 75 people, or so, who intended to stick it out were in party mood. Loudspeakers blared out the Eurovision-style anthem written for the Rose ('It's a part of our history / It's a place of magic and mystery'). Barbara Morris, a senior citizen from Camberwell, who had quickly emerged as one of the Rose heroines, collecting signatures for the petition every day, (transport strikes notwithstanding,) celebrated by doing a jig. Five minutes of silence at midnight marked the Campaign's formal farewell to the site. At midnight, the padlocks were once again changed to mark English Heritage's possession of the site. By 5 a.m. more people gathered in Park Street. Tim Pigott-Smith and Rosemary Harris bought bacon rolls and bagels. It was a token demonstration. Nothing happened, and by 8 a.m. most people had drifted away. The future for the Rose was completely uncertain.

What was certain to both the Museum of London and English Heritage was, that in the first fortnight of flaming June, the remains of the Rose had deteriorated. There were extensive fissures on the surface which, despite constant watering, had dried out in sections. Organic artefacts and ecofacts had started to decay. Before they were sacked, the Museum of London had made plans to cover the site with a metre of soft water-retaining peat. However, the site of the Rose was now in the hands of English Heritage and they proposed covering it with a filter fabric of polymer (terram) and a further 300 mm of washed Buckland sand of a middling Ph level. The sand would be compacted by saturating the amount of air at the surface. Seven water-monitoring points were to be built into the covering (using pipes with a diameter of 68 mm). Ten moisture-sensitive electric cells were to be added to record moisture content and an irrigation system was to be laid in the upper levels of the sand. The sand would then be covered by an impervious polythylene sheet. Finally, the site would be sealed with a 38-50 mm impermeable substance – or concrete, as it turns out to be – (not however MP Clive Soley's proposed specification of two to one. This mix had a ratio more like ten to one).

Professor Barry Cunliffe, a Commissioner at English Heritage, convened a seminar on site on 13 June. Later, Martin Biddle was to refer to this as a 'seminar of very uncertain status'. Although English Heritage's archaeologists (led by John Hinchcliffe) did not know the archaeology of the Rose and were restricting their work to the pre-determined piling positions, they had prepared a press release in advance, announcing support for their proposals. But even Victor Belcher, from English Heritage, was to admit, later, that the backfilling proposal had 'an element of the unknown'. Nevertheless, a collection of archaeologists toured the site and did agree to the plans – as did Simon Hughes, who was in attendance. Privately, archaeologists expressed concern. George Dennis, from the Museum of London was worried about the implications of the load-bearing concrete and Martin Biddle feared that the backfill would cause damage to the remains. The Committee met later that day and debated the possibility of seeking an injunction to stop the English Heritage operation going ahead. Nailing the Museum of London's doubts to a legal certainty, however, was, as George Dennis said, 'like holding water'. In the end, Martin Kramer was asked to write to English Heritage and ask them for a voluntary undertaking not to proceed.

Tension was palpable at this Committee meeting. Defeat exacerbated the internal problems which, by now, had started to bedevil Committee deliberations. It was at this meeting that Ian McKellen *et al* were temporarily evicted. On his return, McKellen was asked if he would address the PosTel board meeting and agreed, pointedly adding that, 'It will be easier talking to them than to you.' It was four weeks after the triumphant victory of 15 May, the site of the Rose was about to be backfilled and the Committee had not found a benefactor. It had failed to raise a significant sum of money. It could not even agree a logo. The EEC elections loomed and Simon Hughes' priorities lay with them. Martin Village proposed co-operating with Imry Merchant by strategic use of the Theatres Trust/Ove Arup scheme. This was blocked. Pat McDonnell urged direct action. This was deflected. The Committee vested everything in Nicholas Ridley's long-anticipated reply to the question of scheduling. At 11.20 p.m. the meeting adjourned so that Hughes could lobby Virginia Bottomley at the House of Commons.

During the night, one of Pat McDonnell's volunteers chained himself to the site. The stunt gained some publicity and gave Timothy Dalton the cue for a long, impassioned speech about the Rose, when he was supposed to be talking to Radio One's Simon Bates about James Bond ('. . . distinguished people from some of the most distinguished companies . . .'). Simon Jenkins was as enraged by the stunt as he was by Martin Kramer's faxed letter asking English Heritage voluntarily to postpone its backfilling operation. It was at this stage that the Campaign lost the battle for Jenkins' ear. He sent back an extremely dusty answer. 'Your campaign chairman, Mr Hughes, was present at Tuesday's meeting and endorsed our proposed action in front of numerous witnesses . . . Could you let us know as soon as possible whether the Rose Committee supports its chairman's views and/or the terms of your letter.' As a libel lawyer, Martin Kramer knows a home truth from a smear and he carefully worded his reply. 'We accept,' he replied, 'that Simon Hughes attended the meeting on June 13th. At that meeting, Mr Hughes commented that the infilling proposed seemed satisfactory so long as it was the safest method of protecting the remains. However his comments were clearly made without any specific expertise in the field and his approval did not extend to the other procedures being proposed by English Heritage.'

The following day, 15 June, finally decided the case of the Rose. In reply to a question from Clive Soley, Nicholas Ridley said that he would not be putting the Rose on his schedule '*at this stage*'. Gerald Bowden, deputy chairman of the Rose Committee applauded the Imry Merchant re-designed 'office on stilts'. Simon Hughes said it was crazy for Ridley to admit that the Rose was schedulable and then, not to go ahead and schedule it. Mark Fisher pointed out that Ridley would end up having preserved a ten-storey office block. Later in the afternoon, the debate over the Rose re-surfaced during one of the House of Common's rare debates on Heritage and the Arts ('We must stop meeting like this, every five years on a European election day' said Tony Banks, 'to discuss arts and heritage.'). Terry Dicks, dubbed 'Alf Garnett's vicar on earth' by Patrick Cormack, claimed that 'Sir Richard this, Sir Michael that – this well known actor, that world-acclaimed actress ... the millionaires who had made a fortune from the public sector – had held a whip-round and come up with the masterly sum of £200'. Mark Fisher urged Virginia Bottomley to give way, but she was obdurate. There was to be no further reprieve for the Rose.

Tuesday's adjourned Committee meeting re-convened that evening. Simon Hughes was in a jaunty mood, sporting a yellow silk rose on the cream lapels of his election suit, but the mood of the meeting was fractious. The issue of the logo dominated. Any move to incorporate the image or name of William Shakespeare was implacably opposed by representatives from the ISGC, who feared that the market for Shakespeare-led Appeals was limited. John Burns acidly counter-proposed that the Campaign's logo should adopt the head of Sam Wanamaker. Sand was due to arrive in the morning and Pat McDonnell said that people were planning another confrontation with the sand lorries. He was

THE CAMPAIGN TO SAVE THE ROSE THEATRE

we're a thorn
in their Site

45. Logo designed for tee-shirts by Windhorse Associates, withdrawn after opposition from the ISGC to the representation of Shakespeare by a rival fundraising body. 'Perhaps the head of Sam Wanamaker could be used instead?' said a disenchanted campaigner.

begged to prevent direct action and reminded of the criticism that Hughes couldn't control his Committee. 'He can't,' agreed McDonnell, 'look at Gerry Bowden's remarks this afternoon.' Ruth Richardson persuaded the Committee to back the demonstration if it could be turned into responsible action and on Friday, 16 June, Ian McKellen linked arms in a token human chain, temporarily blocking one of the lorries. Wired up to BBC's *Breakfast TV*, he was told by Simon Jenkins, sitting in the studio, that, 'What Ian can't admit, is that he has won a great victory.'

Timothy Dalton raced down to the site at the news that sand was being distributed by machine. He talked to reporters for a brief while and then disappeared into the Portacabin for a chat with Pat McDonnell. McDonnell handed him a mug of tea, with globules of milk fat swimming in its hot liquid (the Portacabin's fridge did not operate well in the heatwave). Dalton was outraged at this turn of events. 'The press are lining up the government,' he said cryptically, hissing 'scab' under his breath, at the view of English Heritage archaeologists working on the site of the Rose. He launched into an impassioned diatribe '. . . distinguished people from some of the most distinguished companies . . .' It was strangely familiar. It was Dalton repeating himself. McDonnell interrupted him with a tape-recording of the Simon Bates' interview and Dalton settled down to hear himself in full flow before racing off to catch a plane. The sandblowers continued and, by the end of the day, the patient was no longer in coma. The Rose was buried, swathed in an impermeable shroud. The withered flowers on the fence were gathered into one wreath. Was the Rose a Sleeping Beauty? Or was she a Juliet, dead in her tomb?

The main focus of the Campaign now shifted from Park Street to the more public arenas provided by politics and the law. It was imperative for the Campaign to prove that the 'office on stilts', far from protecting the Rose, would cause serious damage to the remains. In the weeks immediately after English Heritage took control of the site, nothing much was found in the 'keyhole' excavations. Piling on the north site threw up a bone, handed in by a passer-by to the Campaign office. At first this grisly object was thought to be human and the Committee toyed with the idea of embarrassing Imry Merchant by making it a police matter. Subsequent lab analysis proved it to be a bear's femur. Either way, its casual discovery highlighted the problem posed by excavating the piling positions. 'There was a tremendous amount of pedantry over what might be found in the piling positions,' said Simon Jenkins. 'Even if there was nothing there except mud, the Campaign insisted that it couldn't be touched. At every meeting Seifert conceded something but there was no configuration of piling that the Campaign were prepared to accept.'

'Almost every day,' said Simon Jenkins, 'until planning permission was granted there would be a new row about piling positions. Lots of people – Southwark Council, the Theatres Trust – got involved and brought in their engineers to second-guess Seifert's engineers and that upset Seifert's no end. The Theatres Trust proposal which took the piles right out into the street resolved itself into a genuine engineering argument. A span of beam that width holding up a building of that weight would have been gargantuan and fantastically expensive. I became an expert on the nature of piling.' Piling is a heavy crude operation whereby heavy steel casing has to be forced 55 metres into the ground either by high frequency vibration or by repeated impact. Inevitably such a procedure threatens damage to any archaeological remains it encounters. Martin Stockwell, Field Officer for the York Archaeological Trust, has said in the past that disruption caused by modern piling to archaeological remains 'may extend up to 0.25m from the pile.' Alan Baxter, a consultant civil and structural engineer advising the Campaign, called for the even more generous tolerances of one metre between the theoretical face of the pile and the outside face of the Rose Theatre as a minimum requirement, but added that one and a half metres was more sensible still. Only three of the Imry Merchant redesigned piling positions were at least one metre away. The other three were dangerously close to the outer perimeter walls of the Rose, so even a 0.05 metre gain on a piling position was vital for the Campaign, and piling positions changed almost daily. Simon Jenkins was not the only one to become an expert on the nature of piling.

Nicholas Ridley had finally put in writing his reasons for not scheduling the Rose on 15 June and this meant that Martin Kramer could now seek leave to test his decision in law. On 22 June, Mr Justice Kennedy was sufficiently convinced by the persuasive eloquence of Jeremy Sullivan QC, that the Campaign had a case and he gave it leave to apply for judicial review. He expedited the hearing without setting a date and given the backlog in the courts, the Campaign understood that the case might not be heard until the next legal term in October. In the meantime there was Southwark to consider. 22 June was also the day set aside by Southwark Council for its statutory Public Consultation over Imry Merchant's new planning application. Southwark Borough Council (Motto – United to Serve) does not often hit the national news. When it does it's often for sad and squalid failures in its social services. Its poverty is all the more striking because it is situated so close to the ostentatious affluence of the City. Historically, the City may have lost the battle for political control of Southwark, but in planning terms, it is largely the financial clout of the City that calls the tune south of London Bridge. In the matter of the Rose Theatre, the City held the trump card. Its engineer' depot occupied a strategic wedge-shaped site sandwiched in between the proposed office block and Southwark Bridge. Two-fifths of the Rose Theatre remains lie underneath it, unexcavated. By stalling on all decisions concerning this site, the City played straight into Imry Merchant's hands.

The three component areas that make up Southwark are all radically different from one another. 'Three disparate lumps,' says Hilary Wines, Liberal Democrat Councillor for Cathedral Ward, the electoral area which includes Bankside. North Southwark (Liberal Democrat) has a high proportion of elderly people and families drawn from both Irish and Asian communities. Peckham (Labour) has large numbers of Afro/Caribbeans and a transient population. Leafy Dulwich (Tory), is home to Margaret Thatcher and a cluster of expensive fee-paying schools. Long-term residents of North Southwark don't call their home patch North Southwark. They'll say they live in the Borough or the Blue or Bermondsey – even Bankside – but not North Southwark. Traditional jobs were in printing, building, manufacturing, warehousing and all related docks industries. Courage Brewery and Hay's Wharf once were major employers. Today North Southwark tops the list for inner city deprivation. Prosperity has ebbed. The previously settled community has broken up and the last census revealed a dwindling population. The loss of industry and lack of investment is not compensated by the regeneration of Docklands owing to a serious skills mis-match between the new industries and the resident work-force.

'It's a constituency,' says Simon Hughes, 'that's been washed up.' Statistics to do with North Southwark make for grim reading. In 1961 there were nearly 184,000 jobs in the borough. Today this has slumped to less than 107,000. It has the third highest incidence of unemployment in London. It has the highest number of handicapped people in inner London. It has the third highest percentage of single-parent families and pensioners. 'You've only got to walk down Long Lane,' says Cllr Geoff Williams, Chairman of Southwark Planning Committee and Labour's representative for Cathedral Ward, 'and look at some of the estates to see the poverty. Just count the windows without curtains.'

The problems that face Southwark Borough Council are immense. Southwark has the largest number of dwellings under municipal control in London. It owns over 60,000 housing units, many of them unfit to live in and it is estimated that £0.5 billion is needed to bring the housing stock up to a reasonable standard. Large estates, like the Aylesbury, house people with multiple disadvantages, half of whom live on benefit. The government has chosen to benefit only a strip of Southwark by developing the Docklands. New arrivals into these expensive properties are attracted by the easy proximity to the City or the West End and are changing Southwark's demography. 'It's changing more than other constituencies,' says Simon Hughes, looking forward to an uncertain political future. 'The Docks were closed as a process of deliberate re-structuring by property owners,' says Geoff Williams, 'They moved into the Docks area and brought about its closure. Property values in Southwark have risen dramatically. The rental value for the Rose site is probably £30-£35 per square foot. A 130-140,000 square feet office block will raise over £1 million a year. Capitalise that however crudely and you're talking about a development worth £60-70 million. The Council is not in a position to buy out an office developer.'

'When I first came to Bankside in the late 1960s,' said Theo Crosby, the ISGC architect from Pentagram, 'it was derelict. Most of the warehouses were boarded up and unused. Nothing was working. Industry had collapsed. It was ripe for development. From a town planning point of view, I loved the idea of leavening a landscape of office blocks with something on a human scale. The historic city is our biggest resource so when Sam Wanamaker showed me his model theatre, it made sense for Bankside.' Southwark Council, however, had housing plans for the land that the ISGC earmarked as the site for their reconstruction of the Globe Theatre. An enormously long saga of planning permissions granted and then rescinded finally ended after court action forced Southwark to lease the site to the ISGC at a peppercorn rent. 'It's a tremendously valuable gift from the people of Southwark,' says Crosby. 'A hundred yards from the City! It's a giveaway!' 'Southwark was never against Shakespeare *per se*,' says Geoff Williams, 'our North Southwark Plan just registered a different priority for Bankside.'

The original pro-office development North Southwark Plan of the late 1970s had been rejected in 1982 by an incoming Labour group, more radical and left-wing than its predecessors. They drafted a new Plan, restrictive in its approach to office building which was summarily rejected by the Secretary of State for the Environment resulting in Southwark's planning decisions lacking legal validity at Public Inquiry. The result is that its record of winning planning cases on Appeal is not good. 'The planning philosophy of central government,' says Williams, 'is not addressing local needs. The recent Strategic Guidance articulates a market-led approach in which all planning controls are seen as impediments. Close by the site of the Rose, for example, in Thrale Street, there are some brand new industrial workshops developed by the former GLC and now under the control of the London Residuary Body. The LRB intends to demolish the workshops and sell the site for development. Southwark are relatively powerless to block the LRB. If we refuse planning permission, we would lose on Appeal. To knock down these buildings which offer real opportunities for local employment, is, to my mind, a major scandal. It's unfortunate the media are not interested in this sort of story.'

It was against this background that Southwark's Public Consultation took place on 22 June. About a hundred people attended although the register did not show many with SE1 addresses. Representatives from both Imry Merchant and English Heritage were among them. Steven Williams, English Heritage's press officer, arrived hot and bothered from the annual *débâcle* at Stonehenge. Geoff Williams chaired the meeting in an informal way, inviting people to use first names. Stacking chairs lined the walls. Posters, advertising benefits for AIDS and Chile, covered the dreary cream and green paintwork. Robin Thompson, the chief planning officer, told the Campaigners that the Council could consider any number of proposals for the site and invited alternatives to be submitted. The Campaign spokespersons emphasised the planning rather than the emotional arguments against Imry Merchant's new application. Four days later, on 26 June, everyone went through the debate again, but this time in the baronial splendour of the Grand Committee Room in the House of Commons. Outside in the streets of Westminster there was a massive photo-opportunity; Twiggy, Susan Hampshire, Ray Cooney, Richard Briers, Jane Lapotaire and Miriam Karlin joined the familiar Rose supporters to lobby MPs. A fair number of tourists, who were there anyway, followed everyone in to find out what was going on. In the low key discussion which followed the set speeches, a young American expressed his bewilderment at the government's indifference to the fate of the Rose, 'I mean, I come from a country which bought London Bridge.' Peggy Ashcroft sitting next to James Fox, murmured that it was all like *Alice in Wonderland*.

The next day, on 27 June, the committee met to consider their strategy for Southwark's Planning Committee on 3 July. It aimed to get Imry Merchant's planning application deferred until after the judicial review was heard and it considered lodging an application for Jon Greenfield's Option One design. It even talked about filing the Theatres Trust/Ove Arup scheme. Its main concern focused on the extant planning permission that Imry Merchant already had. Outside the meeting room in Bear Gardens Museum, a mechanical digger was already scooping out earth from the proposed piling positions. Rumours in the City about an imminent takeover bid for Imry Merchant made people fear that the company might, at this stage, go for a show of strength and start building work in advance of Southwark's meeting.

By now the financial pages were seething with speculation about the rumoured takeover of Imry Merchant. 'To bid for Imry Merchant or not to bid?' asked Geoff Foster in the *Daily Mail*, still enjoying the sport of quoting the Bard. It was reported that a European consortium or one from the Far East were about to make a bid. However it was Paul Cheesewright of the *Financial Times* who guessed correctly that Stephan Wingate, the entrepreneur behind Marketchief, was the man behind the sporadic buying of shares. The Campaign Committee chose this moment to take pre-emptive action. On

Friday, 30 June, Peter Village, the Campaign's junior counsel, convinced Mr Justice Nolan that building work on both north and south sites should stop. Costs were reserved. It was not a good time for the Campaign to be hitting a property developer for losses of £30,000 a day.

Whilst it is one thing to get an injunction served late on a Friday afternoon, before the respondents have their opportunity to put the opposing case, it is quite another thing to sustain it when all parties get the chance to meet. Mr Justice Schiemann, the following Monday, 3 July, was less convinced by the Campaign's case. He discharged the injunction and ordered the Campaign to pay costs. Many supporters hearing this news believed the Campaign had lost its main court case. It had certainly lost morale and had to put on a brave face for Southwark's Planning meeting in the evening. Barbara Morris in a hat trimmed with silk roses and Dr Urmilla Khan in a day-glo pink sari, formed part of the Campaign Committee's deputation. Peggy Ashcroft and James Fox ensured a high profile. 'This isn't the most important issue in Southwark,' said Cllr Rose Colley, 'The camera crews should be here when homelessness is being discussed.' Nevertheless the meeting was not hostile to the Rose. The Borough solicitor, Dr Clive Grace, advised Southwark on the two main legal grounds which would support deferral until the end of the month. The conflicting statements made by the Museum of London and English Heritage needed to be resolved, and secondly Imry Merchant's application should be called in by the Secretary of State for his decision. Once again, councillors asked the Campaign to submit alternative planning applications. Meanwhile, outside the Chamber, a group of council tenants wearing face masks and pushing a wheelbarrow full of litter and dogshit, staged an environmental protest.

Next day, 4 July, the men in wigs went back to court to ask Lord Donaldson, Master of the Rolls, to set a date for the judicial review before the end of the legal term. Diaries were cross-referenced and 10 July was agreed. This was the date that the Campaign had been waiting for. Its entire strategy had been to get the Rose scheduled or, failing that, to test the Secretary of State's decision in law. But before the judicial review could go ahead, the Campaign suffered two major setbacks. Imry Merchant's solicitors, Linklaters and Paines, asked the Campaign to make a cross-undertaking in damages, failure to do so meant lifting the corporate veil of the Rose Theatre Trust Company, and making its individual members financially liable. The Campaign Committee, by now, had set up both a charitable trust and a company limited by guarantee; the former gave the tax advantages, the latter provided its profit-making arm. Startable Ltd, an off-the-shelf company, had been purchased and its name duly changed to the Rose Theatre Trust Company. Only two directors had been appointed, Anthony Grayling and Martin Village.

All Campaign work had been undertaken on a voluntary basis. Stars donated their celebrity status. Volunteers donated a range of skills. The ISGC donated office space. Theodore Goddard donated legal services as did the Campaign's counsels, Jeremy Sullivan QC and Peter Village. Windhorse Associates donated logo designs. Pentagram donated alternative architectural plans. Imagination, the firm that staged the 11 June Rally, donated staging, sound system and wine tents backstage. Yet there were expenses. The telephone bill, for one, was enormous. And there were costs yet to come. The bill for the injunction would have to be met. The fee for lodging a planning application would have to be found. Money had come in from a number of sources. Theatres, like the RSC, held regular collections. Buckets were passed round at the big Rallies. Tee-shirts were sold. Collecting tins were filled each day on site. An advertising agency persuaded several national newspapers to donate space for a fund-raising message. Leaflets were produced. A video was made. Coral Stringfellow flew to America to talk personally to a number of well-heeled individuals. Bank accounts were opened in London, New York and Los Angeles.

Altogether a steady, though not a large income, had been raised. The big rally on 11 June, for example, brought in £7,000, but the bulk of the Campaign's income came from individuals pledging large amounts. Lord Olivier donated £1,000. Timothy Dalton underwrote the costs of the Press Conference. Steven Spielberg and Amy Irving donated $50,000. In all, by the time accounts were presented in the autumn, the Campaign had raised £59,353. But at the Committee meeting on 8 July, the Campaign believed it had only £6,000 in the bank. The long-awaited judicial review could not go ahead unless the Committee could give an undertaking that it had the money to meet Linklaters and Paines' bill, in the event of their case not succeeding. Linklaters and Paines may only have been sabre-rattling but it had an effect. It was not a good time for a property developer to be hitting a campaign for £40,000 of security.

In the end, the Committee found out it had at least £19,000 in the bank and that, plus the Spielberg's money, allowed the undertaking to be given in Crypt Court One on 10 July, a warm and cloudy day. £45,000 was transferred into a frozen account to be held at Theodore Goddards'. However, there was still another major setback to be overcome. Linklaters and Paines queried the Campaign's status. Did it have any standing in law to pursue the case at all? Did it have *locus standi?* The modern philosophy on *locus standi*, until the Rose, had been flexible. Effectively, Lord Denning had virtually given *locus* to every Tom, Dick and Harry, believing that it would be a grave mistake if outdated technical rules on *locus* got in the way of a challenge to unlawful conduct. For most of the 1980s, the High Court accepted that 'sufficient interest' was enough to enable a judicial review to go ahead. But, as Peter Goldsmith QC, counsel for Imry Merchant, put his case to Mr Justice Schiemann, 'sufficient interest' was now, legally not to be enough. 'How odd,' said Schiemann on more than one occasion, 'how odd that the more people who are interested, the less likely they are to have an interest.' 'How odd,' he said again, 'that a collection of Joe Bloggses can object to a butcher's shop in the High Street, but a collection of eminent archaeologists do not have sufficient standing in law to object to the Secretary of State's ruling on the Rose Theatre. Prove Martin Biddle's *locus* and you're home and dry.' It was not to be that easy.

A judicial review is a clubby kind of activity made even more so, in the case of the Rose, by virtue of the fact that Jeremy Sullivan QC, counsel for the Rose Campaign, and Andrew Collins QC, counsel for the Secretary of State for the Environment, shared the same chambers. Lined up in front of Mr Justice Schiemann were four legal teams. Ranged against Sullivan were a trio of expensive briefs. As well as Collins and Peter Goldsmith, Stephen Sedley QC, counsel for PosTel, the owners of the site, weighed in against the Rose. All four had their juniors, and backing them were teams of scurrying solicitors passing messages to and fro. Crypt Court One was crammed. Collins, representing Nicholas Ridley was most reluctant to discredit the Campaign's *locus*. 'I can well understand,' said Schiemann, 'that the Secretary of State would not want the odium that could be attached to him, if it could be said that though he had acted unlawfully yet no one had the right to take him to court.' Goldsmith was the one barrister truly motivated to discredit the Campaign's standing, calling it variously a collection of 'busybodies . . . Joe Bloggses . . . the world and his wife . . . cranks, mischief-makers. Simon Hughes,' he pointed out, 'is not a licensed litigant.' Martin Myers said, well after the event, 'The Save the Rose people were a pain in the butt. Without them we'd have negotiated the same outcome for the Rose. In many ways they delayed and hindered things. Costs rose and the problems were exacerbated.'

The Campaign's counsel, taken by surprise that *locus* should be challenged at all, pleaded their case on a number of grounds. Under the 1979 Act, anybody is allowed to make representations at the point of Scheduled Monument Consent. Therefore, Jeremy Sullivan argued, the Act implies that representation is also an expectation before the stage of SMC is reached. In addition, Nicholas Ridley, by giving considered replies in writing to the Campaign, *de facto* accorded them standing. No other party claimed to represent the public in relation to the Rose Theatre. If the Campaign's application failed, Sullivan's argument concluded, then Ridley's decision not to schedule – which may be unlawful – was unlikely to ever be tested in the courts. In his judgement, which Mr Justice Schiemann promised 'may well surprise many laymen and some lawyers', he said the law in general provides that 'even an unlawful decision is to be treated as lawful' until proven otherwise. If Ridley's letter was to be taken as proof of *locus*, then decision-makers in future would be deterred from being helpful in their answers to the general public. Under the relevant statute, Schiemann said, an applicant has to have statutory rights. 'I can therefore consider the question of standing,' wrote Schiemann in his judgement, 'by considering whether an individual of acknowledged distinction in the field of archaeology – of which the Campaign has several amongst its members – has sufficient standing to move for a judicial review of a decision not to schedule.' ('Prove Martin Biddle, and you're home and dry.') A strange gap then occurs in Schiemann's written judgement, because he does not go on to impart the results of his consideration, and so the Campaign was never entirely clear why their *locus* failed.

Evidently though Martin Biddle was not proved. The Campaign was not home and dry. Mr Justice Schiemann did not view the function of the courts to be there for every Tom, Dick or Harry. 'My decision on standing may well leave an unlawful act by a minister unrebuked and indeed unrevealed,' he sonorously concluded. 'We all expect our decision-makers to act lawfully. We are not all given the right to apply for judicial review.' Schiemann's decision caused a stir in legal circles. On this alone, the Campaign had clear grounds to go to Appeal but by then Schiemann had also delivered his verdict on the substantive case and ruled against that as well. As Simon Hughes said at the next Committee meeting, 'It is some consolation to know that even if we'd won on *locus*, we'd still have lost the judicial review'.

A judicial review is a handy legal measure which has grown popular in the last five years. In 1989, as well as the Rose's judicial review, headlines were made by a group of Muslims who sought this form of redress to review the laws on blasphemy, and a convent of nuns who sought to overturn an order which threatened to exterminate their flock of salmonella-carrying hens. Judicial review is a mechanism which allows the courts to review administrative decisions made by statutory bodies. The courts have the power to quash decisions but not the power to substitute alternatives. A judicial review covers decisions of Ministers, local authorities, public boards, inferior courts and tribunals, criminal law, civil law, revenue decisions, immigration decisions, planning, public transport, prison visitors and treaties. Judicial review has often been used to mount political attacks on decisions and policies made at local and national level. The knowledge that it exists has so far operated as a check to the abuse of administrative power.

'There's more bureaucracy in our lives now,' says Simon Hughes, 'the courts have developed the idea that there is a remedy.' 'It's relatively quick, simple and cheap', agrees solicitor Martin Kramer, 'It's all done on affidavits and there are no pleadings.' It was the Campaign's intention to prove that 'in coming to his decision the Secretary of State took into account irrelevant considerations, failed to take into account relevant considerations, misdirected himself in law and acted unreasonably'. But first the Secretary of State had to be persuaded to give his reasons for not scheduling the Rose under Section 1 (3) of the 1979 Act as clarified in paragraph 49 of Circular 8/87 (Historic Buildings and Conservation Area – Policy and Procedures) and Section 61 (12) (b) of the same Act and he did not do so until the end of the four week moratorium. It was not until 15 June, the day that Ridley once again told the House of Commons that he would not be scheduling the Rose, that T.E. Radice, the head of the Heritage Sponsorship Division at the DoE, gave the Campaign the reasons *in extenso*. But his statement that 'scheduling could give rise to claims for compensation' was the main peg on which the Campaign hung its legal case. Radice gave other reasons behind Ridley's decision. He wrote of the competing pressures between archaeology and re-development and said that the re-designed building protected the remains, and that the developers had voluntarily co-operated to produce this. The Campaign believed that all the reasons given were either unreasonable or irrelevant. On 3 July, Jeremy Sullivan and Peter Village's joint opinion to the Committee had been that: 'Whilst the seas of litigation are, so far as our researches reveal, uncharted . . . we consider the Applicant's chances of success are good.'

In Court, Jeremy Sullivan argued that the possibility of compensation was only relevant at the stage of SMC. It was an irrelevant factor in the decision to schedule itself. Of the competing pressures between archaeology and redevelopment, he said that a balancing exercise again was only of relevance at the SMC stage. The re-design, said Sullivan, could not protect the remains since the remains had not yet been fully excavated. Scheduling a site does not in itself preclude the voluntary co-operation of the site owner. Nicholas Ridley had fettered his discretion in reaching the decision not to schedule by considering that only if the Rose were under threat, would he be justified in so doing since no such pre-condition exists under the 1979 Act. Such a fetter is, therefore, unlawful and *ultra vires*. Sullivan argued that it was Parliament's intention that nationally important remains should be scheduled. Ridley, he said, was unreasonable in not scheduling a site which he admitted met all the criteria for scheduling. Mr Justice Schiemann did not buy any of this. He agreed with Peter Goldsmith's interpretation of the 1979 Act as a discretionary measure and that it was relevant for the Secretary of State to consider compensation as a consequence of scheduling.

Although his judgement was not given for another week, the mood amongst Campaigners was bleak when the two-day case came to an end on 11 July, compounded further by the news of Lord Olivier's death, announced from every news-stand along the Strand. The media made much of Olivier's last public gesture. 'A few days from death,' wrote *The Guardian*, 'he was there – on tape – defending the Rose Theatre.' James Fox wrote to the *Evening Standard*, 'Would it not be the most perfect epitaph to that great man if the Government agreed with all despatch to his last wish?' Neither the government nor Mr Justice Schiemann were to be in sentimental mood.

For the first time the Committee got into a direct confrontation with Imry Merchant over its plans to lay a wreath for Olivier on the site of the Rose, which Martin Landau said was provocative and unseemly. In the end a compromise was reached when a wreath was positioned on the perimeter fence by Canon Peter Challen from Southwark Cathedral, on 14 July, the day of Olivier's funeral. Landau's tetchiness was fully explained on 17 July when the news finally broke of the £314 million cash takeover bid by Marketchief for Imry Merchant. Marketchief was set up specifically to take over Imry Merchant. Its shareholders are Eagle Star Insurance Co. Ltd., the merchant banking affiliates of Prudential-Bache Capital Funding, and the Development and Realisation Trust Ltd. (D & RT), owned by Eagle Star, Mercury Asset Management Ltd, Kleinwort Benson Investment Management Ltd. and George Soros. At first, hopes were raised that Marketchief might prove more sympathetic to the Rose than had Imry Merchant. *The Stage* came up with the completely erroneous suggestion that Stephan Wingate who heads Marketchief was the brother of Richard Wingate, whose company Chesterfield operates the West End's second largest theatre chain.

Unfortunately he was not and, anyway, Marketchief had taken on the Imry Merchant management team, so the Committee was stuck with the same old adversaries. On 17 July, the same day as the takeover was announced, Mr Justice Schiemann ruled that Nicholas Ridley's decision not to schedule the Rose Theatre was within the law. Costs were awarded to both the DoE and Imry Merchant and the Campaign Committee was given just three days to decide whether to appeal. It met in quarrelsome mood on the evening of 17 July, even though out on the street a band was setting up equipment for a party. The legal advice was strongly against pursuing the matter through the Courts of Appeal. After a round of applause, Martin Kramer and Nicholas Armstrong left to the sound of gospel singers wailing in the deep black velvet sky.

The Committee's main strategy had now failed. The only hope for the Campaign lay with Southwark Council. Its Leader, Anne Matthews, had said repeatedly that Southwark wanted to see alternative plans submitted but the Committee had just one week to file an application before Southwark Planning Committee met on 25 July to make their deferred decision. Previously Jon Greenfield, Pentagram's architect, had resisted the Committee's earlier move to lodge an application for the outline design on Option One, because he felt that it clashed with Theo Crosby's design for similar facilities at the ISGC. The Theatres Trust was anxious that the design drawn up by Ove Arup should be formally considered and they urged the Committee to adopt their scheme, modified by Greenfield (because of the Theatres Trust constitution, it is unable to lodge its own application). The Theatres Trust/Ove Arup scheme was broadly similar to the Imry Merchant proposal whilst containing far more benefits for displaying the Rose. Greenfield proposed that the Committee should go for this. The timescale, he said, was too short for Southwark to be able to consider anything that was radically different.

The Committee's objections to the Theatres Trust scheme, even at this stage, were partly financial and partly political. The Theatres Trust scheme was a detailed application which would cost £3800 to lodge and, after the court case, the Campaign had only £2500 in the bank. Costs for both the injunction and the judicial review loomed large. And there were still enough people solid for Option One to resist this proposal. Ruth Richardson for one, was convinced that a benefactor would turn up at the last minute.

Events, in the end, conspired to thwart the Committee's plans to file plans with Southwark Council when NALGO went on strike which meant that the application could not be processed in time for Southwark's meeting on 25 July. Meanwhile on Saturday, 22 July the Committee was offered yet another design for the site of the Rose, one that radically re-thought the issue. Ronald Denny, of the British Property Federation, had suggested at the National Theatre debate, that a replica of the Rose should be built elsewhere, only for a heckler to tell him to build a replica of the office block instead. Indeed, Mark Fisher had made much the same point when he said that, 'If the Secretary of State does not urgently reconsider his decision not to schedule, he will preserve a 10-storey office block but he will not preserve the Rose.' It was an unspoken assumption amongst Rose supporters that all office blocks are dreary and unremarkable buildings. Richard Seifert, architect for the Imry Merchant office block, who built Centrepoint in 1966, has perhaps done more to change London's landscape than anyone else since Christopher Wren. Some Seifert buildings, like the 1980 NatWest Tower which dominates the skyline from Bankside, are real landmark architecture. Others like the stained and stumpy block in Long Acre are just buildings. Seifert's original design for the Imry Merchant development was basically a glass box with exceptionally long elevations fronting Southwark Bridge and facing the *Financial Times'* smokey glass box opposite. It wasn't so much architecture as a straightforward exercise in lettable area.

Architects love tall towers but most Londoners prefer the London of St Paul's. Prince Charles had voiced a popular sentiment, when in 1984, he described the planned extension to the National Gallery as 'a monstrous carbuncle on the face of a much beloved friend,' and begun an aggressive crusade against modernist design. Although modern architecture is supposed to be economical and functional, these buildings made of glass, concrete and steel begin to decay after twenty years. The original Southbridge House for example, erected in 1957, was tired and obsolete by 1987 and the best thing the Campaign could say for the Seifert replacement was that it too would come down in 30 years. No doubt Simon Jenkins too shared the same view. 'Modernism is entiled to the affection of conservationists,' Jenkins has written, 'but it has less and less to do with modern architecture,' The humanised urban landscape using traditional forms and materials is part of a counter-revolution which includes St Mary Overie's Dock. This redevelopment on Bankside, with its neo-Georgian lines and honey-coloured brick is considered the acceptable face of modern architecture. Some people, not naturally drawn to the cause of an Elizabethan theatre, supported the Campaign if for no other reason than that it got in the way of office development. And then on 22 July, Ruth Richardson introduced to the Committee yet another architect. John Burrell. He put up the hackles of many by

223

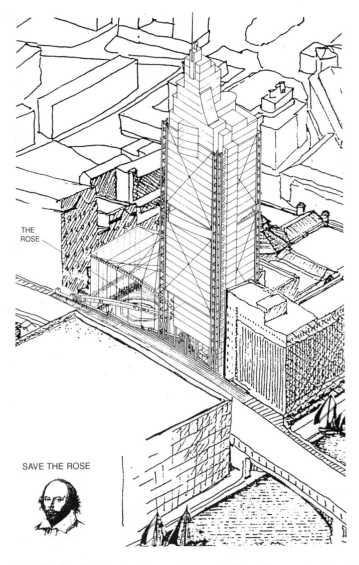

THE
ROSE

SAVE THE ROSE

46. The Burrell Foley Associates solution to the Rose Theatres site, viewed from the north.

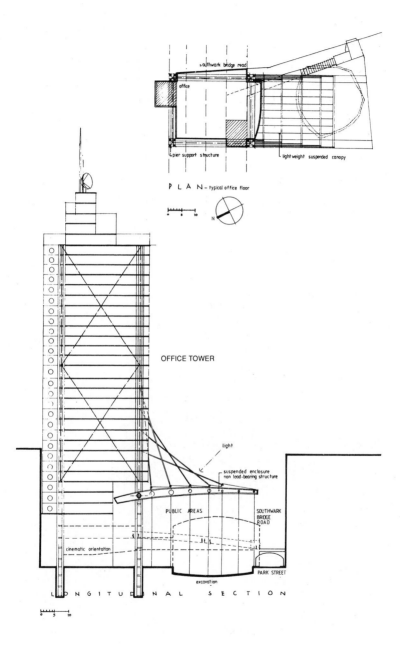

southwark bridge road

office

4 pier support structure

lightweight suspended canopy

P L A N – typical office floor

0   5   10

N

OFFICE TOWER

light

suspended enclosure
non load-bearing structure

PUBLIC AREAS

SOUTHWARK
BRIDGE
ROAD

cinematic orientation

PARK STREET

excavation

L O N G I T U D I N A L   S E C T I O N

0   5   10

47.   Longitudinal section of the Burrell Foley design viewed from Rose
Alley.

225

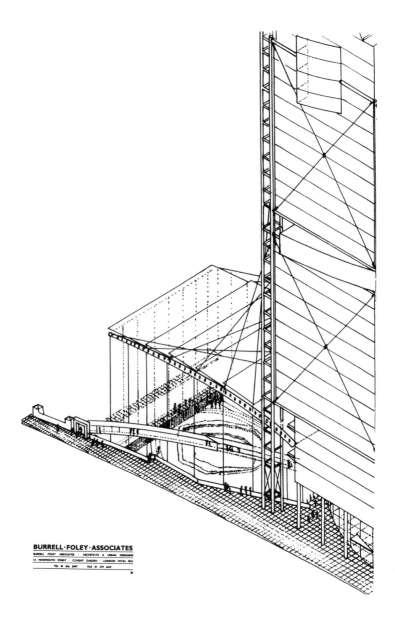

48. An impression of the Rose on display in the Burrell Foley office block, viewed from Southwark Bridge.

defending the aesthetics of modernist architecture and distributed around the table another solution to the problem of the Rose site. It was a witty and elegant design which married both past and present without pastiche.

Twenty-six storeys soared needle sharp into the air. The north site was developed and the south – the site of the Rose – was left clear; a glass cantilevered roof protected the Rose with six storeys of head room, seemingly hanging from its tall neighbour. It was a variant of Option Two, which Fletcher King, the chartered surveyors, had originally dismissed as economically unviable. At twelve storeys it *was*; 26 storeys changed the arithmetic. It was also a stunning building in its own right and would draw the eye to Southwark's skyline in dramatic fashion. Enormous prejudice would have had to be overcome for John Burrell's plan to have got anywhere because although in theory there are no restrictions against tall buildings, in practice architects don't get away with designing towers like that. The Committee was stunned on 22 July. After angry exchanges, it finally agreed that the Burrell design would be put into the public domain as yet another facet of the planning issue, another reason why Southwark should defer its decision yet again.

Between Saturday's committee meeting on 22 July and Southwark's Planning meeting on 25 July, another principal player in the drama of the Rose was re-cast. Nicholas Ridley fell victim to Margaret Thatcher's re-shuffle. He had not had a good summer. The surprising results for the Greens in the EEC elections had made everyone much more sensitive to the Secretary of State for the Environment's many blunders. Everything from water pollution to Rottweilers seemed to turn into a Ridley own goal. Southwark's Planning Committee met on Tuesday 25 July in its usual informal way. Chief Planning Officer, Robin Thompson, arrived with a bike pump sticking out of a bag. Cllr. Patricia Matheson carried a fretful baby around the Chamber. Simon Tait of *The Times* was there with his thick handlebar moustache and even thicker notepad. The saturnine Alan Parness, project architect for Richard Seifert, was there. Julian Bowsher, from the Museum of London, was there in bow tie and striped blazer. Victor Belcher, tall and languid, from English Heritage, was there. Firm and erect and five minutes late, Dame Peggy Ashcroft was there. It was like a gathering of old friends.

'Planning,' Robin Thompson had said on a previous occasion, 'is the art of the possible.' The Imry Merchant re-design – the 'office on stilts' – had come two-thirds of the way along a possible route marked out by Thompson since the application was deferred on 3 July. Piles, 8 feet in diameter, would still be driven within 18 inches of the Rose remains, although they were now positioned just slightly outside its perimeter. The final re-design involved an additional storey which added 1717 square metres. With a height of 47 metres and its considerable elevation, this would be a substantial building. In addition, the re-design incorporated a two-storey extension in the north west which created a further 119 square metres of lettable space. The Rose Theatre was allowed a maximum ceiling height of 22 feet which in places was considerably less, owing to the solid steel beams 12 feet away from the excavated remains. Overall, the additions made to the proposed office block which compensated for the loss of the ground floor, increased its capacity by 3.6%. Robin Thompson had successfully negotiated with Richard Seifert to move the lift shaft and service core to a less insensitive position. No progress had been made on ceiling heights. On archaeological matters, opinion was still in conflict. English Heritage had declined to attend a meeting set up by Southwark Council with the Museum of London.

By contrast to the Imry Merchant design, the Theatres Trust/Ove Arup plan (not before the Planning Committee) would have increased the lettable area by 7.25% and it allowed the Rose a ceiling height of 36 feet. The load of the office block was transferred right to the extreme perimeter of the site with open girders measuring 3 feet x 90 feet running north/south.

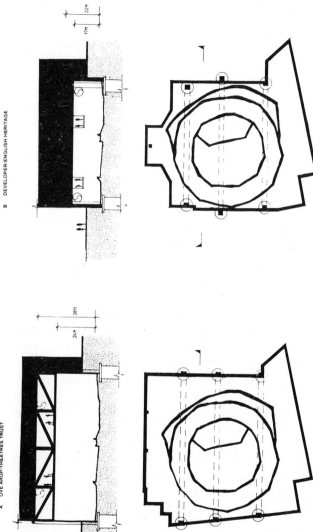

A OVE ARUP/THEATRES TRUST

B DEVELOPER/ENGLISH HERITAGE

49. A comparison between the final 'office on stilts' design, as presented to Southwark Council on 25 July 1989, and the Theatres Trust/Ove Arup plan. Note the difference in ceiling height.

229

The girders were 14 feet deep and allowed viewing walkways and service ducts to pass through them. In planning terms there was little to choose between them except that Imry Merchant owned the land, and the Campaign did not, and Imry Merchant had a planning application for Southwark to consider, and the Campaign did not. If planning is the art of the possible then clearly it was not possible for Southwark to impose the more Rose-friendly design Theatres Trust/Ove Arup plan on Imry Merchant. A local planning authority cannot oblige an applicant to build outside his own site, as the alternative proposed.

Robin Thompson said that Nicholas Ridley's refusal to schedule had left a decision of national importance to an authority not geared to deal with such an issue. Confines of planning law require reasons other than lack of ceiling height for not approving an application. The advice of the statutory body, English Heritage, was emphatic. Part of the Imry Merchant building was already under construction and there existed a valid planning permission. After seven weeks of almost daily negotiations, he said, there were no further modifications that Seifert was prepared to make. The application, said Thompson, subject to stringent conditions under Section 52, should now be approved.

In the discussion that followed, English Heritage got most of the flak. George Dennis from the Museum of London brandished the bone, now known to have come from a European Brown Bear, as evidence that the spoil produced by piling was not being recorded by English Heritage. Simon Hughes said that Southwark Council had achieved more than English Heritage in their discussions with the developer. John Burns said that under English Heritage's monitoring, the site was strewn with mounds of earth and heavy machinery. Harvey Sheldon said that English Heritage had not yet passed on their records to the Museum of London. Cllr. Frank Pemberton asked Victor Belcher if he was satisfied that the re-design would not damage the Rose and Belcher replied, 'We are satisfied'.

Frank Pemberton moved that Southwark should once again defer. Dr Clive Grace, the borough solicitor, advised that a second deferral would stand up in law. Because Imry Merchant had already got a valid planning permission, any further delay in building work on their part could not make Southwark liable for costs. Nevertheless Pemberton's motion was defeated by three votes to seven and Cllr. Nick Snow's motion that the application be approved, won with seven votes for, two abstentions and one vote against. Geoff Williams commended the Campaign for putting the issue on the agenda. In due course, he said, the officers would make a report, on the basis of which, representations would be made to the government about the relationship of archaeology and planning, and the respective responsibilities of the Secretary of State and local authorities. And that was it. The end of the road. The 'office on stilts' could go ahead. That very night pile driving started in the south west corner of the site. 'With hindsight,' said Simon Hughes, 'I think we could have got the Theatres Trust Proposal accepted by Imry Merchant, but the Committee always solidly voted for Option One.'

There was one final sting in the tail for the Campaign. Among the documents considered by Southwark prior to reaching its decision, was a letter from Sam Wanamaker of the ISGC. 'The issue of the Rose,' he wrote, 'has been protracted over many months and has caused some confusion and a serious deflection of effort from our own fund-raising and educational activities. With the additional revisions now proposed, we strongly urge your Committee to act decisively to approve the Imry application so that we can move on to the many urgent issues regarding the future development of Bankside.'

CODA

Bitter in-fighting characterised the dog days of the summer when the Campaign Committee felt their defeat the most. By the early autumn the Rose Campaign and the ISGC had split. Both organisations have expressed their interest in taking responsibility for the Rose once it is re-excavated and put on display in the 22 feet basement of what is now called Rose Court. The Rose Campaign has commissioned a feasibility study from Heritage Projects, the people behind Jorvik Viking Centre, and whoever wins the Rose, will in the immediate future have to focus on serious long term fund-raising. The Campaign Committee, through natural wastage and the incomprehensible Single Transferable Vote system set up by Simon Hughes, slimmed itself down to a more manageable number. Court costs were finally settled in mid-November 1989 when Linklaters and Paines agreed to have their original bill of £83,000 trimmed to a more acceptable £45,920.95. The DoE has not yet presented the Campaign with its bill. There again at the time of writing, it has not yet presented Imry Merchant with its million pounds.

And just when everyone thought it safe to venture down Park Street once more, yet another Elizabethan theatre was excavated from the Bankside earth – Shakespeare's Globe. In a classic public relations exercise, Hansons plc (an £8.6 billion conglomerate) fronted by Michael Shea, former PR advisor to the Queen, unveiled three wall foundations of the familiar chalk blocks to the world's press on 12 October. Planning permission has been delayed pending full excavation and Hansons and the Museum of London have jointly asked the new Secretary of State to schedule the monument. This fragment of the Globe found in the north west of Courage Brewery's old car park may be the only excavation to be undertaken. Probably 40% of it lies underneath Southwark Bridge Road and can therefore never be excavated. 14% in the east has been destroyed by nineteenth century construction work. The remaining 30% that is likely to have survived lies under the Grade II listed Anchor Terrace. The Georgian Group would almost certainly block any attempt to demolish Anchor Terrace in order to excavate the Globe. Besides, archaeologists are reluctant to expose the site whilst preservation techniques for the Rose are still far from settled.

The ISGC immediately stopped building work on its proposed reconstruction of the Globe replica and is pressing for complete excavation of the original. They have a lot at stake. £20 million is about to be spent on a twenty-four-sided polygon and the lessons from the archaeology of the Rose though, suggest that regularity in the architecture of Elizabethan playhouses cannot be assumed. Preliminary scanning of the site seems also to indicate that the Globe's diameter may very well turn out to be much smaller than anticipated. Meanwhile, on the site of the Rose, Costains got on with building what was to be called Rose Court and it was sad to walk the hundred yards from the site of the carefully excavated Globe to the churned up site of the Rose. Angry graffiti had been scrawled on the perimeter fence by those who felt most betrayed by the way the Campaign had turned out. 'Simon "Lapdog" Hughes' and 'Sam "The Sham" Wanamaker' were singled out for particular blame.

And written on a gap in the fence was the bitter caption – 'A window on the world of big business, corruption and greed'.

Underneath its concrete crust ('the impermeable membrane') the Rose lies in its tomb, monitored by Huntington Technical Services whilst English Heritage continued 'keyhole' excavation in the autumn amidst the turmoil of the building work. A bear skull was found in late August among the disturbed debris in the north. Less dramatic but more significant was the discovery of more chalk remains and 'robbed out' foundations in the south east, which suggested the one remarkably long wall making up an irregular thirteen-sided polygon. More modifications then had to be made to the Imry Merchant design to move the piling half a metre south outside the newly defined perimeter of the theatre. At the end of October, John Cholmley's victualling house was unearthed in the south west where Imry Merchant had re-positioned the lift shaft and service core. Fragments of decorated ceramic tiles, stone, chalk and brick foundations have been removed for further study. 'I doubt,' said English Heritage archaeologist John Hinchcliffe, 'if any piece of rubble has ever received so much attention.'

Basically, there are three options for the long-term future of the remains; continued burial, replacement and minimum intervention, that is if the Rose remains survive the vibrations and disturbance caused by piling and building work. The Campaign to save the Rose in the summer heatwave nearly posed as big a threat to the remains as the proposed development itself. Once re-excavated, the main danger to the Rose will come from the drying out of the clay-rich deposits, the decomposition of wooden structural materials, and the decay of organic artefacts and ecofacts. Many experts favour continued burial until such time as a known and proved conservation technology can be applied. Some would opt for total excavation and replacement with a fibreglass cast. Even re-excavation itself will be hazardous. The full area of the site will have to be exposed in the course of what could be a year's digging. A controlled atmosphere to slow down any deterioration of the remains will have to be maintained throughout that year. The rising water table will be an added aggravation.

A Symposium was organised by English Heritage at Fortress House on 9 October 1989 to discuss various solutions for preserving the Rose, all of which are wholly experimental. Techniques in dealing with water-logged timbers have scarcely advanced in the last decade since the discovery of the *Mary Rose*. If left entirely alone, the exposed Rose Theatre has a life expectancy of between four and ten years, and in that period there would be rapid vegetable growth on site. All its components parts, the wood, mud, brick and chalk, need different sorts of treatments and environments. Professor G. Toracca from the University of Rome who has experience of mud brick conservation suggested that a 95% humidity environment would avoid cracking and that the three metres of alluvial clay beneath the Rose would act as a natural damp course. Dr G. Chiari from the University of Turin advised that a nitrogen atmosphere with periodic ultra-violet radiation would minimise the risk of biological infection. The optimum solution would seem to be to keep the site wet whilst enclosing it in a large atmospherically controlled sealed glass box, which Toracca urged should be 'beautiful'. Although low in capital costs, this could run to a maintenance charge of about £200,000 a year. Set against this option of minimal interference, is the costlier proposal to extricate the remains from the site, treat them in a laboratory and replace the Rose on a 'raft'. After this treatment, maintenance is expected to be low in price. The technical problems of conservation are severe, although it has been said that some expert conservationists can't even pickle onions, and that the problems they highlight are politically linked to a vested interest in leaving the Rose permanently underneath its impermeable membrane. Without re-excavation, the Campaign to Save the Rose Theatre in 1989 will have been utterly pointless.

There are, of course, lessons to be learned and morals pointed from the summer of 1989. The Campaign to Save the Rose marked a jump forward in archaeological philosophy. Until the excavation of the Rose, the Museum of London had agreed with current thinking: that recording discoveries was the main priority and it worked within the consequences of planning decisions which allowed for the destruction of remains because British planning law works on the assumption that all necessary information is available when an application is made. But whereas site use, density, height, volume, traffic implications, and visual aesthetics can be projected in advance, archaeology is the only material consideration which cannot. The Queen's Hotel in York, Huggin Hill in the City of London and the Rose Theatre in Southwark are all recent examples of sites that could not have informed the original planning permission. Increasingly, the Museum of London had become concerned at the prospect of 'rescue archaeology' as techniques for preservation and display became possible. The case of the Rose brought these concerns into the open.

In 1988, and again in 1989, the Museum of London submitted a strategic plan to English Heritage which stressed the need for the provision of better information to planning authorities and urged the preparation of constraint maps indicating areas of prime archaeological deposits where piling should be restricted. New technology, particularly remote sensing devices, can give accurate evaluation of what lies beneath the ground. On a site in the Fleet Valley, for example, the Museum of London was able to indentify individual skeletons that lay entombed beneath an intact concrete slab. Although not all remains are worth preserving, some will have the importance and the 'tingle factor' of the Rose, but evaluation which can pre-determine this is not on its own enough. AAIs have to be increased and funding made mandatory. Developers could take out insurance against surprise finds. This would prevent the recurrence of another Rose Campaign by obviating the need for unexpected discoveries to be underwritten from the public purse, but only if legislation is changed.

In his article in *The Times* on 12 May 1989, Simon Jenkins had said that the Rose Theatre was a 'wholly extraordinary discovery, which no amount of legislation could have foreseen'. Even if legislation had, the Secretary of State's refusal to schedule the Rose, illustrates, as George Dennis said at the RESCUE conference on 17 February 1990, 'how our national antiquities legislation is at present mothballed'. The credibility of English Heritage amongst British archaeologists was seriously threatened by the Rose Campaign, which revealed English Heritage's ties to the government at a time when what was most needed was balanced and impartial advice. Throughout the Campaign, English Heritage claimed its impartiality by citing its resolute defence of 1, Poultry, against the redevelopment proposals of Arts Council supremo, Peter Palumbo. Once again, a judicial review turned down the request by a pressure group, SAVE British Heritage, to overturn the DoE's decision and save the listed Mappin and Webb building (although later, SAVE won on Appeal). Simon Jenkins, who gave evidence for SAVE in court, was in the process of seeking parliamentary powers on English Heritage's behalf for a wider scope in legal interventions, before his resignation as Deputy Chairman of English Heritage early in 1990.

But how much in reality would English Heritage intervene in the future over a second Rose controversy, since its policies on archaeology seem to grow ever more conformable to the developer's interest? In October 1989, English Heritage revealed a policy which 'does not recommend the Government to schedule sites in the centres of historic towns and cities'. As English Heritage's Inspector of Ancient Monuments in Yorkshire, Dr David Fraser, said, 'To schedule would place a very great constraint on any future development'. On 15 November 1989 – six months to the day since the major public outcry about the Rose Theatre – English Heritage issued a press release which called for 'a reduction in the need for expensive excavations, the costs incurred by developers, and the kind of crisis which occurred at the Rose Theatre'. Faced with the Museum of London's intransigence over the Rose, English Heritage seem to wish to break the Museum of London's monopoly on archaeology in 23 of the 32 London boroughs by removing a £380,000 establishment grant and replacing it with contract archaeology on an American model. If they succeed, they will have smashed the one organisation that can bring coherence to most of subterranean London and provide evaluative advice to local authorities. It is hard not to think that the name, English Heritage, like the term, 'rescue archaeology' largely turns out to mean the opposite.

At the end of the Campaign, the ball finally rested in Southwark's court. If tougher legislation is needed at national level (as well as the political will to execute it) then it would also seem that legislation is needed at local level to give planning authorities the right to insist on early archaeological evaluation, in line with the EEC principles of Environmental Impact Assessment. At present, the DoE's 1/85 Circular, which indicates that archaeology is best dealt with during development, is a good recipe for further conflict and confrontation. Other aspects of the 1979 Act were effectively 'mothballed' when AAI designation for North Southwark was rejected by the DoE in 1988, resulting in the decision over the Rose having to be made at local level. Certainly, in Southwark, the planning authority had the political will to protect the site, but lacked the cash, if compensation became an issue. Southwark's forward-thinking archaeological conditions have anyway already been thrown out at least once by DoE Inspectors on Appeal. Meanwhile archaeologists in London who have been long awaiting more coherent guidance promised by the DoE were referred back to the old Voluntary Code and the 1/85 Circular in the recently issued Strategic Planning Guidance for London (July 1989). 'This does not begin to advise Southwark or any other council if something like the Rose theatre is discovered', said Simon Hughes.

'What is needed is simple', wrote Simon Jenkins in the easier days before he headed English Heritage. 'It is a regulation requiring the inspection by experts of the demolition and excavation of any London construction site which might be of archaeological importance. There should then be a compulsory delay in further building operations if anything of significance is found.

Such a delay will obviously cost the developer money. But I cannot see why he should be spared the cost – any more than a man who inhabits a historic building must forego the profit he could get by pulling it down.

Certain things about a city are more important than a developer's profit. And this is one of them.'

Politically the future of the Rose now lies with Southwark Council. The Section 52 conditions were agreed in early September 1989. *Inter alia*, Section 52 states that the agreement is binding on Imry Merchant only for as long as Imry Merchant retain their interest in Rose Court. It covenants Imry Merchant to apply for scheduling once building work is finished. It puts a duty on Imry Merchant to continue negotiating for the City depot site and requires Imry Merchant to make a donation of £180,000 towards the eventual costs of displaying the Rose. Southwark retains the absolute discretion of approving the body that takes control of the Rose. But just how do you display a 'hole in the ground'? Can the public take its history neat or will the Rose have to be gift-wrapped in heritage packaging?

Epilogue

Martin Myers has a wonderful view of the trees in St James's Square from his office window on the third floor and if he gets bored with the trees, he can contemplate the watercolours opposite his desk. Evidently, Martin Myers is a man who likes looking at things other than a balance sheet and St James's Square, with Christie's just across the road, is well situated for the businessman who seriously wants to invest in blue chip art. Imry Merchant ended up spending £10 million on re-designing an 'office on stilts' in order to safeguard the foundations of the Rose Theatre, and for that sum the company could have picked up the foundations of a solid art collection. In the summer of 1989, Braque's *L'Arlequin*, Matisse's *Nu aux Souliers Roses*, Léger's *Contrastes de Formes* and Picasso's *Guitar et Compotier Rose*, all came under the hammer at Christie's for a little over £10 million. Art in the private marketplace commands a precise valuation whilst art in the public domain is a devalued activity. David Selbourne in the *Sunday Times* described the Campaign to save the Rose as 'strange one . . . a kind of madness-for-art'.

The confrontation in Park Street between the property developers, the building workers paid to execute their plans, and the demonstrators, over the excavation of an Elizabethan playhouse, illustrated the way in which art reveals the divisions within contemporary culture. Four hundred years ago, a new play at the Rose would have attracted a mass audience composed of the powerful, the lowly and the intellectual. The writers who wrote for the Rose would have been very surprised at the notion of a theatre which put on anything other than new plays. Yet, ironically, in the summer of 1989, the Royal Court, the main flagship for contemporary writing, was reduced to closing its Theatre Upstairs and selling condoms in the foyer; a twentieth-century variant of John Cholmley's ancillary activities. Arts Council-led marketing strategies are transforming the arts into loss leaders for big business, and the classics, which draw on a defined tradition of past works, are considered the most reliable loss leaders of them all. New writing is associated merely with loss. Indeed, the classics, like blue chip art, can be profitable in their own right. In the summer of 1989, Shakespeare made big business at the box offices in the West End. After all, Shakespeare is part of 'our heritage', and 'our heritage' is one of Britain's more marketable assets.

Everyone was agreed that the Rose Theatre, billed as 'Shakespeare's theatre', was a part of 'our heritage'. Margaret Thatcher has probably never seen a play by William Shakespeare in all her ten years of office, but even she was prepared to lend her weight to save the Rose Theatre. Martin Myers wrote to protesters to say, 'rest assured that as an Englishman, lover of our heritage and tradition . . .' The sign outside his building site proclaimed, 'Revealing today's heritage, building tomorrow's'. The Tory MP, Michael Marshall was clear that the Rose is 'our heritage' and Labour MP, Eric Heffer, found himself in agreement; the Rose is part of 'our English heritage'. Given this political consensus about what constitutes 'our heritage', it is inevitable that all solutions to the Rose are going to be doomed to symbolic totemisation. As Robbie Barnett, circus performer and street entertainer, said of the impromptu performances given to the crowd in Park Street on 14 May; 'The Rose was a theatre where the working class sweated into the armpits of the middle class. The Rose was not about the RSC's po-faced performances. None of them represented the traditions of the Rose.'

Defining 'our heritage' is a highly selective activity. Conflate the first syllable of 'heirloom' and the last syllable of 'nostalgia', and you get not only the same sort of sound as 'heritage' but also the twin meanings embodied in that word; a combination of the inherited glory of the past and the enthralment to values it is held to represent. The chief value of 'our heritage' is to remind us of the immutability of the human condition. Colin Moynihan, for example, spoke of Southwark Cathedral testifying 'to continuing values in a constantly changing world'. 'Our heritage' has come to represent the fraudulence of a nostalgia divorced from history. To save the Rose, its values and traditions were subtly re-written, erasing uncomfortable evidence from the past.

On aesthetic grounds, the 1957 concrete stumps which were driven into the basic geometry of the Rose, are to be removed. Yet they are an essential part of the historical archive and provide interesting links between both Elizabethan ages. Southbridge House and Philip Henslowe's Rose were both built by societies energised by a tremendous belief in renewal. John Stow, the archivist, like all true nostalgists, thought his age 'the most scoffing, respectless and unthankful age that ever was' and hated 'the bad and greedy men of spoil', such as Henslowe, who were re-building London, and, who in the process built 'our heritage'. The mirthless merriment prompted by the Imry Merchant sign ('Revealing today's heritage, building tomorrow's') is a symptom of our age which, riddled with John Stows, is more interested in the idea of a living past than a seemingly dead future. It is inconceivable amongst latter day nostalgists that we can create any heirlooms for the future and so the concrete stumps must go.

'What other country would be prepared to bury the heritage that we link to Shakespeare's name, a name which is famous throughout the world?', asked Mark Fisher, Labour's shadow spokesman on the arts. If rubbing out the 1957 stumps is one thing, then writing in the idea that the Rose is 'Shakespeare's theatre' is quite another. Shakespeare is the supreme iconic figure in our culture. Synonymous with Britain, Human Nature and Our Heritage. 'We can all,' says the critic Terry Eagleton, 'identify with Shakespeare even if we have only the dimmest idea of what he is rattling on about.' Indeed when Access, the credit card firm, wanted an image which would be instantly recognisable at home and abroad and was British, they lighted upon the face of Shakespeare ('In addition, as a security measure, Shakespeare's image appears in a hologram'). In fact, as the *Mail on Sunday* revealed, the image of the Bard is actually a photograph of Greg Bell, a 42 year old Californian rat catcher. Why should it matter? No one knows what Shakespeare looked like. Some people doubt if Shakespeare wrote 'Shakespeare'. It does not matter how many revelations are made about the 'true' Shakespeare. He will never be discredited, because grappling with Shakespeare, as Eagleton says, is like 'grappling with a cross between a state industry and a major religious cult'.

Ben Jonson may have written that he honoured Shakespeare 'this side of idolatry' but it wasn't long before idolatry took over. The process of apotheosis really set in when a statue of Shakespeare was allowed in 1741 to penetrate that most potent symbol of the Establishment, Westminster Abbey. During the Seven Year War with France, Shakespeare was used as a subversive alternative to the hegemony of French neo-classicism. With David Garrick as priest, Shakespeare was finally elevated to the deity in the notorious Jubilee celebrations of 1769, which, tellingly, omitted any of Shakespeare's own words. The subsequent apotheosis could not have been consolidated without suitably transforming his plays. William Kemble's adaptation of *Henry V* in 1789 – the year of the French Revolution – was given a direct political thrust (the same play was used to much the same purpose in the Olivier film of 1944 by cutting all scenes which showed Henry's cruelty to French prisoners of war. The critical reception of Kenneth Branagh's 1989 film version proved how hard it can be to occlude the accretions and recover the original).

British imperialism which propagated the British way of life across the globe placed Shakespeare at the heart of its cultural colonisation and in 1904, Shaw coined the term 'Bardolatry'. The Southwark commentator Robert W. Bower (whom Shaw might well have had in mind when he invented the neologism), expressed the common view that whilst Shakespeare's contemporaries were peddling hack plays, 'little did they know that the greatest of them all was writing noble, pure and healthy works'. Shakespeare's works, perceived as text books for righteous living, have been set texts for almost a century, appropriated by educationalists as the outpourings of our National Poet. Where once schoolchildren learnt Latin and Greek so they could understand the justification for Western Civilisation, now they study Shakespeare to understand the justification for the dominance of Western Civilisation. In 1916, two months before the Battle of the Somme, schools held a 'Shakespeare day', with recitations of the famous scenes and speeches, by the writer who had come to embody the very soul of patriotism.

The tendency of everybody to quote Shakespeare's aphoristic lines, wrenching them out of context, allows Shakespeare to authorise anything at all and each time he is cited, he takes on more of a force within the culture at large. The 'genius' with which he is invested is explained by the very plurality of meanings that can be extrapolated from his work, yet this 'genius' is also said to reside in the 'eternal truths' that his plays embody. Terry Eagleton, however, points out that 'Shakespeare saw nothing wrong with slaughtering foreign peasants, believed strongly in the subordination of women and was a moderate anti-Semite'; scarcely 'continuing values in a constantly changing world' as Moynihan would have it. Although, perhaps it was for these reasons that Nigel Lawson in 1983 put on record, in *The Guardian*, the opinion that Shakespeare would have voted Conservative; '*Coriolanus* was written from a Tory point of view.' This would have come as news to Bertolt Brecht. Shakespeare has come to mirror society's preoccupations and give back to it the narcissistic satisfaction of believing that in its transient social and political values lie eternal truths. And in this way, 'our heritage' is manufactured, to testify to continuing values in a changing world.

Heritage is big business. As Clive Soley said of the Rose, 'If the site were properly developed and enhanced, it would bring in far more money as a tourist attraction than half a dozen office blocks on the land'. At present, the site in Park Street repels the Shakespeare pilgrim. Most of the street is under construction and, although this is a residential area as well as an office zone, it is not a good place to run out of milk in, let alone seek a souvenir tee-shirt or a spare roll of film. Tourists occasionally venture down the road, usually in search of the Anchor Inn, an old establishment (1775) but not so old it can boast a Shakespearean connection. Little, at present, is made of the Bard's tie with Bankside. A dingy brown plaque commemorates the site of the Globe. Further down Southwark Bridge Road there is a modern pub called the Shakespeare Tavern. Inside Southwark Cathedral where Shakespeare's brother Edmund is buried, a recumbent curvaceous Shakespeare carved in alabaster has clung to the wall since 1911. Higher up, a stained glass window installed in 1954 celebrates some of Shakespeare's immortal creations – Falstaff and Portia, Ariel and Othello, Romeo and Juliet *et al*.

Another plaque in the Cathedral tells us that Shakespeare was a citizen of Southwark between 1599 and 1611. This is a much contested issue. History tells us that he was taxed 5s. on land in Southwark valued at £5 in 1593 and seven years later was still being sued for that debt by the Bishop of Winchester – by then it had risen to 13s. 4d. Recent evidence, which came to light during the Rose Campaign, that Shakespeare actually lived next door to the Rose playhouse for fifteen years has been described by Andrew Gurr as 'plausible but indirect'. But once Park Street is developed for tourists, what will matter most – indirect evidence or plausibility?

In 1969 Sam Wanamaker first visited England. 'I was an American,' he said, 'looking for the history of England and as I was most interested in the history of the theatre, Bankside was the obvious place to visit. I couldn't believe that there was only a plaque. The atmosphere around here was terrific and with all the rebuilding that was going to happen I thought it would be a great time to reconstruct the Globe.' With Sam Wanamaker's replica finally going ahead and with the real thing itself – the excavated Rose – 'Bankside,' as Simon Hughes prophesied, 'will one day eclipse Stratford.'

Stratford-upon-Avon is the Mecca for the true pilgrim. From London, in the season, you can get British Rail's Shakespeare Connection, change at Coventry ('Welcome to the City in Shakespeare Country') and catch one of the coaches manned by Guide Friday Ltd., whose tour operators all seem to be incredibly well informed on Elizabethan plumbing. Few serious theatre-goers bother with the tourist trail and few serious tourists bother with the theatre, but between the two and a half million of them, £50 million is spent. Long before Walt Disney dreamt up Disneyland, Stratford-upon-Avon had created the theme park. If history could not confirm the fact that William Shakespeare was born in a thatched cottage in the market town of Stratford-upon-Avon, right in the geographical heart of England, then history would have to invent it.

Long before Garrick's Jubilee celebrations, tourists had been invading the town. In 1759, The Rev. Francis Gastrell then living in Shakespeare's retirement home, New Place, petitioned the town council to lower his rates to compensate for the nuisance value of residing in a place of pilgrimage. When they refused, he demolished it. In 1847 Shakespeare's actual birthplace was put up for auction. The estate agents made much of the fact that Mrs Hart, who had sold the property in 1806 for £200, was a descendant of Shakespeare's sister. Their poster proclaimed: 'The most truly heart stirring relic of a most glorious period of England's immortal Bard. The most honoured monument of the greatest genius that ever lived.' Victorian society was determined to purchase this heart stirring relic for the nation. An Appeal went up headed by Prince Albert, Alfred Lord Tennyson, Lord Macaulay and Charles Dickens. Benefits were arranged. Dickens took part in a production of the *Merry Wives of Windsor*. A musical extravaganza was held at the Adelphi entitled *This House to Be Sold (The Property of The*

Late William Shakespeare) Inquire Within. As a result of all the fund-raising, the house in Henley Street was knocked down to the nation for an inflationary £3000.

Subsequently the Shakespeare Birthplace Trust has gone on to acquire four other associated properties; Anne Hathaway's Cottage, New Place, Hall's Croft and Mary Arden's House. For a £5 inclusive ticket and an extra £3.50 for the guided tour, you can visit them all. They are beautifully maintained and furnished with appropriate *objets*. In Anne Hathaway's Cottage – the twelfth most-visited place in Britain – tourists peer solemnly at an electric kettle in the dairy. It has an air of solid reality about it. One could imagine Anne Hathaway buying an electric kettle for her dairy, rather than the expensive antiques thoughtfully provided for her by the Birthplace Trust. A Japanese tourist lost in a time-warp tries to buy a post card with an old pound note. Ah! Instant nostalgia! Here, in the gift shop cunningly sited by the exit, you can buy a tea towel (£2.40) or a placemat (£1.50), a Coalport figurine (£79.95) or, at the other end of the scale, a bookmark (25p). You can even buy books. Some are by William Shakespeare but a large number though, with titles like *Flowers in Shakespeare* or *Birds in Shakespeare*, turn out to be by Dr Levi Fox, the chairman of the Shakespeare Birthplace Trust.

The rest of the town is given over to Shakespeare. There are the Hathaway Tea Rooms and the As You Like It Disco. There's the Heritage Theatre where for £1.25 you can watch a twenty minute audio/visual presentation of Good Queen Bess's journey to Kenilworth. And of course, there is the Royal Shakespeare Company, the town's main loss leader for the endless purveying of honey, handknits, floral sprigged table cloths, Crabtree and Evelyn preserves, fine china and all the other paraphernalia of 'olde worlde Englande', the theme of 'Shakespeare Country'. No wonder Southwark Council are suspicious of tourism. Amongst all the interesting street names in North Southwark, Disney Street SE1 strikes an ominous note. British Rail has announced plans to dig up the area between the power station and the river to use as a construction site (and future ventilation shaft) for the Channel Tunnel underground link between Peckham and King's Cross. Once the tunnel is complete the whole site could then be made available for development – one of the largest sites still undeveloped on the Thames.

Theo Crosby, the ISGC architect, has very definite ideas for this part of London. 'The river was the main artery of London in the sixteenth-century and it should be the main tourist route today.' Crosby sees the future for England as one of tourism. He anticipates 40 million annual visitors to London by the end of the century. By 1994 the Department of Employment who have taken over tourism from the Department of Trade and Industry, forecast that 176 million visitors to the country as a whole, spending £246 billion, will need to be catered for. Tourism, indissolubly linked around 'our heritage', is now in many places the only alternative to heavy industry, which has long since disappeared. 'Other businesses will die,' says Theo Crosby; 'Would you prefer sitting in a factory putting widgets together? What is work anyway? Mostly it's just talking on the telephone.' Crosby's speculative plan for the power station site includes an opera house, hotel, conference centre, tube station and museum. The complex, if it came to fruition, would be connected to the City by a new footbridge over the river to St Paul's as part of an infrastructure to take the tourist away from existing attractions. 'They're wearing out the historic places. You've only got to look at the staircases in Westminster Abbey. Bankside is going to play a critical part in the future because of its evocative nature, its romance.'

Tied in with Theo Crosby's forecast, is the future of the ISGC, whose foundations were dug in 1989. Its brochure promises 'An exciting place of entertainment and leisure for Londoners and visitors alike'. It anticipates 500,000 visitors paying £4 each in its first year, arriving at a rate of 1700 an hour.

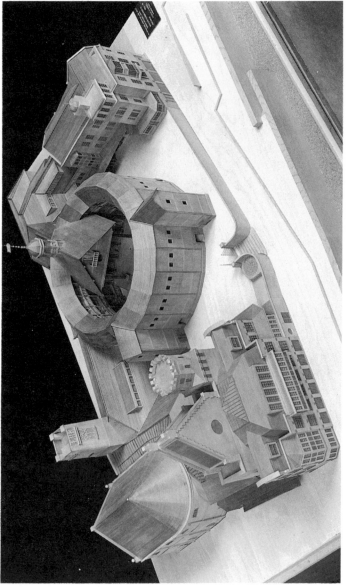

50. A model of the International Shakespeare Globe Centre made by students at Hertfordshire College of Art and Design. (Andy Fulgoni)

The whole centre, with the reconstructed Globe as its focus, features a series of inter-connected buildings including flats, shops, a pub, restaurant and cafeteria. On the lower level a 20,000 square feet exhibition hall will recreate the life of an Elizabethan playhouse with young actors, garbed suitably in doublet and hose, acting as guides. A smaller 250-seater theatre, based on Inigo Jones's unrealised plans in 1616 for the Phoenix Theatre in Drury Lane, will be open all year. The reconstructed Globe will be used only seasonally. Based on the first pre-fire Globe of 1599-1613, it will stand on a piazza formed from the roof of the exhibition hall. Raised above ground level, its twenty-four-sided white polygon will be visible from across the river.

Everything has been done to ensure authenticity although modern fire regulations will limit the capacity of the twentieth-century Globe to 1500 and not even Sam Wanamaker can control the aeroplanes flying overhead. Plays will be performed in natural light unaided by modern technology or amplification. If it rains the groundlings will indeed get authentically wet. The building will be constructed using the traditional methods of seasoned oak, wattle and daub. Art schools and technical colleges have started work on the decorative details. Yet with the real Globe still unexcavated, the only true part of 'our heritage' on Bankside comes from the excavation of the Rose, the theatre that isn't Shakespeare's. But if Bankside is to eclipse Stratford then clearly the Rose has to play its part in the major state industry – the heritage industry.

Heritage is big business. Museums can no longer afford to present themselves as 'ghastly charnel houses of murdered evidence', as Flinders Petrie once called them. Instead, in parts of the country, miners made forcibly redundant, dress up as miners to help tourists experience what life was like down the pit. It's all in keeping with the 'empathy' exercises which are replacing historical knowledge on GCSE History courses. In Stratford-upon-Avon at the Heritage Theatre you can 'Travel Back in time to the World of Shakespeare – a £1,000,000 Family Entertainment'. The brochure promises that 'You are a bystander and actually experience – the excitement of bear-baiting – the horrors of the plague cellar – the spectacle of royal fireworks'. A developer like Ken King who started life in a Hertfordshire council house has invested £1 million to become Lord of Avebury Manor in Wiltshire, a sixteenth-century house situated in the middle of Avebury's sacred circle of prehistoric stones. For a further £250,000 he has restored the house against local opposition and is creating an 'Elizabethan experience' in a 'living museum'.

York Archaeological Trust's experience of charging the public 35p each to watch them excavate the Viking village led them to invest £2.5 million in Jorvik Viking Centre which re-creates Viking life for popular consumption. So far, £3.5 million has been recouped and a further £800,000 earned for archaeology in York during 1989. It is said that the Centre has generated another £20 million of business in and around York and that Jorvik's gift shop has a higher turnover than the local Woolworth. Heritage Projects Ltd., who designed the Centre, are experts in the field and this year Jorvik Viking Centre was number nine in Britain's Top Ten of museum attendance. Its popularity threatens to outstrip the more traditional experience of visiting a museum and since its opening in 1984 beneath Coppergate shopping centre, nearly five million visitors have taken the twelve minute funfair ride through a recreation of a tenth century Viking settlement. Heritage Projects have installed tableaux of domestic life and for added authenticity wafted the amoniac tang of urine into the air.

'The Rose has all the things going for it that Jorvik had and very much more,' said Dr Peter Addyman, the director of the York Archaeological Trust. 'The Rose developers, Imry Merchant, need their heads screwing on if they can't see how the theatre remains could be turned to profit.' Since then Heritage Projects Ltd. have been commissioned by the Rose Campaign to prepare a £26,000 feasibility study to show how a 'hole in the ground' can be displayed. Martin Myers has never been impressed by the financial argument. 'The commercial possibility of the Rose is another classic,' he said. 'We were going to make millions by taking money at the turnstiles. People wrote to me and said, so you think you're a businessman and you don't realise how much money you stand to make. Apart from the fact that museum charges are immoral, if anyone thinks they can make money out of the Rose and conform to Section 52, then good luck to them. We will give it to them. We will give it to the nation. If it turns out I am wrong, we will have given away millions.'

Interpretation of a site is the key to the boom in heritage centres. 'Without it,' says Martin Myers, 'the average tourist is

going to ask what all the fuss was about.' Simon Jenkins
suggests that partial reconstruction of the Rose will have to take
place to give the site meaning. Conservationists are talking
about the need to extract the remains, treat them with chemicals
and then replace them, perhaps in a fibre-glass moulding. Yet
the Rose's biggest asset is what Campaign Committee member
Martin Village calls the 'tingle factor': its 'sense of place' – that
this is the place where one can empathise that Shakespeare once
trod. 'I stood on the spot where the stage was,' says Simon
Jenkins, 'and it does give you a funny kind of feeling – why not
re-create the stage so that everyone can stand on it?' The actual
connection that Shakespeare has with the Rose is that *Titus
Andronicus* was performed on its stage and quite possibly, so
too was *Henry VI Part III*. Any evidence that the young William
Shakespeare once trod its boards can only be said to be plausible
but indirect. It would be a shame if the Rose Theatre was saved
from being buried under hardcore only to disappear from view
once more, buried this time under the weight of a heritage that
neither it – nor, for that matter, the Globe – really represents.

WHO'S WHO

AAI: Area of Archaeological importance.

AMAA: the 1979 Ancient Monuments and Archaeological Areas Act.

Nicholas Armstrong, solicitor with Theodore Goddard and for the Campaign to Save the Rose.

Dame Peggy Ashcroft, celebrated classical actress who played a leading role in saving the Rose.

Tony Banks, MP (Newham North West), former Chairman of the GLC's Arts Committee.

Robbie Barnett, actor, clown and street entertainer.

John Barton, Associate Director with the RSC.

Lauryn Beer, member of Campaign Committee to Save the Rose and studying for PhD in English at Oxford University.

Victor Belcher, Head of London Division's Survey and General branch with English Heritage.

Professor Martin Biddle, archaeologist at Oxford University.

Simon Blatherwick, archaeologist and co-site director for the Museum of London's excavation of the Rose Theatre.

Virginia Bottomley, Under Secretary of State for the Environment during the Campaign to Save the Rose.

Gerald Bowden, MP (Dulwich), one time deputy Chairman of Campaign Committee to Save the Rose.

Julian Bowsher, archaeologist and co-site director for the Museum of London's excavation of the Rose Theatre.

John Burns, member of Campaign Committee to Save the Rose and studying for PhD in Archaeology at Oxford University.

Eileen Chivers, member of Campaign Committee to Save the Rose and drama teacher at Alleyn's School.

Martin Clout, member of Campaign Committee to Save the Rose and Shakespeare historian.

Andrew Collins, QC, counsel for the Secretary of State for the Environment.

Theo Crosby, architect with design firm Pentagram and architect for the ISGC.

Professor Barry Cunliffe, Commissioner with English Heritage.

Timothy Dalton, actor most famous for his portrayal of James Bond in recent 'Bond' films.

Mark Dennett, planning officer for Southwark Council.

George Dennis, archaeological planning officer with the Museum of London.

DoE: Department of the Environment.

Dame Edna Everage, a.k.a. Barry Humphries, drag act which portrays an Australian 'megastar'.

Ralph Fiennes, RSC actor prominent in the organisation of the events of 14/15 May.

Mark Fisher, MP (Stoke on Trent, Central). Old Etonian Labour shadow spokesman on the Arts.

James Fox, member of Campaign Committee to Save the Rose and filmstar.

Theodore Goddard, legal firm that acted for the Campaign to Save the Rose.

Peter Goldsmith, QC, counsel for Imry Merchant.

Dr Clive Grace, borough solicitor for Southwark Council.

Leslie Grantham, actor most famous for his portrayal of the womanising Den ('Dirty Den') in the BBC's soap opera *EastEnders*.

Dr Anthony Grayling, member of Campaign Committee to Save the Rose and philosopher at Oxford University.

GLC: Greater London Council.

Jon Greenfield, architect with design firm Pentagram, project architect for the ISGC and member of Campaign Committee to Save the Rose.

John Griffiths, secretary to the Campaign Committee to Save the Rose and political researcher.

Professor Andrew Gurr, of the University of Reading and advisor to the ISGC.

Sir Peter Hall, director, formerly artistic director of the National Theatre.

Rosemary Harris, actress and member of the Campaign Committee to Save the Rose.

John Hinchcliffe, Head of the Central Excavations Unit at English Heritage.

C. Walter Hodges, Shakespearean scholar and illustrator and advisor to the ISGC.

Michael Holden, theatre consultant and advisor to the ISGC.

Roger Howells, RSC production manager at Stratford upon Avon.

Simon Hughes, MP (Bermondsey and North Southwark) Chairman of the Campaign Committee to Save the Rose.

ISGC, International Shakespeare Globe Centre, headed by Sam Wanamaker which aims to reconstruct the Globe Theatre on Bankside.

Simon Jenkins, former Deputy Chairman of English Heritage, currently editor of *The Times*.

Jennifer Jones, Marketing and Public Relations Officer at ISGC and member of Campaign Committee to Save the Rose.

Dr Urmilla Khan, from the University of Delhi, member of the Campaign Committee to Save the Rose.

Martin Kramer, solicitor with Theodore Goddard and for the Campaign to Save the Rose.

Martin Landau, Deputy Chairman of property company, Imry Merchant.

Linklaters and Paines, legal firm that acted for property company, Imry Merchant.

Iain Mackintosh, theatre consultant, member of Theatres Trust, advisor to the ISGC.

Pat McDonnell, member of Campaign Committee to Save the Rose, and actor.

Ian McKellen, celebrated classical actor who activated the events of 14/15 May 1989 in support of the Rose Theatre.

Councillor Anne Matthews, leader of Southwark Council.

Lord Montagu of Beaulieu, chairman of English Heritage.

Barbara Morris, enthusiastic pensioner who collected signatures for petitions to Save the Rose.

Colin Moynihan, Secratary of State for the Environment in 1988.

Gerard Murphy, actor and director with the RSC.

Martin Myers, chief executive of property firm, Imry Merchant.

Caro Newling, press officer for the RSC.

Trevor Nunn, former Artistic Director of the RSC.

Lord Olivier, celebrated classical actor and patron of the Rose Theatre Trust.

Professor John Orrell, from the University of Alberta, advisor to the ISGC.

Philip Ormond, member of Campaign Committee to Save the Rose and director of Theatre Despatch, a theatre PR firm.

Brian de Palma, director of cult *genre* films such as *Carrie, Blow Out* and *Get to Know Your Rabbit.*

John Peter, theatre critic for the *Sunday Times.*

Heather Pickering, founder member of Southwark Heritage and member of the Campaign Committee to Save the Rose.

Tim Pigott-Smith, actor active in the Campaign to Save the Rose.

Vanessa Redgrave, celebrated actress and international film star.

RESCUE: The British Archaeological Trust.

Dr Ruth Richardson, member of Campaign to Save the Rose and historian at London University.

Nicholas Ridley, Secretary of State for the Environment during the Campaign to Save the Rose.

RADA: the Royal Academy of Dramatic Art.

RSC: Royal Shakespeare Company.

SMC: Scheduled Monument Consent.

Mr Justice Schiemann, judge who heard the judicial review.

Harvey Sheldon, Head of Greater London Archaeology at the Museum of London.

Richard Seifert, architect for Imry Merchant.

Margaret Slythe, Head of the Wodehouse Library at Dulwich College.

Nicola Smith, librarian with Southwark's Local History library.

Clive Soley, MP (Hammersmith).

Coral Stringfellow, nightclub owner and member of the Campaign Committee to Save the Rose.

Jeremy Sullivan, QC, counsel for the Campaign to Save the Rose.

Simon Tait, arts correspondent on *The Times*.

Robin Thompson, chief planning officer for Southwark Council.

Barbara Todd, member of Campaign Committee to Save the Rose and Registrar at RADA.

Martin Village, member of Campaign Committee to Save the Rose and property consultant specialising in historic buildings.

Peter Village, brother to Martin and junior counsel for the Campaign to Save the Rose.

Dr Geoff Wainright, senior archaeologist from English Heritage.

Sam Wanamaker, international film star, founder member of the ISCG and now its Executive Vice Chairman.

Alex Wilbraham, translator and member of the Campaign Committee to Save the Rose.

Councillor Geoff Williams, Labour member of Southwark Council for Cathedral Ward and Chairman of Planning Committee.

Richard Williams, theatre director.

Councillor Hilary Wines, Liberal Democrat member of Southwark Council for Cathedral Ward and a member of the Campaign Committee to Save the Rose.

Stephan Wingate, heads Marketchief the property consortium that took over Imry Merchant.

Bibliography

Chapters One and Two

The main source books consulted for the history of the Rose Theatre are *The Theatrical Manager in England and America* edited by Joseph W. Donohue Jnr (Princeton University Press, 1971), *Henslowe's Diary* edited by R.A. Foakes and R.T. Rickert (Cambridge University Press, 1961), *The Life and Times of Edward Alleyn* by G.L. Hosking (Cape, 1952), *Henslowe's Rose* by Ernest L. Rhodes (The University Press of Kentucky, 1976) and *Documents of the Rose Playhouse* by Carol Chillington Rutter (Manchester University Press, 1984).

The background to Elizabethan and Jacobean theatres came from: *To Present the Pretence* by John Arden (Eyre Methuen, 1977), *The Rise of the Common Player* by M.C. Bradbrook (London, 1962), *The Elizabethan Stage* by E.K. Chambers (Oxford, 1923), *At the Sign of the Swan* by Judith Cook (Harrap, 1986), *Acting Women* by Lesley Ferris (Macmillan, 1990), *The Age of Shakespeare* edited by Boris Ford (Penguin, 1955), *The Shakespearean Stage* by Andrew Gurr (Cambridge, 1970), *Shakespeare* by F.E. Halliday (Thames and Hudson, 1956), *Shakespeare's Audience* by Alfred Harbage (New York, 1941), *Elizabethan Drama* edited by Ralph J. Kaufmann (Oxford University Press, 1961), *Marlowe: The Critical Heritage* edited by Millar MacLure (Routledge and Kegan Paul Ltd, 1979), *Shakespeare and the Idea of the Play* by Anne Righter (Chatto and Windus, 1962), *The England of Elizabeth* by A.L. Rowse (Macmillan and Company Ltd, 1951), *William Shakespeare: A Documentary Life*, by S. Schoenbaum (Oxford, 1975), *Shakespeare's Theatre* by Peter Thomson (Routledge and Kegan Paul Ltd, 1953). The novels *No Bed for Bacon* by Caryl Brahms and S.J. Simon (Hogarth Press, 1986) and *Nothing Like the Sun* by Anthony Burgess (William Heinemann Ltd, 1964) are fictional treatments of the same subject.

The history of Southwark came from *Southwark and the City* by David Johnson (Oxford University Press, 1969), *Neighbourhood and Society: a London Suburb in the Seventeenth Century* by Jeremy Boulton (Cambridge University Press, 1987), the London Borough of Southwark's Neighbourhood Histories pamphlets, *Sketches of Southwark Old and New*, privately printed by Robert W. Bower in 1902 and The Bankside Volume in the LCC's *Survey of London* (1950).

Author's interviews with Andrew Gurr, Heather Pickering, Margaret Slythe and Nicola Smith.

Bibliography

Chapter Three

Background to archaeology came from the following: *Archaeological Papers from York* edited by P.V. Addyman and V.E. Black (York Archaeological Trust, 1984), *Roman Burials from Southwark* by Martin Dean and Michael Hammerson (1981), *Excavations beneath the Choir of Southwark Cathedral* by Michael Hammerson (1977), *Rescuing the Past in Southwark* by Harvey Sheldon (1982), *Recent Dendrochronological Work in Southwark and its Implications* by Harvey Sheldon and Ian Tyers (1983) and *Excavations at Winchester Palace, Southwark* by Brian Yule (1989).

The discussion of playhouse architecture is drawn from: *The History of the Greek and Roman Theater* by Margaret Bieber (Princeton University Press, revised and enlarged 1961), *Raising a Playhouse from the Dust*, a paper by S.P. Cerasano (in the edition of Shakespeare Quarterly, vol 40, no 4, 1989), *The Globe that Shakespeare Knew*, a privately printed paper by Martin Clout, (1987), *The Globe Playhouse, its Design and Equipment* by J. Cranford Adams (Harvard University Press, 1942), *Rebuilding Shakespeare's Globe* by Andrew Gurr and John Orrell (Weidenfeld and Nicolson, 1989), *What the Rose Can Tell Us* by Andrew Gurr and John Orrell (Antiquity vol 63, no 240, 1989), the ISGC transcripts of a symposium held on 22 April 1989, *The Fortune Contract and Vitruvian Symmetry* by R.C. Kohler (Shakespeare Studies, vol 6, 1970), *Excavating Henslowe's Rose*, a paper by R.C. Kohler (Shakespeare Quarterly, Vol 40, No 4, 1989), *The Development of the English Playhouse* by Richard Leacroft (Methuen, 1973), *This Golden Round* by Ronnie Mulryne and Margaret Shewring (Jolly & Barber Ltd, 1989) and the private correspondence of Jon Greenfield, Andrew Gurr, C. Walter Hodges, Michael Holden, Iain Mackintosh and John Orrell. Author's interviews with Julian Bowsher, Martin Clout, Theo Crosby, Ralph Fiennes, Jon Greenfield, Andrew Gurr, John Hinchcliffe, Roger Howells and Harvey Sheldon.

Chapters Four and Five

Coverage of the Campaign came from first hand observation and the following sources: Theatre Despatch's daily newsletters, minutes of the Campaign Committee's meetings and debates in the House of Commons and House of Lords reported by Hansard (24 June 1988, 9 May 1989, 11 May 1989, 15 May 1989, 15 June 1989, 27 July 1989).

The Campaign itself was extensively reported throughout the media. Important articles were by the following (Simon Tait of *The Times* being its most assiduous reporter): Simon Jenkins in *The Times* (12 May 1989), Alex Renton in *The Independent* (20 May 1989), Ian McKellen in the *Daily Mail* (20 May 1989), Julie Birchill in *The Mail on Sunday* (21 May 1989), David Randall in the *Observer* (21 May 1989), Elizabeth Grice and Hugh Pearman in *The Sunday Times* (21 May 1989), John Peter and David Selbourne *The Sunday Times* (28 May 1989), Simon Tait in *The Times* (2 June 1989), Herbert Kretzmer in *The Evening Standard* (3 July 1989) and David Keys in *The Independent* (17 October 1989).

Participants on both sides of the Campaign described their involvement in the following publications, Victor Belcher in English Heritage's magazine

(Issue 7, September 1989), Geoff Wainwright in *Antiquity* (Vol 63, 1989), Iain Mackintosh in *Arts Management* (Summer 1989) and again in *Cue International* (Autumn, 1989) and George Dennis in a paper entitled *Archaeology into the 1990s* given to a conference organised by RESCUE on 17 February 1990.

Key documents are: Core Bundle in The Queen v The Secretary of State for the Environment ex parte Rose Theatre Trust Company in the High Court of Justice, Queen's Bench Division (Ref. CO/994/89), draft judgement by Mr Justice Schiemann, English Heritage's Report and Accounts 1988-9, Imry Merchant Developers plc Annual Report 1989, Southwark's Inner Area Programme Annual Report 1987-8, report to the planning committee of the London Borough of Southwark (Ref 3rd July 1989 Item 31 pp 177-194), 'The Rose Theatre – a preliminary description of the way to develop Southbridge House and to save the Rose Theatre' (Theatres Trust 1989) and minutes of a Symposium on Long-Term Preservation of the Rose organised by English Heritage on 9 October 1989.

Author's interviews with Nicholas Armstrong, Robbie Barnett, Julian Bowsher, Eileen Chivers, Martin Clout, Mark Dennett, George Dennis, Ralph Fiennes, James Fox, Anthony Grayling, Jon Greenfield, Andrew Gurr, Simon Hughes, Simon Jenkins, Martin Kramer, Pat McDonnell, Martin Myers, Caro Newling, Ruth Richardson, Harvey Sheldon, Geoff Williams, Richard Williams, Stephen Williams and Hilary Wines.

Epilogue

The discussion of the politics of heritage drew upon the following: *Shakespearean Constitutions: Politics, Theatre, Criticism 1730-1830* by Jonathan Bate (Oxford University Press, 1989), *The Royal Shakespeare Company: A History of Ten Decades* by Sally Beauman (Oxford University Press, 1982) Robert Hewison's *The Heritage Industry* (Methuen, 1987) and *Shakespeare: A Celebration*, edited by T.S.B. Spencer (Penguin 1964).

Author's interviews with Theo Crosby, Simon Hughes, Jennifer Jones, Heather Pickering and Sam Wanamaker.

INDEX

Index